THE NEW FOLGER LIBRARY SHAKESPEARE

Designed to make Shakespeare's great plays available to all readers, the New Folger Library edition of Shakespeare's plays provides accurate texts in modern spelling and punctuation, as well as scene-by-scene action summaries, full explanatory notes, many pictures clarifying Shakespeare's language, and notes recording all significant departures from the early printed versions. Each play is prefaced by a brief introduction, by a guide to reading Shakespeare's language, and by accounts of his life and theater. Each play is followed by an annotated list of further readings and by a "Modern Perspective" written by an expert on that particular play.

Barbara A. Mowat was Director of Research *emerita* at the Folger Shakespeare Library, Consulting Editor of *Shakespeare Quarterly,* and author of *The Dramaturgy of Shakespeare's Romances* and of essays on Shakespeare's plays and their editing.

Paul Werstine is Professor of English at the Graduate School and at King's University College at Western University. He is a general editor of the New Variorum Shakespeare and author of *Early Modern Playhouse Manuscripts and the Editing of Shakespeare* and of many papers and articles on the printing and editing of Shakespeare's plays.

The Folger Shakespeare Library

The Folger Shakespeare Library in Washington, D.C., a privately funded research library dedicated to Shakespeare and the civilization of early modern Europe, was founded in 1932 by Henry Clay and Emily Jordan Folger, and incorporated as part of Amherst College in Amherst, Massachusetts, one of the nation's oldest liberal arts colleges, from which Henry Folger had graduated in 1879. In addition to its role as the world's preeminent Shakespeare collection and its emergence as a leading center for Renaissance studies, the Folger Shakespeare Library offers a wide array of cultural and educational programs and services for the general public.

EDITORS

BARBARA A. MOWAT
Former Director of Research emerita
Folger Shakespeare Library

PAUL WERSTINE
Professor of English
King's University College
at Western University, Canada

Folger SHAKESPEARE LIBRARY

The Winter's Tale

By
WILLIAM SHAKESPEARE

Edited by Barbara A. Mowat
and Paul Werstine

Simon & Schuster Paperbacks
NEW YORK LONDON TORONTO SYDNEY NEW DELHI

Simon & Schuster
1230 Avenue of the Americas
New York, NY 10020

This Simon & Schuster trade paperback edition September 2021

SIMON & SCHUSTER and colophon are registered trademarks of Simon & Schuster, Inc.

For information about special discounts for bulk purchases, please contact Simon & Schuster Special Sales at 1-866-506-1949 or business@simonandschuster.com.

The Simon & Schuster Speakers Bureau can bring authors to your live event. For more information or to book an event, contact the Simon & Schuster Speakers Bureau at 1-866-248-3049 or visit our website at www.simonspeakers.com.

Manufactured in the United States of America

10 9 8 7 6 5 4 3

ISBN 978-1-9821-2250-8
ISBN 978-1-5011-3689-4 (ebook)

From the Director of the Folger Shakespeare Library

It is hard to imagine a world without Shakespeare. Since their composition more than four hundred years ago, Shakespeare's plays and poems have traveled the globe, inviting those who see and read his works to make them their own.

Readers of the New Folger Editions are part of this ongoing process of "taking up Shakespeare," finding our own thoughts and feelings in language that strikes us as old or unusual and, for that very reason, new. We still struggle to keep up with a writer who could think a mile a minute, whose words paint pictures that shift like clouds. These expertly edited texts, presented here with accompanying explanatory notes and up-to-date critical essays, are distinctive because of what they do: they allow readers not simply to keep up, but to engage deeply with a writer whose works invite us to think, and think again.

These New Folger Editions of Shakespeare's plays and poems are also special because of where they come from. The Folger Shakespeare Library in Washington, D.C., where the Editions are produced, is the single greatest documentary source of Shakespeare's works. An unparalleled collection of early modern books, manuscripts, and artwork connected to Shakespeare, the Folger's holdings have been consulted extensively in the preparation of these texts. The Editions also reflect the expertise gained through the regular performance of Shakespeare's works in the Folger's Elizabethan Theatre.

I want to express my deep thanks to editors Barbara Mowat and Paul Werstine for creating these indispensable editions of Shakespeare's works, which incorporate the best of textual scholarship with a richness of commentary that is both inspired and engaging. Readers who want to know more about Shakespeare and his plays can follow the paths these distinguished scholars have trod by visiting the Folger itself, where a range of physical and digital resources (available online) exists to supplement the material in these texts. I commend to you these words, and hope that they inspire.

Michael Witmore
Director, Folger Shakespeare Library

Contents

Editors' Preface   ix
Shakespeare's *The Winter's Tale*   xiii
Reading Shakespeare's Language:
   The Winter's Tale   xv
Shakespeare's Life   xxx
Shakespeare's Theater   xl
The Publication of Shakespeare's Plays   xlix
An Introduction to This Text   liii

The Winter's Tale
   Text of the Play with Commentary   1

Longer Notes   237
Textual Notes   251
The Winter's Tale: A Modern Perspective
   by Stephen Orgel   257
Further Reading   273
Key to Famous Lines and Phrases   291

Editors' Preface

In recent years, ways of dealing with Shakespeare's texts and with the interpretation of his plays have been undergoing significant change. This edition, while retaining many of the features that have always made the Folger Shakespeare so attractive to the general reader, at the same time reflects these current ways of thinking about Shakespeare. For example, modern readers, actors, and teachers have become interested in the differences between, on the one hand, the early forms in which Shakespeare's plays were first published and, on the other hand, the forms in which editors through the centuries have presented them. In response to this interest, we have based our edition on what we consider the best early printed version of a particular play (explaining our rationale in a section called "An Introduction to This Text") and have marked our changes in the text—unobtrusively, we hope, but in such a way that the curious reader can be aware that a change has been made and can consult the "Textual Notes" to discover what appeared in the early printed version.

Current ways of looking at the plays are reflected in our brief prefaces, in many of the commentary notes, in the annotated lists of "Further Reading," and especially in each play's "Modern Perspective," an essay written by an outstanding scholar who brings to the reader his or her fresh assessment of the play in the light of today's interests and concerns.

As in the Folger Library General Reader's Shakespeare, which this edition replaces, we include explanatory notes designed to help make Shakespeare's language clearer to a modern reader, and we place the notes on the page facing the text that they explain. We also follow the earlier edition in including illustrations—of objects, of clothing, of mythological figures—from books and manuscripts in the Folger Library collection. We provide fresh accounts of the life of Shakespeare, of the publishing of his plays, and of the theaters in which his plays were performed, as well as an introduction to the text itself. We also include a section called "Reading Shakespeare's Language," in which we try to help readers learn to "break the code" of Elizabethan poetic language.

For each section of each volume, we are indebted to a host of generous experts and fellow scholars. The "Reading Shakespeare's Language" sections, for example, could not have been written had not Arthur King, of Brigham Young University, and Randall Robinson, author of *Unlocking Shakespeare's Language,* led the way in untangling Shakespearean language puzzles and shared their insights and methodologies generously with us. "Shakespeare's Life" profited by the careful reading given it by the late S. Schoenbaum, "Shakespeare's Theater" was read and strengthened by Andrew Gurr and John Astington, and "The Publication of Shakespeare's Plays" is indebted to the comments of Peter W. M. Blayney. Among the texts we consulted, we found Stephen Orgel's edition in the Oxford series especially helpful. We are immensely grateful to Robert K. Turner for allowing us to consult in manuscript the commentary to his New Variorum edition. We, as editors, take sole responsibility for any errors in our editions.

We are grateful to the authors of the "Modern Perspectives"; to Leeds Barroll and David Bevington for their generous encouragement; to the Huntington and Newberry Libraries for fellowship support; to King's College for the grants it has provided to Paul Werstine; to the Social Sciences and Humanities Research Council of Canada, which provided him with a Research Time

Stipend for 1990–91; to R. J. Shroyer of the University of Western Ontario for essential computer support; to the Folger Institute's Center for Shakespeare Studies for its fortuitous sponsorship of a workshop on "Shakespeare's Texts for Students and Teachers" (funded by the National Endowment for the Humanities and led by Richard Knowles of the University of Wisconsin), a workshop from which we learned an enormous amount about what is wanted by college and high-school teachers of Shakespeare today; and especially to Steve Llano, our production editor at Pocket Books, whose expertise and attention to detail are essential to this project.

Our biggest debt is to the Folger Shakespeare Library—to Werner Gundersheimer, Director of the Library, who made possible our edition; to Deborah Curren-Aquino, who provides extensive editorial and production support; to Jean Miller, the Library's Art Curator, who combs the Library holdings for illustrations, and to Julie Ainsworth, Head of the Photography Department, who carefully photographs them; to Peggy O'Brien, former Director of Education at the Folger and now Director of Education Programs at the Corporation for Public Broadcasting, who gave us expert advice about the needs being expressed by Shakespeare teachers and students (and to Martha Christian and other "master teachers" who used our texts in manuscript in their classrooms); to Jessica Hymowitz and Wazir Shpoon for their expert computer support; to the staff of the Academic Programs Division, especially Amy Adler, Mary Tonkinson, Kathleen Lynch, Keira Roberts, Carol Brobeck, Kelleen Zubick, Toni Krieger, and Martha Fay; and, finally, to the generously supportive staff of the Library's Reading Room.

Barbara A. Mowat and Paul Werstine

Shakespeare's *The Winter's Tale*

The Winter's Tale, one of Shakespeare's very late plays, puts onstage a story so filled with improbabilities that the play occasionally seems amused at its own audacity. Near the story's end, for example, as incredible details accumulate, one character says "This news which is called true is so like an old tale that the verity [i.e., the truth] of it is in strong suspicion"; he has just exclaimed "Such a deal of wonder is broken out within this hour that ballad makers [the tabloid writers of Shakespeare's day] cannot be able to express it." As the "old tale" spins to its remarkable conclusion, another character tells us that what we are about to see, "Were it but told you, should be hooted at / Like an old tale."

The sense of the incredible and the wonderful seems built into the design of the play, as the play's title indicates. And the play's dialogue forces upon us an awareness of the title's significance. "Pray you sit by us / And tell 's a tale," Queen Hermione says early in the play to her young son Mamillius, who replies, "A sad tale's best for winter. I have one / Of sprites and goblins." The tale that the play tells, like that promised by Mamillius, is indeed of "sprites and goblins"—of ferocious and murderous passions, of man-eating bears, of princes and princesses in disguise, of death by drowning and by grief, of Greek oracles, of betrayal, and of unexpected joy. And the play draws much of its power from its heavy dependence on Greek myths of loss and of transformation.

Yet the story the play tells is at the same time solidly

grounded in the everyday, while the play itself is closely tied to Shakespeare's earlier, more straightforward, tragedies and comedies. The monstrous jealousy that descends upon Leontes, for example, is mythlike in its resemblance to the madness sent by the gods to punish Hercules in classical drama, but it seems not unfamiliar as an emotional state that can threaten anyone who loves someone else and who is thus vulnerable to loss and betrayal. Leontes' actions are so extreme that one at first discounts them as rather un-Shakespearean, yet his story is recognizably a retelling of Othello's (with the Iago-figure here incorporated into the hero's own psyche), as well as being a retelling of the Claudio-Hero plot in *Much Ado About Nothing*.

A "winter's tale" is a story to be told or read in front of a fire on a long winter's night. Paradoxically, this *Winter's Tale* is ideally seen rather than read. Its sudden shift from tragedy to comedy, its playing with disguise, its startling exits and transformations seem addressed to theater audiences, not readers. But the imagination can do much to transform words into living characters and stage directions into vivid action, and thus to turn this play that is quintessentially for the stage back into a tale of wonder, a tale "of sprites and goblins."

After you have read the play, we invite you to turn to the essay printed at the back of this book, *"The Winter's Tale:* A Modern Perspective," by Professor Stephen Orgel of Stanford University.

Reading Shakespeare's Language:
The Winter's Tale

For many people today, reading Shakespeare's language can be a problem—but it is a problem that can be solved. Those who have studied Latin (or even French or German or Spanish), and those who are used to reading poetry, will have little difficulty understanding the language of Shakespeare's poetic drama. Others, though, need to develop the skills of untangling unusual sentence structures and of recognizing and understanding poetic compressions, omissions, and wordplay. And even those skilled in reading unusual sentence structures may have occasional trouble with Shakespeare's words. Four hundred years of "static" intervene between his speaking and our hearing. Most of his immense vocabulary is still in use, but a few of his words are not, and, worse, some of his words now have meanings quite different from those they had in the sixteenth and seventeenth centuries. In the theater, most of these difficulties are solved for us by actors who study the language and articulate it for us so that the essential meaning is heard—or, when combined with stage action, is at least *felt*. When reading on one's own, one must do what each actor does: go over the lines (often with a dictionary close at hand) until the puzzles are solved and the lines yield up their poetry and the characters speak in words and phrases that are, suddenly, rewarding and wonderfully memorable.

Shakespeare's Words

As you begin to read the opening scenes of a play by Shakespeare, you may notice occasional unfamiliar words. Some are unfamiliar simply because we no longer use them. In the opening scenes of *The Winter's Tale*, for example, you will find the words *sneaping* (i.e., nipping), *bawcock* (i.e., fellow), *pash* (i.e., head), and *hoxes* (i.e., cuts the hamstring muscles). Words of this kind are explained in notes to the text and will become familiar the more of Shakespeare's plays you read.

In *The Winter's Tale*, as in all of Shakespeare's writing, more problematic are the words that we still use but that we use with a different meaning. In the opening scenes of *The Winter's Tale*, for example, the word *embassies* has the meaning of "messages," *subject* is used where we would say "people," *jar o' th' clock* is used where we would say "tick of the clock," and *fabric* where we would say "edifice." Such words will be explained in the notes to the text, but they, too, will become familiar as you continue to read Shakespeare's language.

Some words are strange not because of the "static" introduced by changes in language over the past centuries but because these are words that Shakespeare is using to build a dramatic world that has its own space, time, and history. In the opening scenes of *The Winter's Tale*, for example, Shakespeare conjures up the "magnificence" (meaning "splendid ceremony, liberal expenditure, and good taste") with which "Sicilia" (i.e., King Leontes) has been entertaining his lifelong friend "Bohemia" (i.e., King Polixenes) for "nine changes of the wat'ry star," or nine months. ("Sicilia" and "Bohemia" are used to name both the kingdoms and, on occasion, their kings.) The conversation among Leontes, his queen, Hermione, and the couple's friend Polixenes recalls the kings' "unfledged days," when they were "pretty lordings." Then suddenly for no good reason Leontes suspects an affair between Hermione and his friend Polixenes; he drops out of the three-way conversation, heaps abuse on Hermione as a "slippery" wife, a "hobby-horse," and a "bed-swerver," and describes the covert sexual activity of the couple—"paddling palms," "meeting noses," "horsing foot on foot." Leontes' queen and court suffer intolerably as they are subjected to his "dangerous unsafe lunes," "tyrannous passion," "humor," and "weak-hinged fancy."

Then as suddenly as Leontes' court is transformed by his insane jealousy, the world of the play is transformed again when the scene shifts from Sicilia to the fictional seacoast and countryside of Bohemia. First, Bohemia is created as the site of terrifying natural disasters with terms such as "grimly" skies, "blusters," and "creatures of prey." Shortly thereafter, the play's language constructs it as beautiful and desirable, a place where "gillyvors," the "crown imperial," and the "flower-de-luce" grow, and the people perform in "Whitsun pastorals."

Shakespeare's Sentences

In an English sentence, meaning is quite dependent on the place given each word. "The dog bit the boy" and "The boy bit the dog" mean very different things, even though the individual words are the same. Because English places such importance on the positions of words in sentences, on the way words are arranged, unusual arrangements can puzzle a reader. Shakespeare frequently shifts his sentences away from "normal" English arrangements—often to create the rhythm he seeks, sometimes to use a line's poetic rhythm to emphasize a particular word, sometimes to give a character his or her own speech patterns or to allow the character to speak in a special way. When we attend a good performance of the play, the actors will have worked out the sentence structures and will articulate

PANDOSTO
The Triumph
of Time.

VVHEREIN IS DISCOVERED
by a pleafant Hiftorie, that although by the
meanes of finifter fortune Truth may be concealed, yet by Time in fpite offortune it
is moft manifeftly reuealed.

*Pleafant for age to auoyd drovvfie thoughts, profitable
for youth to efchue other vvanton paftimes, and
bringing to both a defired content.*

Temporis filia veritas.

By Robert Greene Maifter of Artes *in Cambridge.*

Omne tulit punctum qui mifcuit vtile dulci.

Imprinted at London for I.B. dwelling at the figne of the
Bible, neare vnto the North doore of Paules.
1 5 9 2

Title page of the novel dramatized in *The Winter's Tale.*
From Robert Greene, *Pandosto; The Triumph
of Time* . . . (1592).

Father Time. (4.1)
From Jean de Serres, *A generall historie
of France* . . . (1611).

the sentences so that the meaning is clear. (Sometimes the language of *The Winter's Tale* steadfastly resists being reduced to any clear meaning. But the actors will, nonetheless, clarify as far as the words and sentence structure allow.) In reading for yourself, do as the actor does. That is, when you become puzzled by a character's speech, check to see if words are being presented in an unusual sequence.

Shakespeare often, for example, rearranges subjects and verbs (i.e., instead of "He goes" we find "Goes he"). In *The Winter's Tale*, when Leontes says "So stands this squire" (1.2.214–15), he is using such a construction. Shakespeare also frequently places the object before the subject and verb (i.e., instead of "I hit him," we might find "Him I hit"). Hermione's "This satisfaction the bygone day proclaimed" (1.2.40–41) is an example of such an inversion, as is her "Th' offenses we have made you do we'll answer" (1.2.105). (The "normal" order would be "The bygone day proclaimed this satisfaction" and "We'll answer the offenses we have made you do.")

Inversions are not the only unusual sentence structures in Shakespeare's language. Often in his sentences words that would normally appear together are separated from each other. Again, this is often done to create a particular rhythm or to stress a particular word. Take, for example, Hermione's "But *I*, though you would seek t' unsphere the stars with oaths, *should* yet *say* 'Sir, no going'" (1.2.60–63). Here, the clause "though you would seek t' unsphere the stars with oaths" separates subject ("I") from verb ("should . . . say"), while the adverb "yet" divides the two parts of the verb "should say." Or take Leontes' lines to Camillo:

> Ay, and *thou,*
> His cupbearer—whom I from meaner form
> Have benched and reared to worship, who mayst see

Plainly as heaven sees earth and earth sees heaven
How I am galled—*mightst bespice* a cup
To give mine enemy a lasting wink.

(1.2.379–84)

Here, the subject and verb "thou mightst bespice" are interrupted by the insertion of the appositive "His cupbearer" and by two extensive clauses that emphasize, first, Leontes' past promotion of Camillo and, second, what Leontes believes is the obviousness of the offense against him. In order to create for yourself sentences that seem more like the English of everyday speech, you may wish to rearrange the words, putting together the word clusters ("I should say 'Sir, no going'"; "Thou mightst bespice a cup"). You will usually find that the sentence will gain in clarity but will lose its rhythm or shift its emphasis.

Locating and then rearranging words that "belong together" is especially necessary in passages that repeatedly separate basic sentence elements by long delaying or expanding interruptions, a common feature of dialogue in *The Winter's Tale*. One prominent example is Leontes' question to Camillo ("Ha' not you seen or heard or thought my wife is slippery?"), which becomes rather difficult to grasp because Leontes keeps interrupting himself to insist that it is impossible for Camillo not to have noticed:

LEONTES   *Ha' not you seen,* Camillo—
But that's past doubt; you have, or your eyeglass
Is thicker than a cuckold's horn—*or heard*—
For to a vision so apparent, rumor
Cannot be mute—*or thought*—for cogitation
Resides not in that man that does not think—
My wife is slippery?

(1.2.329–35)

Often in *The Winter's Tale,* rather than separating basic sentence elements, Shakespeare simply holds them back, delaying them until other material to which he wants to give greater emphasis has been presented. Shakespeare uses a version of this construction more than once in the speech in which Camillo attempts to answer Leontes' accusation that he has been negligent, foolish, and cowardly:

CAMILLO   In your affairs, my lord,
    If ever I were willful-negligent,
    It was my folly; if industriously
    I played the fool, *it was my negligence,*
    Not weighing well the end; if ever fearful
    To do a thing where I the issue doubted,
    Whereof the execution did cry out
    Against the non-performance, *'twas a fear*
    Which oft infects the wisest.

                                    (1.2.315–23)

Because Camillo does not know what he has failed to do, he is not about to confess to the accusation that Leontes has leveled against him, but Camillo is too accomplished a courtier to suggest in any way that his monarch is making a false accusation. Camillo's solution is to admit the possibility that he has failed his king in all kinds of ways, but to admit his failure only as a possibility, not as a demonstrated fact. He emphasizes the as yet only provisional status of the king's accusations by beginning each part of his excuse with a conditional clause (*"If* ever I were willful-negligent"; *"if* industriously I played the fool"; *"if* ever fearful to do a thing where I the issue doubted, whereof the execution did cry out against the non-performance").

Finally, in many of Shakespeare's plays, sentences are sometimes complicated not because of unusual structures or interruptions but because Shakespeare omits words and parts of words that English sentences normally require. (In conversation, we, too, often omit words. We say, "Heard from him yet?" and our hearer supplies the missing "Have you.") Even among Shakespeare's later plays, in all of which words are frequently omitted, *The Winter's Tale* stands out for the frequency of its omissions. Ellipsis (omission of words) is particularly evident in many of the rapid conversational exchanges that take place between characters. The following is just one example:

LEONTES   Didst note it?
CAMILLO
  He would not stay at your petitions, made
  His business more material.
LEONTES   Didst perceive it?
                                        (1.2.265–68)

To fill in these ellipses, making Leontes say "Didst [thou] note it?" and "Didst [thou] perceive it?" and having Camillo say "[He] made his business more material," not only would destroy the rhythm of the verse but would also purge the dialogue of its conversational flavor. To an extraordinary extent throughout *The Winter's Tale*, Shakespeare depends on the omission of explicit subjects before verbs to achieve an informal tone.

But he also employs ellipsis to create rising excitement in speeches. Leontes' description of what he believes has transpired between Hermione and Polixenes becomes increasingly elliptical as it proceeds:

LEONTES   Is whispering nothing?
  Is leaning cheek to cheek? Is meeting noses?
  Kissing with inside lip? Stopping the career

Of laughter with a sigh?—a note infallible
Of breaking honesty. Horsing foot on foot?
Skulking in corners? Wishing clocks more swift?
Hours minutes? Noon midnight?

(1.2.347–53)

This speech begins with a complete sentence ("Is whispering nothing?"), and this sentence provides the model for the rest of the sentences in the speech even though no other sentence fully embodies the model. Instead, as the speech goes on, its sentences become progressively more elliptical. The first sentence element to disappear is the word "nothing": "Is leaning cheek to cheek [nothing]? Is meeting noses [nothing]?" Then the verb "is" drops out so that the sentences consist only of their subjects: "[Is] kissing with inside lip [nothing]? . . . [Is] skulking in corners [nothing]? [Is] wishing clocks more swift [nothing]?" Finally, words are omitted from the subjects of the sentences as well: "[Is wishing that] hours [were] minutes [nothing]? [Is wishing that] noon [were] midnight [nothing]?" But the progression toward greater and greater ellipsis is so brilliantly controlled by the dramatist that the meaning is always clear, and the force of the (purely imaginary) intimate details that Leontes is itemizing is all the more powerful when they are unencumbered by needless repetition of other sentence elements.

Shakespearean Wordplay

Shakespeare plays with language so often and so variously that entire books are written on the topic. Here we will mention only two kinds of wordplay, puns and metaphors. Puns in *The Winter's Tale* usually play on the multiple meanings of a single word. While puns can convey a speaker's sense of superiority or delight in language, they can also appear in quite different contexts. When, for example, Leontes puns early in the play, shortly after he has been overtaken by delusions about his wife's infidelity, his wordplay conveys bitter irony. He addresses these words to his young son: "Go play, boy, play. Thy mother plays, and I / Play too, but so disgraced a part, whose issue / Will hiss me to my grave" (1.2.234–36). The meaning of the word *play* in this speech repeatedly shifts as Leontes puns on it. In "play, boy, play," it means only "amuse yourself"; but in "thy mother plays," *plays* means "amorously plays" or "has sexual intercourse," referring to the adultery of which Leontes mistakenly thinks his queen, Hermione, is guilty. Finally, when Leontes says "I play . . . so disgraced a part," the meaning of *play* changes once again in another pun, for now Leontes uses it to mean "play or act a part or role onstage." More challenging to reader and editor alike than these puns on *play* is Leontes' possible pun on *issue* when he says that the "issue [of the part I play] will hiss me to my grave." Three meanings of *issue* are at work in this speech: (1) outcome; (2) offspring; (3) exit. As a consequence, Leontes says three somewhat different things all at the same time: (1) "The *outcome* of my playing the part of the betrayed husband will be that I am hissed to my grave"; (2) "My *offspring* or descendants will hiss me to my grave because of the part I've played"; (3) "My *exit* (from the imaginary stage on which I have played my part) will be that I am hissed to my grave." Such complex linguistic play illustrates both the difficulty and the richness of *The Winter's Tale*'s language.

When Autolycus puns, his tone, in contrast to Leontes', is delight at his own superiority over those not as clever as he. In one case, for example, he steals the purses of the Shepherd's Son and his friends, who were so busy learning a song that they were unaware of the theft. He speaks of his victims as "my choughs" at "the chaff," punning on the two meanings of *choughs:* "easily captured birds" and "rustics" or "simple country people." Autolycus also puns when he is directly addressing those he regards as his inferiors. Identifying himself as a courtier, Autolycus directs the attention of the Shepherd and the Shepherd's Son to his clothes: "Seest thou not the air of the court in these enfoldings? . . . Receives not thy nose court odor from me?" (4.4.858–60). At first his phrase "air of the court" seems to mean simply "style of the court," but when he goes on to mention "court odor," then "air of the court" also comes to acquire the additional meaning "smell of the court."

A metaphor is a play on words in which one object or idea is expressed as if it were something else, something with which it shares common features. For instance, when Camillo says of the young Prince Mamillius that he "physics the subject," Camillo is using metaphorical language to describe Mamillius as, by his very existence, providing restorative medicine (then called "physic") to the subjects of Leontes' kingdom. Leontes too employs a metaphor when he says to Hermione "Three crabbèd months had soured themselves to death / Ere I could make thee open thy white hand / And clap thyself my love" (1.2.130–33). In this wordplay Leontes expresses the harshness of months of anxious waiting by, in effect, turning them into sour-tasting crabapples.

While there are many metaphors in *The Winter's Tale* and while many of them can be understood as easily as the two just analyzed, not all of them can be so readily grasped. *The Winter's Tale* contains some metaphorical passages that have successfully withstood efforts by centuries of editors and commentators to explain them. One such famous passage is Leontes' metaphorical representation of "affection":

Affection, thy intention stabs the center.
Thou dost make possible things not so held [i.e.,
    things thought impossible],
Communicat'st with dreams—how can this be?
With what's unreal thou coactive art,
And fellow'st [i.e., share in] nothing.

                                    (1.2.175–79)

All interpreters agree that Leontes is using a metaphor when he speaks of "affection" having both an "intention" and the power to stab. This metaphor is a personification because it endows the abstraction "affection" with capacities that are unique to human beings. "Center," in the first line, is also a metaphor, but it is not at all clear what this "center" is. Nor is it clear what meanings are to be attached to either "affection" or "intention." Some commentators understand Leontes to be commenting abstractly in this speech on the power of emotion (one possible meaning of "affection") to find out the truth, or to be commenting, again abstractly, on the power of passionate love (another meaning of "affection") to pierce the soul and "make possible things not so held." Others think that Leontes is addressing his own "affection"—his emotions, or passions: more specifically, his jealousy of Hermione. On this interpretation, "intention" may refer to the intensity of his feeling, and "center," according to this way of reading the passage, could mean Leontes' center, his heart, which is wounded by his jealousy—or it could even mean the center of the earth, which is shaken, for him, by his belief in Hermione's adultery. These suggestions about how to read this passage by no means exhaust the readings to which it is susceptible. (For more, see our longer note on page 238.) Irreducible uncertainty about the meaning of this passage and a

number of others in *The Winter's Tale* has led Stephen
Orgel to locate in this play a "poetics of incomprehensibility."

Implied Stage Action

Finally, in reading Shakespeare's plays we should always
remember that what we are reading is a performance
script. The dialogue is written to be spoken by actors
who, at the same time, are moving, gesturing, picking
up objects, weeping, shaking their fists. Some stage
action is described in what are called "stage directions"; some is suggested within the dialogue itself. We
must learn to be alert to such signals as we stage the
play in our imaginations. When, in *The Winter's Tale*
2.3.208–10, Leontes orders Antigonus to "Swear by this
sword / Thou wilt perform my bidding" and Antigonus
replies "I will, my lord," it is clear that a sword is placed
before Antigonus and that he places his hand on the
sword's hilt (which is in the form of a cross) as he obeys
Leontes' command to swear. When, a few lines later at
2.3.226, Antigonus says "Come on, poor babe," it is
equally clear that he then picks up a prop representing
the infant Perdita.

Occasionally in *The Winter's Tale*, signals to the reader
are not quite so clear. Earlier in the same scene in
which Antigonus picks up Perdita, for example, Leontes
repeatedly orders his attendants, and Antigonus in particular, to remove Paulina. "Away with that audacious
lady" (2.3.50), Leontes commands. Paulina remains.
"Force her hence" (76) says Leontes, and Paulina tells
his attendants: "Let him that makes but trifles of his eyes
/ First hand me. On mine own accord I'll off, / But first
I'll do my errand" (77–79). And so she does, in spite of

Leontes' exclamations: "Out! / A mankind witch! Hence with her, out o' door" (83–84). Finally, Leontes is obeyed. When he says, "Away with her!" (159), Paulina's words indicate that his lords are moving to eject her: "I pray you do not push me; . . . What needs these hands?" (160–62). It is possible to stage this scene in several ways either in a theater or in one's imagination: perhaps Leontes' lords repeatedly lay hands on her in response to the king's orders and a physically powerful Paulina resolutely, or even violently, resists their efforts until she has done her "errand." Or perhaps her words combined with her looks freeze Leontes' attendants in their places, and they never presume to approach her until just before she takes her leave. And there are a number of other possible stagings of the action. We as editors have inserted (bracketed) stage directions at what seemed to us the most probable places, but these are ultimately matters that directors and actors—and readers in their imaginations—must decide. Learning to read the language of stage action repays one many times over when one reaches a crucial scene like the statue scene in 5.3, in which implied stage action vitally affects our response to the play.

It is immensely rewarding to work carefully with Shakespeare's language—with the words, the sentences, the wordplay, and the implied stage action—as readers for the past four centuries have discovered. It may be more pleasurable to attend a good performance of a play—though not everyone has thought so. But the joy of being able to stage one of Shakespeare's plays in one's imagination, to return to passages that continue to yield further meanings (or further questions) the more one reads them—these are pleasures that, for many, rival (or at least augment) those of the performed text, and certainly make it worth considerable effort to "break the code" of Elizabethan poetic drama and let free the remarkable language that makes up a Shakespeare text.

Shakespeare's Life

Surviving documents that give us glimpses into the life of William Shakespeare show us a playwright, poet, and actor who grew up in the market town of Stratford-upon-Avon, spent his professional life in London, and returned to Stratford a wealthy landowner. He was born in April 1564, died in April 1616, and is buried inside the chancel of Holy Trinity Church in Stratford.

We wish we could know more about the life of the world's greatest dramatist. His plays and poems are testaments to his wide reading—especially to his knowledge of Virgil, Ovid, Plutarch, Holinshed's *Chronicles,* and the Bible—and to his mastery of the English language, but we can only speculate about his education. We know that the King's New School in Stratford-upon-Avon was considered excellent. The school was one of the English "grammar schools" established to educate young men, primarily in Latin grammar and literature. As in other schools of the time, students began their studies at the age of four or five in the attached "petty school," and there learned to read and write in English, studying primarily the catechism from the Book of Common Prayer. After two years in the petty school, students entered the lower form (grade) of the grammar school, where they began the serious study of Latin grammar and Latin texts that would occupy most of the remainder of their school days. (Several Latin texts that Shakespeare used repeatedly in writing his plays and poems were texts that schoolboys memorized and recited.) Latin comedies were introduced early in the lower form; in the upper form, which the boys entered at age ten or eleven, students wrote their own Latin orations and declamations, studied Latin historians and rhetoricians, and began the study of Greek using the Greek New Testament.

Since the records of the Stratford "grammar school" do not survive, we cannot prove that William Shakespeare attended the school; however, every indication (his father's position as an alderman and bailiff of Stratford, the playwright's own knowledge of the Latin classics, scenes in the plays that recall grammar-school experiences—for example, *The Merry Wives of Windsor,* 4.1) suggests that he did. We also lack generally accepted documentation about Shakespeare's life after his schooling ended and his professional life in London began. His marriage in 1582 (at age eighteen) to Anne Hathaway and the subsequent births of his daughter Susanna (1583) and the twins Judith and Hamnet (1585) are recorded, but how he supported himself and where he lived are not known. Nor do we know when and why he left Stratford for the London theatrical world, nor how he rose to be the important figure in that world that he had become by the early 1590s.

We do know that by 1592 he had achieved some prominence in London as both an actor and a playwright. In that year was published a book by the playwright Robert Greene attacking an actor who had the audacity to write blank-verse drama and who was "in his own conceit [i.e., opinion] the only Shake-scene in a country." Since Greene's attack includes a parody of a line from one of Shakespeare's early plays, there is little doubt that it is Shakespeare to whom he refers, a "Shake-scene" who had aroused Greene's fury by successfully competing with university-educated drama-

CATECHISMVS

paruus pueris primùm Latinè
qui ediscatur, proponendus
in Scholis.

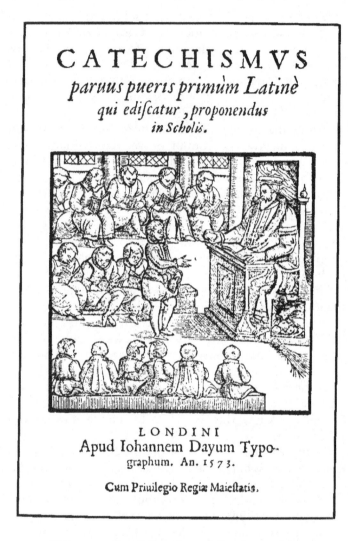

LONDINI
Apud Iohannem Dayum Typo-
graphum. An. 1573.

Cum Priuilegio Regiæ Maieſtatis.

Title page of a 1573 Latin and Greek catechism
for children.

tists like Greene himself. It was in 1593 that Shakespeare became a published poet. In that year he published his long narrative poem *Venus and Adonis;* in 1594, he followed it with *The Rape of Lucrece.* Both poems were dedicated to the young earl of Southampton (Henry Wriothesley), who may have become Shakespeare's patron.

It seems no coincidence that Shakespeare wrote these narrative poems at a time when the theaters were closed because of the plague, a contagious epidemic disease that devastated the population of London. When the theaters reopened in 1594, Shakespeare apparently resumed his double career of actor and playwright and began his long (and seemingly profitable) service as an acting-company shareholder. Records for December of 1594 show him to be a leading member of the Lord Chamberlain's Men. It was this company of actors, later named the King's Men, for whom he would be a principal actor, dramatist, and shareholder for the rest of his career.

So far as we can tell, that career spanned about twenty years. In the 1590s, he wrote his plays on English history as well as several comedies and at least two tragedies (*Titus Andronicus* and *Romeo and Juliet*). These histories, comedies, and tragedies are the plays credited to him in 1598 in a work, *Palladis Tamia*, that in one chapter compares English writers with "Greek, Latin, and Italian Poets." There the author, Francis Meres, claims that Shakespeare is comparable to the Latin dramatists Seneca for tragedy and Plautus for comedy, and calls him "the most excellent in both kinds for the stage." He also names him "Mellifluous and honey-tongued Shakespeare": "I say," writes Meres, "that the Muses would speak with Shakespeare's fine filed phrase, if they would speak English." Since Meres also mentions Shakespeare's "sugared sonnets among

A stylized representation of the Globe theater.
From Claes Jansz Visscher, *Londinum florentissima
Britanniae urbs . . .* (c. 1625).

his private friends," it is assumed that many of Shakespeare's sonnets (not published until 1609) were also written in the 1590s.

In 1599, Shakespeare's company built a theater for themselves across the river from London, naming it the Globe. The plays that are considered by many to be Shakespeare's major tragedies (*Hamlet, Othello, King Lear,* and *Macbeth*) were written while the company was resident in this theater, as were such comedies as *Twelfth Night* and *Measure for Measure*. Many of Shakespeare's plays were performed at court (both for Queen Elizabeth I and, after her death in 1603, for King James I), some were presented at the Inns of Court (the residences of London's legal societies), and some were doubtless performed in other towns, at the universities, and at great houses when the King's Men went on tour; otherwise, his plays from 1599 to 1608 were, so far as we know, performed only at the Globe. Between 1608 and 1612, Shakespeare wrote several plays—among them *The Winter's Tale* and *The Tempest*—presumably for the company's new indoor Blackfriars theater, though the plays seem to have been performed also at the Globe and at court. Surviving documents describe a performance of *The Winter's Tale* in 1611 at the Globe, for example, and performances of *The Tempest* in 1611 and 1613 at the royal palace of Whitehall.

Shakespeare wrote very little after 1612, the year in which he probably wrote *King Henry VIII.* (It was at a performance of *Henry VIII* in 1613 that the Globe caught fire and burned to the ground.) Sometime between 1610 and 1613 he seems to have returned to live in Stratford-upon-Avon, where he owned a large house and considerable property, and where his wife and his two daughters and their husbands lived. (His son Hamnet had died in 1596.) During his professional years in London, Shakespeare had presumably derived income from the acting

company's profits as well as from his own career as an
actor, from the sale of his play manuscripts to the acting
company, and, after 1599, from his shares as an owner of
the Globe. It was presumably that income, carefully
invested in land and other property, which made him the
wealthy man that surviving documents show him to
have become. It is also assumed that William Shakespeare's growing wealth and reputation played some part
in inclining the crown, in 1596, to grant John Shakespeare, William's father, the coat of arms that he had so
long sought. William Shakespeare died in Stratford on
April 23, 1616 (according to the epitaph carved under his
bust in Holy Trinity Church) and was buried on April 25.
Seven years after his death, his collected plays were published as *Mr. William Shakespeares Comedies, Histories, &
Tragedies* (the work now known as the First Folio).

The years in which Shakespeare wrote were among
the most exciting in English history. Intellectually, the
discovery, translation, and printing of Greek and
Roman classics were making available a set of works
and worldviews that interacted complexly with Christian texts and beliefs. The result was a questioning, a
vital intellectual ferment, that provided energy for the
period's amazing dramatic and literary output and that
fed directly into Shakespeare's plays. The Ghost in
Hamlet, for example, is wonderfully complicated in part
because he is a figure from Roman tragedy—the spirit
of the dead returning to seek revenge—who at the same
time inhabits a Christian hell (or purgatory); Hamlet's
description of humankind reflects at one moment the
Neoplatonic wonderment at mankind ("What a piece of
work is a man!") and, at the next, the Christian dispar-
agement of human sinners ("And yet, to me, what is
this quintessence of dust?").

As intellectual horizons expanded, so also did geographical and cosmological horizons. New worlds—

both North and South America—were explored, and in them were found human beings who lived and worshiped in ways radically different from those of Renaissance Europeans and Englishmen. The universe during these years also seemed to shift and expand. Copernicus had earlier theorized that the earth was not the center of the cosmos but revolved as a planet around the sun. Galileo's telescope, created in 1609, allowed scientists to see that Copernicus had been correct; the universe was not organized with the earth at the center, nor was it so nicely circumscribed as people had, until that time, thought. In terms of expanding horizons, the impact of these discoveries on people's beliefs—religious, scientific, and philosophical—cannot be overstated.

London, too, rapidly expanded and changed during the years (from the early 1590s to around 1610) that Shakespeare lived there. London—the center of England's government, its economy, its royal court, its overseas trade—was, during these years, becoming an exciting metropolis, drawing to it thousands of new citizens every year. Troubled by overcrowding, by poverty, by recurring epidemics of the plague, London was also a mecca for the wealthy and the aristocratic, and for those who sought advancement at court, or power in government or finance or trade. One hears in Shakespeare's plays the voices of London—the struggles for power, the fear of venereal disease, the language of buying and selling. One hears as well the voices of Stratford-upon-Avon—references to the nearby Forest of Arden, to sheep herding, to small-town gossip, to village fairs and markets. Part of the richness of Shakespeare's work is the influence felt there of the various worlds in which he lived: the world of metropolitan London, the world of small-town and rural England, the world of the theater, and the worlds of craftsmen and shepherds.

That Shakespeare inhabited such worlds we know from surviving London and Stratford documents, as

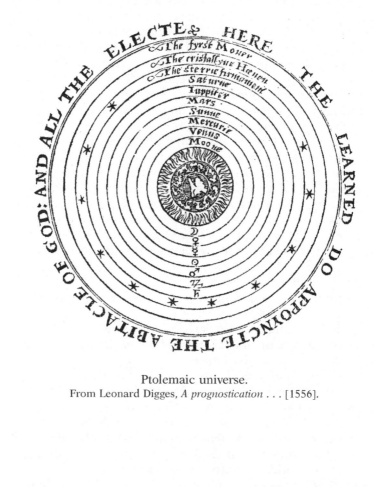

Ptolemaic universe.
From Leonard Digges, *A prognostication* . . . [1556].

well as from the evidence of the plays and poems themselves. From such records we can sketch the dramatist's life. We know from his works that he was a voracious reader. We know from legal and business documents that he was a multifaceted theater man who became a wealthy landowner. We know a bit about his family life and a fair amount about his legal and financial dealings. Most scholars today depend upon such evidence as they draw their picture of the world's greatest playwright. Such, however, has not always been the case. Until the late eighteenth century, the William Shakespeare who lived in most biographies was the creation of legend and tradition. This was the Shakespeare who was supposedly caught poaching deer at Charlecote, the estate of Sir Thomas Lucy close by Stratford; this was the Shakespeare who fled from Sir Thomas's vengeance and made his way in London by taking care of horses outside a playhouse; this was the Shakespeare who reportedly could barely read but whose natural gifts were extraordinary, whose father was a butcher who allowed his gifted son sometimes to help in the butcher shop, where William supposedly killed calves "in a high style," making a speech for the occasion. It was this legendary William Shakespeare whose Falstaff (in *1* and *2 Henry IV*) so pleased Queen Elizabeth that she demanded a play about Falstaff in love, and demanded that it be written in fourteen days (hence the existence of *The Merry Wives of Windsor*). It was this legendary Shakespeare who reached the top of his acting career in the roles of the Ghost in *Hamlet* and old Adam in *As You Like It*—and who died of a fever contracted by drinking too hard at "a merry meeting" with the poets Michael Drayton and Ben Jonson. This legendary Shakespeare is a rambunctious, undisciplined man, as attractively "wild" as his plays were seen by earlier generations to be. Unfortunately, there is no trace of evidence to support these wonderful stories.

Perhaps in response to the disreputable Shakespeare of legend—or perhaps in response to the fragmentary and, for some, all-too-ordinary Shakespeare documented by surviving records—some people since the mid–nineteenth century have argued that William Shakespeare could not have written the plays that bear his name. These persons have put forward some dozen names as more likely authors, among them Queen Elizabeth, Sir Francis Bacon, Edward de Vere (earl of Oxford), and Christopher Marlowe. Such attempts to find what for these people is a more believable author of the plays is a tribute to the regard in which the plays are held. Unfortunately for their claims, the documents that exist that provide evidence for the facts of Shakespeare's life tie him inextricably to the body of plays and poems that bear his name. Unlikely as it seems to those who want the works to have been written by an aristocrat, a university graduate, or an "important" person, the plays and poems seem clearly to have been produced by a man from Stratford-upon-Avon with a very good "grammar-school" education and a life of experience in London and in the world of the London theater. How this particular man produced the works that dominate the cultures of much of the world almost four hundred years after his death is one of life's mysteries—and one that will continue to tease our imaginations as we continue to delight in his plays and poems.

Shakespeare's Theater

The actors of Shakespeare's time are known to have performed plays in a great variety of locations. They played at court (that is, in the great halls of such royal

residences as Whitehall, Hampton Court, and Green-
wich); they played in halls at the universities of Oxford
and Cambridge, and at the Inns of Court (the residences
in London of the legal societies); and they also played in
the private houses of great lords and civic officials.
Sometimes acting companies went on tour from London into the provinces, often (but not only) when
outbreaks of bubonic plague in the capital forced the
closing of theaters to reduce the possibility of contagion
in crowded audiences. In the provinces the actors
usually staged their plays in churches (until around
1600) or in guildhalls. While surviving records show
only a handful of occasions when actors played at inns
while on tour, London inns were important playing
places up until the 1590s.

The building of theaters in London had begun only
shortly before Shakespeare wrote his first plays in the
1590s. These theaters were of two kinds: outdoor or
public playhouses that could accommodate large numbers of playgoers, and indoor or private theaters for
much smaller audiences. What is usually regarded as
the first London outdoor public playhouse was called
simply the Theatre. James Burbage—the father of Richard Burbage, who was perhaps the most famous actor in
Shakespeare's company—built it in 1576 in an area
north of the city of London called Shoreditch. Among
the more famous of the other public playhouses that
capitalized on the new fashion were the Curtain and
the Fortune (both also built north of the city), the Rose,
the Swan, the Globe, and the Hope (all located on the
Bankside, a region just across the Thames south of the
city of London). All these playhouses had to be built
outside the jurisdiction of the city of London because
many civic officials were hostile to the performance of
drama and repeatedly petitioned the royal council to
abolish it.

The theaters erected on the Bankside (a region under the authority of the Church of England, whose head was the monarch) shared the neighborhood with houses of prostitution and with the Paris Garden, where the blood sports of bearbaiting and bullbaiting were carried on. There may have been no clear distinction between playhouses and buildings for such sports, for we know that the Hope was used for both plays and baiting and that Philip Henslowe, owner of the Rose and, later, partner in the ownership of the Fortune, was also a partner in a monopoly on baiting. All these forms of entertainment were easily accessible to Londoners by boat across the Thames or over London Bridge.

Evidently Shakespeare's company prospered on the Bankside. They moved there in 1599. Threatened by difficulties in renewing the lease on the land where their first theater (the Theatre) had been built, Shakespeare's company took advantage of the Christmas holiday in 1598 to dismantle the Theatre and transport its timbers across the Thames to the Bankside, where, in 1599, these timbers were used in the building of the Globe. The weather in late December 1598 is recorded as having been especially harsh. It was so cold that the Thames was "nigh [nearly] frozen," and there was heavy snow. Perhaps the weather aided Shakespeare's company in eluding their landlord, the snow hiding their activity and the freezing of the Thames allowing them to slide the timbers across to the Bankside without paying tolls for repeated trips over London Bridge. Attractive as this narrative is, it remains just as likely that the heavy snow hampered transport of the timbers in wagons through the London streets to the river. It also must be remembered that the Thames was, according to report, only "nigh frozen" and therefore as impassable as it ever was. Whatever the precise circumstances of this fascinating event in English theater history, Shakespeare's company was able to begin playing at their new

Globe theater on the Bankside in 1599. After the first Globe burned down in 1613 during the staging of Shakespeare's *Henry VIII* (its thatch roof was set alight by cannon fire called for by the performance), Shakespeare's company immediately rebuilt on the same location. The second Globe seems to have been a grander structure than its predecessor. It remained in use until the beginning of the English Civil War in 1642, when Parliament officially closed the theaters. Soon thereafter it was pulled down.

The public theaters of Shakespeare's time were very different buildings from our theaters today. First of all, they were open-air playhouses. As recent excavations of the Rose and the Globe confirm, some were polygonal or roughly circular in shape; the Fortune, however, was square. The most recent estimates of their size put the diameter of these buildings at 72 feet (the Rose) to 100 feet (the Globe), but we know that they held vast audiences of two or three thousand, who must have been squeezed together quite tightly. Some of these spectators paid extra to sit or stand in the two or three levels of roofed galleries that extended, on the upper levels, all the way around the theater and surrounded an open space. In this space were the stage and, perhaps, the tiring house (what we would call dressing rooms), as well as the so-called yard. In the yard stood the spectators who chose to pay less, the ones whom Hamlet contemptuously called "groundlings." For a roof they had only the sky, and so they were exposed to all kinds of weather. They stood on a floor that was sometimes made of mortar and sometimes of ash mixed with the shells of hazelnuts. The latter provided a porous and therefore dry footing for the crowd, and the shells may have been more comfortable to stand on because they were not as hard as mortar. Availability of shells may not have been a problem if hazelnuts were a favorite food for Shakespeare's audiences to munch on as they watched his plays. Archaeologists who are today unearthing the remains of theaters from this period have discovered quantities of these nutshells on theater sites. Unlike the yard, the stage itself was covered by a roof. Its ceiling, called "the heavens," is thought to have been elaborately painted to depict the sun, moon, stars, and planets. Just how big the stage was remains hard to determine. We have a single sketch of part of the interior of the Swan. A Dutchman named Johannes de Witt visited this theater around 1596 and sent a sketch of it back to his friend, Arend van Buchel. Because van Buchel found de Witt's letter and sketch of interest, he copied both into a book. It is van Buchel's copy, adapted, it seems, to the shape and size of the page in his book, that survives. In this sketch, the stage appears to be a large rectangular platform that thrusts far out into the yard, perhaps even as far as the center of the circle formed by the surrounding galleries. This drawing, combined with the specifications for the size of the stage in the building contract for the Fortune, has led scholars to conjecture that the stage on which Shakespeare's plays were performed must have measured approximately 43 feet in width and 27 feet in depth, a vast acting area. But the digging up of a large part of the Rose by archaeologists has provided evidence of a quite different stage design. The Rose stage was a platform tapered at the corners and much shallower than what seems to be depicted in the van Buchel sketch. Indeed, its measurements seem to be about 37.5 feet across at its widest point and only 15.5 feet deep. Because the surviving indications of stage size and design differ from each other so much, it is possible that the stages in other theaters, like the Theatre, the Curtain, and the Globe (the outdoor playhouses where we know that Shakespeare's plays were performed), were different from those at both the Swan and the Rose.

After about 1608 Shakespeare's plays were staged not

only at the Globe but also at an indoor or private playhouse in Blackfriars. This theater had been constructed in 1596 by James Burbage in an upper hall of a former Dominican priory or monastic house. Although Henry VIII had dissolved all English monasteries in the 1530s (shortly after he had founded the Church of England), the area remained under church, rather than hostile civic, control. The hall that Burbage had purchased and renovated was a large one in which Parliament had once met. In the private theater that he constructed, the stage, lit by candles, was built across the narrow end of the hall, with boxes flanking it. The rest of the hall offered seating room only. Because there was no provision for standing room, the largest audience it could hold was less than a thousand, or about a quarter of what the Globe could accommodate. Admission to Blackfriars was correspondingly more expensive. Instead of a penny to stand in the yard at the Globe, it cost a minimum of sixpence to get into Blackfriars. The best seats at the Globe (in the Lords' Room in the gallery above and behind the stage) cost sixpence; but the boxes flanking the stage at Blackfriars were half a crown, or five times sixpence. Some spectators who were particularly interested in displaying themselves paid even more to sit on stools on the Blackfriars stage.

Whether in the outdoor or indoor playhouses, the stages of Shakespeare's time were different from ours. They were not separated from the audience by the dropping of a curtain between acts and scenes. Therefore the playwrights of the time had to find other ways of signaling to the audience that one scene (to be imagined as occurring in one location at a given time) had ended and the next (to be imagined at perhaps a different location at a later time) had begun. The customary way used by Shakespeare and many of his contemporaries was to have everyone onstage exit at the end of one scene and have one or more different characters enter to begin the next. In a few cases, where characters remain onstage from one scene to another, the dialogue or stage action makes the change of location clear, and the characters are generally to be imagined as having moved from one place to another. For example, in *Romeo and Juliet,* Romeo and his friends remain on- stage in Act 1 from scene 4 to scene 5, but they are represented as having moved between scenes from the street that leads to Capulet's house into Capulet's house itself. The new location is signaled in part by the appearance onstage of Capulet's servingmen carrying napkins, something they would not take into the streets. Playwrights had to be quite resourceful in the use of hand properties, like the napkin, or in the use of dialogue to specify where the action was taking place in their plays because, in contrast to most of today's theaters, the playhouses of Shakespeare's time did not use movable scenery to dress the stage and make the setting precise. As another consequence of this differ- ence, however, the playwrights of Shakespeare's time did not have to specify exactly where the action of their plays was set when they did not choose to do so, and much of the action of their plays is tied to no specific place.

Usually Shakespeare's stage is referred to as a "bare stage," to distinguish it from the stages of the last two or three centuries with their elaborate sets. But the stage in Shakespeare's time was not completely bare. Philip Henslowe, owner of the Rose, lists in his inventory of stage properties a rock, three tombs, and two mossy banks. Stage directions in plays of the time also call for such things as thrones (or "states"), banquets (presum- ably tables with plaster replicas of food on them), and beds and tombs to be pushed onto the stage. Thus the stage often held more than the actors.

The actors did not limit their performing to the stage alone. Occasionally they went beneath the stage, as the Ghost appears to do in the first act of *Hamlet*. From there they could emerge onto the stage through a trapdoor. They could retire behind the hangings across the back of the stage (or the front of the tiring house), as, for example, the actor playing Polonius does when he hides behind the arras. Sometimes the hangings could be drawn back during a performance to "discover" one or more actors behind them. When performance required that an actor appear "above," as when Juliet is imagined to stand at the window of her chamber in the famous and misnamed "balcony scene," then the actor probably climbed the stairs to the gallery over the back of the stage and temporarily shared it with some of the spectators. The stage was also provided with ropes and winches so that actors could descend from, and reascend to, the "heavens."

Perhaps the greatest difference between dramatic performances in Shakespeare's time and ours was that in Shakespeare's England the roles of women were played by boys. (Some of these boys grew up to take male roles in their maturity.) There were no women in the acting companies, only in the audience. It had not always been so in the history of the English stage. There are records of women on English stages in the thirteenth and fourteenth centuries, two hundred years before Shakespeare's plays were performed. After the accession of James I in 1603, the queen of England and her ladies took part in entertainments at court called masques, and with the reopening of the theaters in 1660 at the restoration of Charles II, women again took their place on the public stage.

The chief competitors for the companies of adult actors such as the one to which Shakespeare belonged and for which he wrote were companies of exclusively boy actors. The competition was most intense in the early 1600s. There were then two principal children's companies: the Children of Paul's (the choirboys from St. Paul's Cathedral, whose private playhouse was near the cathedral); and the Children of the Chapel Royal (the choirboys from the monarch's private chapel, who performed at the Blackfriars theater built by Burbage in 1596, which Shakespeare's company had been stopped from using by local residents who objected to crowds). In *Hamlet* Shakespeare writes of "an aerie [nest] of children, little eyases [hawks], that cry out on the top of question and are most tyrannically clapped for 't. These are now the fashion and . . . berattle the common stages [attack the public theaters]." In the long run, the adult actors prevailed. The Children of Paul's dissolved around 1606. By about 1608 the Children of the Chapel Royal had been forced to stop playing at the Blackfriars theater, which was then taken over by the King's Men, Shakespeare's own troupe.

Acting companies and theaters of Shakespeare's time were organized in different ways. For example, Philip Henslowe owned the Rose and leased it to companies of actors, who paid him from their takings. Henslowe would act as manager of these companies, initially paying playwrights for their plays and buying properties, recovering his outlay from the actors. Shakespeare's company, however, managed itself, with the principal actors, Shakespeare among them, having the status of "sharers" and the right to a share in the takings, as well as the responsibility for a part of the expenses. Five of the sharers themselves, Shakespeare among them, owned the Globe. As actor, as sharer in an acting company and in ownership of theaters, and as playwright, Shakespeare was about as involved in the theatrical industry as one could imagine. Although Shakespeare and his fellows prospered, their status under the law was conditional upon the protection of powerful patrons. "Common players"—those who did not have patrons or masters—were classed in the language of the law with "vagabonds and sturdy beggars." So the actors had to secure for themselves the official rank of servants of patrons. Among the patrons under whose protection Shakespeare's company worked were the lord chamberlain and, after the accession of King James in 1603, the king himself.

We are now perhaps on the verge of learning a great deal more about the theaters in which Shakespeare and his contemporaries performed—or at least of opening up new questions about them. Already about 70 percent of the Rose has been excavated, as has about 10 percent of the second Globe, the one built in 1614. It is to be hoped that soon more will be available for study. These are exciting times for students of Shakespeare's stage.

The Publication of Shakespeare's Plays

Eighteen of Shakespeare's plays found their way into print during the playwright's lifetime, but there is nothing to suggest that he took any interest in their publication. These eighteen appeared separately in editions called quartos. Their pages were not much larger than the one you are now reading, and these little books were sold unbound for a few pence. The earliest of the quartos that still survive were printed in 1594, the year that both *Titus Andronicus* and a version of the play now called *2 King Henry VI* became available. While almost every one of these early quartos displays on its title page the name of the acting company that performed the play, only about half provide the name of the playwright, Shakespeare. The first quarto edition to bear the name Shakespeare on its title page is *Love's Labor's Lost* of 1598. A few of these quartos were popular with the book-buying public of Shakespeare's lifetime; for example, quarto *Richard II* went through five editions between 1597 and 1615. But most of the quartos were far from best-sellers; *Love's Labor's Lost* (1598), for instance, was not reprinted in quarto until 1631. After Shakespeare's death, two more of his plays appeared in quarto format: *Othello* in 1622 and *The Two Noble Kinsmen*, coauthored with John Fletcher, in 1634.

In 1623, seven years after Shakespeare's death, *Mr. William Shakespeares Comedies, Histories, & Tragedies* was published. This printing offered readers in a single book thirty-six of the thirty-eight plays now thought to have been written by Shakespeare, including eighteen that had never been printed before. And it offered them in a style that was then reserved for serious literature and scholarship. The plays were arranged in double columns on pages nearly a foot high. This large page size is called "folio," as opposed to the smaller "quarto," and the 1623 volume is usually called the Shakespeare First Folio. It is reputed to have sold for the lordly price of a pound. (One copy at the Folger Library is marked fifteen shillings—that is, three-quarters of a pound.)

In a preface to the First Folio entitled "To the great Variety of Readers," two of Shakespeare's former fellow actors in the King's Men, John Heminge and Henry Condell, wrote that they themselves had collected their dead companion's plays. They suggested that they had seen his own papers: "we have scarce received from him a blot in his papers." The title page of the Folio declared that the plays within it had been printed "according to the True Original Copies." Comparing the Folio to the quartos, Heminge and Condell disparaged the quartos, advising their readers that "before you were abused with divers stolen and surreptitious copies, maimed, and deformed by the frauds and stealths of injurious impostors." Many Shakespeareans of the eighteenth and nineteenth centuries believed Heminge and Condell and regarded the Folio plays as superior to anything in the quartos.

Once we begin to examine the Folio plays in detail, it becomes less easy to take at face value the word of Heminge and Condell about the superiority of the Folio texts. For example, of the first nine plays in the Folio (one quarter of the entire collection), four were essentially reprinted from earlier quarto printings that Heminge and Condell had disparaged; and four have now been identified as printed from copies written in the hand of a professional scribe of the 1620s named Ralph Crane; the ninth, *The Comedy of Errors,* was apparently also printed from a manuscript, but one whose origin cannot be readily identified. Evidently then, eight of the first nine plays in the First Folio were not printed, in spite of what the Folio title page announces, "according to the True Original Copies," or Shakespeare's own papers, and the source of the ninth is unknown. Since today's editors have been forced to treat Heminge and Condell's pronouncements with skepticism, they must choose whether to base their own editions upon quartos or the Folio on grounds other than Heminge and Condell's story of where the quarto and Folio versions originated.

Editors have often fashioned their own narratives to explain what lies behind the quartos and Folio. They have said that Heminge and Condell meant to criticize only a few of the early quartos, the ones that offer much shorter and sometimes quite different, often garbled, versions of plays. Among the examples of these are the 1600 quarto of *Henry V* (the Folio offers a much fuller version) or the 1603 *Hamlet* quarto (in 1604 a different, much longer form of the play got into print as a quarto). Early in this century editors speculated that these questionable texts were produced when someone in the audience took notes from the plays' dialogue during performances and then employed "hack poets" to fill out the notes. The poor results were then sold to a publisher and presented in print as Shakespeare's plays. More recently this story has given way to another in which the shorter versions are said to be re-creations from memory of Shakespeare's plays by actors who wanted to stage them in the provinces but lacked manuscript copies. Most of the quartos offer much better texts than these so-called bad quartos. Indeed, in most of the quartos we find texts that are at least equal to or better than what is printed in the Folio. Many of this century's Shakespeare enthusiasts have persuaded themselves that most of the quartos were set into type directly from Shakespeare's own papers, although there is nothing on which to base this conclusion except the desire for it to be true. Thus speculation continues about how the Shakespeare plays got to be printed. All that we have are the printed texts.

The book collector who was most successful in bringing together copies of the quartos and the First Folio was Henry Clay Folger, founder of the Folger Shakespeare Library in Washington, D.C. While it is estimated that there survive around the world only about 230 copies of the First Folio, Mr. Folger was able to acquire more than seventy-five copies, as well as a large number of fragments, for the library that bears his name. He also amassed a substantial number of quartos. For example, only fourteen copies of the First Quarto of *Love's Labor's Lost* are known to exist, and three are at the Folger Shakespeare Library. As a consequence of Mr. Folger's labors, twentieth-century scholars visiting the

Folger Library have been able to learn a great deal about sixteenth- and seventeenth-century printing and, particularly, about the printing of Shakespeare's plays. And Mr. Folger did not stop at the First Folio, but collected many copies of later editions of Shakespeare, beginning with the Second Folio (1632), the Third (1663–64), and the Fourth (1685). Each of these later folios was based on its immediate predecessor and was edited anonymously. The first editor of Shakespeare whose name we know was Nicholas Rowe, whose first edition came out in 1709. Mr. Folger collected this edition and many, many more by Rowe's successors.

An Introduction to This Text

The Winter's Tale was first printed in the 1623 collection of Shakespeare's plays now known as the First Folio. The present edition is based directly upon that printing.* For the convenience of the reader, we have modernized the punctuation and the spelling of the Folio. Sometimes we go so far as to modernize certain old forms of words; for example, when *a* means "he," we change it to *he;* we change *mo* to *more,* and *ye* to *you.* But it is not our practice in editing any of the plays to modernize words that sound distinctly different from modern forms. For example, when the early printed texts read *sith* or *apricocks* or *porpentine,* we have not modernized to *since, apricots, porcupine.* When the forms *an, and,* or *and if* appear instead of the modern form *if,* we have

---

*We have also consulted the computerized text of the First Folio provided by the Text Archive of the Oxford University Computing Centre, to which we are grateful.

reduced *and* to *an* but have not changed any of these forms to their modern equivalent, *if*. We also modernize and, where necessary, correct passages in foreign languages, unless an error in the early printed text can be reasonably explained as a joke.

Whenever we change the wording of the First Folio or add anything to its stage directions, we mark the change by enclosing it in superior half-brackets (⌐ ⌐). We want our readers to be immediately aware when we have intervened. (Only when we correct an obvious typographical error in the First Folio does the change not get marked.) Whenever we change either the First Folio's wording or its punctuation so that meaning changes, we list the change in the textual notes at the back of the book, even if all we have done is fix an obvious error.

We regularize spellings of a number of the proper names, as is the usual practice in editions of the play. For example, the Folio once calls Florizell "Florizel," but we use the Folio's standard spelling "Florizell" throughout the text. The Folio employs the spellings "Cleomines" and "Autolicus," which we normalize to their standard spellings in classical literature: "Cleomenes" and "Autolycus."

This edition differs from many earlier ones in its efforts to aid the reader in imagining the play as a performance rather than as a series of actual events. Thus stage directions are written with reference to the stage. For example, when in 4.3 the Shepherd's Son names the items that he has been sent to buy for the sheepshearing feast, he appears to be reading a written list: "Three pound of sugar, five pound of currants, rice—what will this sister of mine do with rice?" (39–41). However, many editors are reluctant to include a stage direction to indicate that he is reading because, as is well known, it is most unlikely that an actual early-seventeenth-century shepherd would have been literate. We add the direction *"He reads a paper"* because the dialogue signals that he is, in fact, reading, and we want to present him as the stage shepherd that he is, not as an actual shepherd. Whenever it is reasonably certain, in our view, that a speech is accompanied by a particular action, we provide a stage direction describing the action. (Occasional exceptions to this rule occur when the action is so obvious that to add a stage direction would insult the reader.) Stage directions for the entrance of a character in midscene are, with rare exceptions, placed so that they immediately precede the character's participation in the scene, even though these entrances may appear somewhat earlier in the early printed texts. Whenever we move a stage direction, we record this change in the textual notes. Latin stage directions (e.g., *Exeunt*) are translated into English (e.g., *They exit*).

We expand the often severely abbreviated forms of names used as speech headings in early printed texts into the full names of the characters. We also regularize the speakers' names in speech headings, using only a single designation for each character, even though the early printed texts sometimes use a variety of designations. Variations in the speech headings of the early printed texts are recorded in the textual notes.

In the present edition, as well, we mark with a dash any change of address within a speech, unless a stage direction intervenes. When the *-ed* ending of a word is to be pronounced, we mark it with an accent. Like editors for the past two centuries, we print metrically linked lines in the following way:

HERMIONE
He'll stay, my lord.
LEONTES   At my request he would not.
(1.2.110–11)

However, when there are a number of short verse-lines that can be linked in more than one way, we do not, with rare exceptions, indent any of them.

The Explanatory Notes

The notes that appear on the pages facing the text are designed to provide readers with the help that they may need to enjoy the play. Whenever the meaning of a word in the text is not readily accessible in a good contemporary dictionary, we offer the meaning in a note. Sometimes we provide a note even when the relevant meaning is to be found in the dictionary but when the word has acquired since Shakespeare's time other potentially confusing meanings. In our notes, we try to offer modern synonyms for Shakespeare's words. We also try to indicate to the reader the connection between the word in the play and the modern synonym. For example, Shakespeare sometimes uses the word *head* to mean "source," but, for modern readers, there may be no connection evident between these two words. We provide the connection by explaining Shakespeare's usage as follows: "**head:** fountainhead, source." On some occasions, a whole phrase or clause needs explanation. Then we rephrase in our own words the difficult passage, and add at the end synonyms for individual words in the passage. When scholars have been unable to determine the meaning of a word or phrase, we acknowledge the uncertainty.

THE
WINTER'S TALE

The Names of the Actors.

Leontes, *King of Sicillia.*
Mamillus, *yong Prince of Sicillia.*
Camillo.
Antigonus.
Cleomines.   *Foure*
Dion.   *Lords of Sicillia.*
Hermione, *Queene to Leontes.*
Perdita, *Daughter to Leontes and Hermione.*
Paulina, *wife to Antigonus.*
Emilia, *a Lady.*
Polixenes, *King of Bohemia.*
Florizell, *Prince of Bohemia.*
Old Shepheard, *reputed Father of Perdita.*
Clowne, *his Sonne.*
Autolicus, *a Rogue.*
Archidamus, *a Lord of Bohemia.*
Other Lords, *and Gentlemen, and Seruants.*
Shepheards, *and Shephearddesses.*

From the 1623 First Folio.

Characters in the Play

LEONTES, King of SICILIA
HERMIONE, Queen of Sicilia
MAMILLIUS, their son
PERDITA, their daughter

POLIXENES, King of BOHEMIA
FLORIZELL, his son

CAMILLO, a courtier, friend to Leontes and then to
    Polixenes
ANTIGONUS, a Sicilian courtier
PAULINA, his wife and lady-in-waiting to Hermione
CLEOMENES ⎫
          ⎬ courtiers in Sicilia
DION   ⎭
EMILIA, a lady-in-waiting to Hermione

SHEPHERD, foster father to Perdita
SHEPHERD'S SON
AUTOLYCUS, former servant to Florizell, now a rogue
ARCHIDAMUS, a Bohemian courtier

TIME, as Chorus

TWO LADIES attending on Hermione
LORDS, SERVANTS, and GENTLEMEN attending on Leontes
An OFFICER of the court
A MARINER
A JAILER
MOPSA ⎫
       ⎬ shepherdesses in Bohemia
DORCAS ⎭
SERVANT to the Shepherd

SHEPHERDS and SHEPHERDESSES
Twelve COUNTRYMEN disguised as satyrs

3

THE
WINTER'S TALE

ACT 1

1.1 Archidamus, a Bohemian courtier, exclaims about the magnificent hospitality he has found in Sicilia. Camillo explains about the long friendship between the kings of the two countries. Both noblemen agree that Mamillius, Sicilia's prince, shows promise of greatness.

---

1. **shall:** i.e., should

2–3. **on the . . . foot:** i.e., on an occasion similar to the one in which I am now employed

6. **Bohemia:** i.e., Polixenes, king of Bohemia; **visitation:** friendly visit

8. **Wherein:** i.e., during which; **entertainment:** hospitality

10. **Beseech:** i.e., I beseech

12. **magnificence:** splendid ceremony; liberal expenditure combined with good taste

14. **sleepy drinks:** i.e., **drinks** that will put you to sleep; **unintelligent of:** i.e., unable to perceive

15. **insufficience:** i.e., insufficiency

17. **dear:** i.e., dearly

22–23. **Sicilia . . . Bohemia:** i.e., Leontes . . . Polixenes **over-kind:** too kind

23. **trained:** (1) brought up; (2) made to grow in a particular way, like plants (The gardening metaphor introduced by this second meaning is picked up in **rooted** [line 24] and in **branch** [line 25].)

ACT 1

Scene 1
Enter Camillo and Archidamus.

ARCHIDAMUS If you shall chance, Camillo, to visit Bohemia on the like occasion whereon my services
are now on foot, you shall see, as I have said, great
difference betwixt our Bohemia and your Sicilia.

CAMILLO I think this coming summer the King of   5
Sicilia means to pay Bohemia the visitation which
he justly owes him.

ARCHIDAMUS Wherein our entertainment shall shame
us; we will be justified in our loves. For indeed—

CAMILLO Beseech you—   10

ARCHIDAMUS Verily, I speak it in the freedom of my
knowledge. We cannot with such magnificence—in
so rare—I know not what to say. We will give you
sleepy drinks, that your senses, unintelligent of our
insufficience, may, though they cannot praise us, as 15
little accuse us.

CAMILLO You pay a great deal too dear for what's given
freely.

ARCHIDAMUS Believe me, I speak as my understanding
instructs me and as mine honesty puts it to utter-   20
ance.

CAMILLO Sicilia cannot show himself over-kind to Bohemia. They were trained together in their child-
hoods, and there rooted betwixt them then such an

7

25. **cannot choose:** i.e., cannot help
26–27. **their more mature dignities and royal necessities:** i.e., the positions and duties that come with maturity and kingship
27. **made . . . society:** severed their companionship
28. **personal:** in person; **hath:** i.e., have
29. **attorneyed:** performed by agents
30. **embassies:** messages; **that they:** i.e., so that Leontes and Polixenes
31. **as . . . vast:** i.e., as if over an ocean
32–33. **ends . . . winds:** i.e., widely distant regions (For "Opposed winds," see page 50.)
33. **The heavens:** i.e., "May the heavens . . ."; or, perhaps, "Thus the heavens . . ."
35. **matter:** cause, reason
35–36. **unspeakable:** inexpressible
36. **of your:** i.e., in your; **It:** i.e., he
38. **into my note:** to my notice or knowledge
40. **gallant:** a general term of praise; **physics:** i.e., relieves (literally, provides medicine to)
41. **subject:** subjects, people

1.2 Leontes suddenly grows insanely jealous of the friendship between his queen, Hermione, and his visiting friend Polixenes. Leontes forces Camillo to promise to murder Polixenes. Camillo informs Polixenes of the murder threat and the two plan a hasty departure for Bohemia.

_____

0 SD. **Camillo:** See longer note, page 237.

(continued)

affection which cannot choose but branch now.   25
Since their more mature dignities and royal necessities made separation of their society, their en-
counters, though not personal, hath been royally
attorneyed with interchange of gifts, letters, loving
embassies, that they have seemed to be together   30
though absent, shook hands as over a vast, and
embraced as it were from the ends of opposed
winds. The heavens continue their loves.

ARCHIDAMUS   I think there is not in the world either
malice or matter to alter it. You have an unspeak-   35
able comfort of your young Prince Mamillius. It is a
gentleman of the greatest promise that ever came
into my note.

CAMILLO   I very well agree with you in the hopes of
him. It is a gallant child—one that indeed physics   40
the subject, makes old hearts fresh. They that went
on crutches ere he was born desire yet their life to
see him a man.

ARCHIDAMUS   Would they else be content to die?

CAMILLO   Yes, if there were no other excuse why they   45
should desire to live.

ARCHIDAMUS   If the King had no son, they would desire
to live on crutches till he had one.

They exit.

Scene 2
Enter Leontes, Hermione, Mamillius, Polixenes, Camillo,
⌜*and Attendants.*⌝

POLIXENES
Nine changes of the wat'ry star hath been
The shepherd's note since we have left our throne
Without a burden. Time as long again

1. **wat'ry star:** i.e., the moon, called "wat'ry" because it controls the tides (See page 16.)

2. **note:** sign (of nine months passing); **we, our:** i.e., I, my (Polixenes, Leontes, and Hermione all vary between referring to themselves in the singular ["I," "my"] and using the "royal we.")

3. **Without a burden:** i.e., empty

6–9. **like . . . before it:** In this complicated metaphor, Polixenes (or his **one "We thank you"**) is likened to the numerical zero. Valueless when standing alone, a zero at the end of a number multiplies the value of that which goes **before it.**

10. **Stay:** hold back

13–16. **I am . . . truly:** i.e., I am tormented by anxiety about affairs in my kingdom during my absence **sneaping:** nipping (See longer note, page 237.)

16. **stayed:** i.e., stayed so long as

17. **your Royalty:** perhaps, your Majesty (i.e., you)

19. **you . . . to 't:** i.e., any trial you can make of me

21. **sev'nnight:** week

22. **Very sooth:** i.e., in truth (a very mild oath)

23. **part:** i.e., divide equally; **'s:** i.e., us

24. **I'll:** i.e., I'll endure; **gainsaying:** contradiction

26–28. **There . . . me:** i.e., no one could persuade me more readily than you

32. **whip:** blow (as from a whip)

33. **charge:** burden

Would be filled up, my brother, with our thanks,
And yet we should for perpetuity   5
Go hence in debt. And therefore, like a cipher,
Yet standing in rich place, I multiply
With one "We thank you" many thousands more
That go before it.
LEONTES   Stay your thanks awhile,   10
And pay them when you part.
POLIXENES   Sir, that's tomorrow.
I am questioned by my fears of what may chance
Or breed upon our absence, that may blow
No sneaping winds at home to make us say   15
"This is put forth too truly." Besides, I have stayed
To tire your Royalty.
LEONTES   We are tougher, brother,
Than you can put us to 't.
POLIXENES   No longer stay.   20
LEONTES
One sev'nnight longer.
POLIXENES   Very sooth, tomorrow.
LEONTES
We'll part the time between 's, then, and in that
I'll no gainsaying.
POLIXENES   Press me not, beseech you, so.   25
There is no tongue that moves, none, none i' th'
    world,
So soon as yours could win me. So it should now,
Were there necessity in your request, although
'Twere needful I denied it. My affairs   30
Do even drag me homeward, which to hinder
Were in your love a whip to me, my stay
To you a charge and trouble. To save both,
Farewell, our brother.
LEONTES   Tongue-tied, our queen?   35
    Speak you.

39. **Charge:** exhort, urge

40. **satisfaction:** assurance

41. **The bygone day:** the past day (perhaps, yesterday); **proclaimed:** made known

42. **beat . . . ward:** i.e., soundly defeated **beat:** i.e., beaten **ward:** defensive position

44. **To tell:** i.e., for him to say that; **strong:** i.e., a strong reason for going

47. **distaffs:** staffs used in spinning thread (hence symbolic of female authority) See page 46.

49. **adventure:** risk

50. **borrow:** borrowing

50–51. **When . . . lord:** i.e., when you have Leontes visit you in Bohemia **take:** receive

52. **let him:** i.e., stay, remain

52–53. **behind . . . parting:** beyond the date arranged in advance for his departure

53. **good deed:** indeed

54. **jar:** tick

54–55. **behind . . . lord:** i.e., less than any **lady** whatsoever loves **her lord**

56–108. **No, madam . . . with us:** See longer note, page 237.

58. **verily:** i.e., truly (a very mild oath)

60. **limber:** soft, weak; **vows:** oaths

61. **unsphere the stars:** i.e., dislodge **the stars** and the planets from the crystalline spheres that, according to Ptolemaic astronomy, carried them around the earth (See page xxxviii.)

66. **Force:** i.e., if you force

67. **so you shall:** i.e., you shall; **pay your fees:** As a **prisoner,** he would be expected to pay **fees** to the jailer when released.

HERMIONE
  I had thought, sir, to have held my peace until
  You had drawn oaths from him not to stay. You, sir,
  Charge him too coldly. Tell him you are sure
  All in Bohemia's well. This satisfaction   40
  The bygone day proclaimed. Say this to him,
  He's beat from his best ward.
LEONTES   Well said, Hermione.
HERMIONE
  To tell he longs to see his son were strong.
  But let him say so then, and let him go.   45
  But let him swear so and he shall not stay;
  We'll thwack him hence with distaffs.
  ⌜*To Polixenes.*⌝ Yet of your royal presence I'll
    adventure
  The borrow of a week. When at Bohemia   50
  You take my lord, I'll give him my commission
  To let him there a month behind the gest
  Prefixed for 's parting.—Yet, good deed, Leontes,
  I love thee not a jar o' th' clock behind
  What lady she her lord.—You'll stay?   55
POLIXENES   No, madam.
HERMIONE
  Nay, but you will?
POLIXENES   I may not, verily.
HERMIONE   Verily?
  You put me off with limber vows. But I,   60
  Though you would seek t' unsphere the stars with
    oaths,
  Should yet say "Sir, no going." Verily,
  You shall not go. A lady's "verily" is
  As potent as a lord's. Will you go yet?   65
  Force me to keep you as a prisoner,
  Not like a guest, so you shall pay your fees
  When you depart and save your thanks. How say you?

72. **import offending:** i.e., imply I was guilty of an offense

74. **Than you:** i.e., than it is for you

78. **pretty lordings:** fine little lords

80. **behind:** i.e., in the future

84. **verier wag:** more mischievous boy

86. **changed:** exchanged

87–88. **knew . . . ill-doing:** i.e., had no knowledge of evil

90. **spirits:** invisible, barely material entities carried throughout the body in the veins, arteries, and nerves; **higher reared:** i.e., made more active

91. **stronger blood:** i.e., the hotter and thicker **blood** of the mature male

91–92. **we . . . heaven:** i.e., we would have been able to answer God (The reference is to the Christian concept of a judgment after death of our actions on earth.)

93–94. **the imposition . . . ours:** i.e., innocent even of original sin; or, innocent except for original sin **the imposition cleared:** (1) freed from the accusation or charge, or (2) except for the accusation or charge **Hereditary ours:** i.e., inherited from Adam and Eve by all humans (See Romans 5.12–21.)

96. **tripped:** i.e., sinned ("Trip" could also mean, specifically, "copulate.")

97. **sacred:** i.e., royal, noble

98. **'s:** i.e., us

101. **playfellow:** playmate

102. **Grace to boot:** i.e., Heaven help us

103. **this:** i.e., this line of reasoning

My prisoner or my guest? By your dread "verily,"
One of them you shall be.　　　　　　　　　　70
POLIXENES　　　　　　　　Your guest, then, madam.
　To be your prisoner should import offending,
　Which is for me less easy to commit
　Than you to punish.
HERMIONE　　　　　　Not your jailer, then,　　75
　But your kind hostess. Come, I'll question you
　Of my lord's tricks and yours when you were boys.
　You were pretty lordings then?
POLIXENES　　　　　　　　　We were, fair queen,
　Two lads that thought there was no more behind　80
　But such a day tomorrow as today,
　And to be boy eternal.
HERMIONE　　　　　　Was not my lord
　The verier wag o' th' two?
POLIXENES
　We were as twinned lambs that did frisk i' th' sun　85
　And bleat the one at th' other. What we changed
　Was innocence for innocence. We knew not
　The doctrine of ill-doing, nor dreamed
　That any did. Had we pursued that life,
　And our weak spirits ne'er been higher reared　90
　With stronger blood, we should have answered
　　heaven
　Boldly "Not guilty," the imposition cleared
　Hereditary ours.
HERMIONE　　　　　By this we gather　　95
　You have tripped since.
POLIXENES　　　　　　　O my most sacred lady,
　Temptations have since then been born to 's, for
　In those unfledged days was my wife a girl;
　Your precious self had then not crossed the eyes　100
　Of my young playfellow.
HERMIONE　　　　　　　Grace to boot!
　Of this make no conclusion, lest you say

105. **answer:** i.e., answer for

106–7. **that ... that:** i.e., if ... if **continue fault:** i.e., continue to offend

119. **tongueless:** not spoken of

120. **waiting upon that:** i.e., accompanying it

121. **ride 's:** perhaps, ride me, or, perhaps, ride women (The sexual implications of **ride** may continue in **kiss, spur,** and **heat.**)

123. **heat ... acre:** perhaps, race one furlong

126. **would:** i.e., I wish; **Grace:** (1) a name for a woman; (2) a gracious deed worthy of praise

127. **But:** only

130. **crabbèd:** harsh (alluding to the sour taste of the crab apple)

132–33. **open ... love:** a reference to the custom of handfasting, in which a couple clasped hands and declared their intention to marry

136. **lo:** look

"The wat'ry star." (1.2.1)
From Laurentius Wolffgang Woyt, . . . *Emblematischer Parnassus* . . . (1728–30).

Your queen and I are devils. Yet go on.
Th' offenses we have made you do we'll answer,   105
If you first sinned with us, and that with us
You did continue fault, and that you slipped not
With any but with us.
LEONTES   Is he won yet?
HERMIONE
He'll stay, my lord.   110
LEONTES   At my request he would not.
Hermione, my dearest, thou never spok'st
To better purpose.
HERMIONE   Never?
LEONTES   Never but once.   115
HERMIONE
What, have I twice said well? When was 't before?
I prithee tell me. Cram 's with praise, and make 's
As fat as tame things. One good deed dying
    tongueless
Slaughters a thousand waiting upon that.   120
Our praises are our wages. You may ride 's
With one soft kiss a thousand furlongs ere
With spur we heat an acre. But to th' goal:
My last good deed was to entreat his stay.
What was my first? It has an elder sister,   125
Or I mistake you. O, would her name were Grace!
But once before I spoke to th' purpose? When?
Nay, let me have 't; I long.
LEONTES   Why, that was when
Three crabbèd months had soured themselves to   130
    death
Ere I could make thee open thy white hand
⌜And⌝ clap thyself my love; then didst thou utter
"I am yours forever."
HERMIONE   'Tis grace indeed.   135
Why, lo you now, I have spoke to th' purpose twice.

137. **one:** i.e., first

138. **friend:** In line 140, Leontes plays with the secondary meaning of **friend** as "lover."

139. **hot:** lustful

140. **mingling bloods:** According to Aristotle, sexual intercourse was the **mingling** of **bloods.**

141. **tremor cordis:** agitation of the heart

142. **entertainment:** i.e., manner of social behavior (The word could also mean "hospitality," "manner of reception," and "spending of time," all of which may be present here and in line 149.)

143. **free:** innocent; **a liberty:** i.e., permission

144. **heartiness:** genuine friendliness; **fertile bosom:** i.e., from a generous heart

145. **well become:** do credit to

146. **paddling:** playfully or fondly fingering

149. **mort . . . deer:** note sounded on a hunter's horn at the death of the **deer**

150. **brows:** In popular thought, the cuckold (the man whose wife is unfaithful) sprouts horns on his forehead. (See page 48.)

153. **I' fecks:** i.e., in faith

154. **bawcock:** fellow (French *beau coq*, "fine bird")

156. **out of:** taken from

157. **neat:** Leontes rejects the adjective **neat**, because, as he makes clear in line 159, the noun **neat** refers to cattle and the word thus reminds him of horns. (See line 150.)

158. **the steer, the heifer, and the calf:** young cattle that have yet to grow horns **steer:** young ox

159. **virginalling:** tapping as on a virginal (a small keyboard instrument)

(continued)

The one forever earned a royal husband,
Th' other for some while a friend.
                    ⌐*She gives Polixenes her hand.*⌐
LEONTES, ⌐*aside*⌐   Too hot, too hot!
To mingle friendship far is mingling bloods.   140
I have *tremor cordis* on me. My heart dances,
But not for joy, not joy. This entertainment
May a free face put on, derive a liberty
From heartiness, from bounty, fertile bosom,
And well become the agent. 'T may, I grant.   145
But to be paddling palms and pinching fingers,
As now they are, and making practiced smiles
As in a looking glass, and then to sigh, as 'twere
The mort o' th' deer—O, that is entertainment
My bosom likes not, nor my brows.—Mamillius,   150
Art thou my boy?
MAMILLIUS   Ay, my good lord.
LEONTES   I' fecks!
Why, that's my bawcock. What, hast smutched thy
    nose?   155
They say it is a copy out of mine. Come, captain,
We must be neat—not neat, but cleanly, captain.
And yet the steer, the heifer, and the calf
Are all called neat.—Still virginalling
Upon his palm?—How now, you wanton calf?   160
Art thou my calf?
MAMILLIUS   Yes, if you will, my lord.
LEONTES
Thou want'st a rough pash and the shoots that I
    have
To be full like me; yet they say we are   165
Almost as like as eggs. Women say so,
That will say anything. But were they false
As o'erdyed blacks, as wind, as waters, false
As dice are to be wished by one that fixes

160. **wanton:** playful; **calf:** a term of endearment

163. **Thou want'st:** i.e., you lack; **pash:** head; **shoots:** branches, i.e., horns (of the cuckold)

165. **full:** entirely

166. **as like as eggs:** Proverbial: "as like as one egg is to another."

167. **false:** inconstant, unstable (Proverbial: "as false as water," "as inconstant as the wind.")

168. **blacks:** perhaps, funeral clothing or hangings (See longer note, page 238.)

170. **bourn:** boundary

172. **welkin:** heavenly, or blue; **villain:** here, a term of endearment

173. **collop:** i.e., child (literally, a piece of flesh); **dam:** mother (a term usually reserved for animals)

175. **Affection . . . center:** Perhaps: Feeling (**affection**), your meaning (**intention**) hits the truth (**center**). (But see longer note, page 238.)

176. **not so held:** i.e., thought to be impossible

179. **fellow'st:** i.e., share in; **credent:** credible

180. **co-join:** i.e., conjoin

181. **beyond commission:** i.e., illicitly

183. **hard'ning . . . brows:** i.e., growing horns

185. **something seems:** i.e., seems somewhat

186. **How:** i.e., how is it

190. **moved:** angry, disturbed

193. **pastime:** diversion, amusement

194. **bosoms:** i.e., hearts; **lines:** contours

196. **unbreeched:** not yet dressed in breeches, but in the coat worn by little children

201. **squash:** unripened pea pod

202. **take eggs for money:** i.e., buy something worthless (proverbial)

No bourn 'twixt his and mine, yet were it true   170
To say this boy were like me. Come, sir page,
Look on me with your welkin eye. Sweet villain,
Most dear'st, my collop! Can thy dam?—may 't
  be?—
Affection, thy intention stabs the center.   175
Thou dost make possible things not so held,
Communicat'st with dreams—how can this be?
With what's unreal thou coactive art,
And fellow'st nothing. Then 'tis very credent
Thou may'st co-join with something; and thou dost,   180
And that beyond commission, and I find it,
And that to the infection of my brains
And hard'ning of my brows.
POLIXENES   What means Sicilia?
HERMIONE
He something seems unsettled.   185
POLIXENES   How, my lord?
LEONTES
What cheer? How is 't with you, best brother?
HERMIONE   You look
As if you held a brow of much distraction.
Are you moved, my lord?   190
LEONTES   No, in good earnest.
How sometimes nature will betray its folly,
Its tenderness, and make itself a pastime
To harder bosoms! Looking on the lines
Of my boy's face, methoughts I did recoil   195
Twenty-three years, and saw myself unbreeched,
In my green velvet coat, my dagger muzzled
Lest it should bite its master and so prove,
As ornaments oft ⌜do,⌝ too dangerous.
How like, methought, I then was to this kernel,   200
This squash, this gentleman.—Mine honest friend,
Will you take eggs for money?
MAMILLIUS   No, my lord, I'll fight.

204. **happy . . . dole:** a proverbial expression for wishing good luck **'s:** his

207. **If at home:** i.e., when I am **at home**

208. **all . . . matter:** i.e., my constant companion **exercise:** habitual employment (**Mirth** and **matter** were often opposed to indicate the whole range of human concerns.)

209–10. **Now . . . all:** i.e., he plays every courtly role

212. **varying childness:** i.e., childlike ways

213. **thick:** i.e., thicken (Thickening of the **blood** was associated with melancholy.)

214–16. **So . . . me:** i.e., such is the role of Mamillius in my life

216. **We two:** i.e., Mamillius and I

217. **graver:** more solemn or serious

219. **dear:** expensive; **cheap:** inexpensive

221. **Apparent:** heir apparent

223. **We are yours:** i.e., you will find us; **Shall 's attend:** i.e., shall we await

226. **give line:** i.e., give scope or latitude (as in "playing" a hooked fish)

227. **Go to:** an expression of disapproval

228. **neb:** mouth (but usually meaning a bird's **bill**)

229. **arms her:** i.e., gives her arm (to Polixenes, as if he were **her husband** [line 230])

230. **allowing:** approving

232–33. **forked one:** i.e., cuckold

234. **plays:** (1) pretends, acts; (2) has sexual intercourse

235. **issue:** (1) outcome; (2) offspring; (3) exit from a stage

LEONTES
You will? Why, happy man be 's dole!—My brother,
Are you so fond of your young prince as we   205
Do seem to be of ours?
POLIXENES   If at home, sir,
He's all my exercise, my mirth, my matter,
Now my sworn friend and then mine enemy,
My parasite, my soldier, statesman, all.   210
He makes a July's day short as December,
And with his varying childness cures in me
Thoughts that would thick my blood.
LEONTES   So stands this
   squire   215
Officed with me. We two will walk, my lord,
And leave you to your graver steps.—Hermione,
How thou lov'st us show in our brother's welcome.
Let what is dear in Sicily be cheap.
Next to thyself and my young rover, he's   220
Apparent to my heart.
HERMIONE   If you would seek us,
We are yours i' th' garden. Shall 's attend you there?
LEONTES
To your own bents dispose you. You'll be found,
Be you beneath the sky. ⌜*Aside.*⌝ I am angling now,   225
Though you perceive me not how I give line.
Go to, go to!
How she holds up the neb, the bill to him,
And arms her with the boldness of a wife
To her allowing husband!   230
      ⌜*Exit Hermione, Polixenes, and Attendants.*⌝
                Gone already.
Inch thick, knee-deep, o'er head and ears a forked
   one!—
Go play, boy, play. Thy mother plays, and I
Play too, but so disgraced a part, whose issue   235

236. **hiss:** perhaps, cause me to be hissed (by the displeased audience)

240. **present:** i.e., present moment

242. **sluiced:** The metaphor that begins here and continues through line 247 compares an unfaithful wife to a **pond fished** by a poaching **neighbor.** (The words "sluice," **pond,** and **gates** were all used to refer to female genitalia.)

243. **pond:** private fishpond; **next:** nearest

245. **gates:** floodgates of the private fishpond (but also **gates** of a city, opened to **the enemy** of line 254)

248. **revolted:** i.e., faithless

249. **Physic:** medicine, remedy

250–51. **It . . . predominant:** Perhaps: "Lust is like a **bawdy planet** that influences everyone when in the ascendant." **strike:** blast, destroy as a superhuman power (The word could also mean "to copulate.")

253. **barricado:** barricade; **belly:** womb

255. **on 's:** i.e., of us

256. **Have the disease:** i.e., are cuckolds

259. **What:** an interjection introducing a question

262. **great sir:** i.e., Polixenes

264. **cast out:** i.e., dropped the **anchor; still came home:** i.e., kept being dragged from its hold

Will hiss me to my grave. Contempt and clamor
Will be my knell. Go play, boy, play.—There have
   been,
Or I am much deceived, cuckolds ere now;
And many a man there is, even at this present,   240
Now while I speak this, holds his wife by th' arm,
That little thinks she has been sluiced in 's absence,
And his pond fished by his next neighbor, by
Sir Smile, his neighbor. Nay, there's comfort in 't
Whiles other men have gates and those gates   245
   opened,
As mine, against their will. Should all despair
That have revolted wives, the tenth of mankind
Would hang themselves. Physic for 't there's none.
It is a bawdy planet, that will strike   250
Where 'tis predominant; and 'tis powerful, think it,
From east, west, north, and south. Be it concluded,
No barricado for a belly. Know 't,
It will let in and out the enemy
With bag and baggage. Many thousand on 's   255
Have the disease and feel 't not.—How now, boy?
MAMILLIUS
   I am like you, ⌜they⌝ say.
LEONTES   Why, that's some comfort.—
   What, Camillo there?
CAMILLO, ⌜*coming forward*⌝ Ay, my good lord.   260
LEONTES
   Go play, Mamillius. Thou'rt an honest man.
                                    ⌜*Mamillius exits.*⌝
   Camillo, this great sir will yet stay longer.
CAMILLO
   You had much ado to make his anchor hold.
   When you cast out, it still came home.
LEONTES   Didst note it?   265

267. **material:** important
269. **They're . . . me:** i.e., they know I am a cuckold (See longer note, page 239.)
270. **rounding:** whispering, muttering
271. **so-forth:** i.e., you-know-what
271–72. **'Tis . . . last:** Proverbial: "The cuckold is the last to know." **gust:** taste
272. **came 't:** i.e., did it come about
276. **so it is:** i.e., as the case stands; **taken:** understood, apprehended
278. **conceit:** understanding; **soaking:** i.e., absorbent
279. **blocks:** i.e., minds (usually slang for "heads")
280. **of:** i.e., by; **severals:** individuals
281. **headpiece:** intellect; **Lower messes:** i.e., those of inferior rank
282. **purblind:** totally blind; or, perhaps, mentally dull
294. **chamber-counsels:** i.e., private affairs
294–96. **priestlike . . . reformed:** Camillo is figured here as a priest who has heard the confession of Leontes, the **penitent**, given him absolution (**cleansed** [his] **bosom**), and counseled him to amend or "reform" his life.

CAMILLO
  He would not stay at your petitions, made
  His business more material.
LEONTES   Didst perceive it?
  ⌐Aside.⌐ They're here with me already, whisp'ring,
    rounding: 270
  "Sicilia is a so-forth." 'Tis far gone
  When I shall gust it last.—How came 't, Camillo,
  That he did stay?
CAMILLO   At the good queen's entreaty.
LEONTES
  "At the queen's" be 't. "Good" should be pertinent,   275
  But so it is, it is not. Was this taken
  By any understanding pate but thine?
  For thy conceit is soaking, will draw in
  More than the common blocks. Not noted, is 't,
  But of the finer natures, by some severals   280
  Of headpiece extraordinary? Lower messes
  Perchance are to this business purblind? Say.
CAMILLO
  Business, my lord? I think most understand
  Bohemia stays here longer.
LEONTES
  Ha?   285
CAMILLO   Stays here longer.
LEONTES   Ay, but why?
CAMILLO
  To satisfy your Highness and the entreaties
  Of our most gracious mistress.
LEONTES   Satisfy?   290
  Th' entreaties of your mistress? Satisfy?
  Let that suffice. I have trusted thee, Camillo,
  With all the nearest things to my heart, as well
  My chamber-counsels, wherein, priestlike, thou
  Hast cleansed my bosom; I from thee departed   295
  Thy penitent reformed. But we have been

297. **in:** i.e., regarding
300. **bide:** dwell
301. **that way:** i.e., toward honesty
302. **Which:** i.e., which cowardice; **hoxes honesty behind:** hamstrings **honesty**
303. **From . . . required:** i.e., from the direction honesty should take
305. **grafted . . . trust:** i.e., completely in my confidence
307. **home:** i.e., to the end
307–8. **stake drawn:** i.e., bet won
315. **Sometime puts forth:** i.e., (he) sometimes displays; or, perhaps, (these weaknesses) sometimes appear
316. **willful-negligent:** i.e., willfully or perversely negligent
317. **industriously:** intentionally, designedly
320. **the issue doubted:** i.e., mistrusted or feared the outcome
321–22. **execution . . . non-performance:** i.e., accomplishment of the act was a reproach to my hesitation
324. **allowed:** permitted
325. **free of:** exempt from
329. **Ha':** i.e., have
330. **eyeglass:** crystalline lens of the eye

Deceived in thy integrity, deceived
In that which seems so.
CAMILLO   Be it forbid, my lord!
LEONTES
To bide upon 't: thou art not honest; or,   300
If thou inclin'st that way, thou art a coward,
Which hoxes honesty behind, restraining
From course required; or else thou must be
    counted
A servant grafted in my serious trust   305
And therein negligent; or else a fool
That seest a game played home, the rich stake
    drawn,
And tak'st it all for jest.
CAMILLO   My gracious lord,   310
I may be negligent, foolish, and fearful.
In every one of these no man is free,
But that his negligence, his folly, fear,
Among the infinite doings of the world,
Sometime puts forth. In your affairs, my lord,   315
If ever I were willful-negligent,
It was my folly; if industriously
I played the fool, it was my negligence,
Not weighing well the end; if ever fearful
To do a thing where I the issue doubted,   320
Whereof the execution did cry out
Against the non-performance, 'twas a fear
Which oft infects the wisest. These, my lord,
Are such allowed infirmities that honesty
Is never free of. But, beseech your Grace,   325
Be plainer with me; let me know my trespass
By its own visage. If I then deny it,
'Tis none of mine.
LEONTES   Ha' not you seen, Camillo—
But that's past doubt; you have, or your eyeglass   330

331. **horn:** See note on 1.2.150. (There is also perhaps wordplay on the thin **horn** used as a transparent protective covering.)

332. **to:** i.e., in response to; **vision:** object of sight

335. **slippery:** unchaste

336–37. **else . . . thought:** i.e., otherwise insolently deny that you have either **eyes, ears,** or **thought**

338. **hobby-horse:** unchaste woman, prostitute

339. **rank:** indecent, coarse; **flax-wench:** i.e., a girl who is a flax-worker (hence, lower class, and represented as therefore low in morals); **puts to:** begins (to be sexually active)

340. **troth-plight:** solemn promise to marry

343. **present:** immediate; **'Shrew my heart:** literally, may my heart be cursed (a mild oath)

344. **did become you less:** i.e., was less appropriate to you

346. **deep:** heinous; **that:** perhaps, her supposed adultery; or, perhaps, your accusation; **though true:** i.e., even if it were **true**

348. **meeting noses:** i.e., in the act of kissing

349. **career:** course

350. **note:** sign

351. **honesty:** chastity; **Horsing foot on foot:** setting his foot on hers, hers on his

354. **the pin and web:** i.e., cataracts

357. **Bohemia:** i.e., the king of Bohemia, Polixenes

361. **betimes:** soon; before it is too late

363. **Say it be:** i.e., suppose it is (dangerous)

Is thicker than a cuckold's horn—or heard—
For to a vision so apparent, rumor
Cannot be mute—or thought—for cogitation
Resides not in that man that does not think—
My wife is slippery? If thou wilt confess—   335
Or else be impudently negative
To have nor eyes nor ears nor thought—then say
My wife's a ⌐hobby-horse,⌐ deserves a name
As rank as any flax-wench that puts to
Before her troth-plight. Say 't, and justify 't.   340
CAMILLO
I would not be a stander-by to hear
My sovereign mistress clouded so without
My present vengeance taken. 'Shrew my heart,
You never spoke what did become you less
Than this, which to reiterate were sin   345
As deep as that, though true.
LEONTES   Is whispering nothing?
Is leaning cheek to cheek? Is meeting noses?
Kissing with inside lip? Stopping the career
Of laughter with a sigh?—a note infallible   350
Of breaking honesty. Horsing foot on foot?
Skulking in corners? Wishing clocks more swift?
Hours minutes? Noon midnight? And all eyes
Blind with the pin and web but theirs, theirs only,
That would unseen be wicked? Is this nothing?   355
Why, then the world and all that's in 't is nothing,
The covering sky is nothing, Bohemia nothing,
My wife is nothing, nor nothing have these nothings,
If this be nothing.
CAMILLO   Good my lord, be cured   360
Of this diseased opinion, and betimes,
For 'tis most dangerous.
LEONTES   Say it be, 'tis true.

367. **gross:** stupid, dull
368. **hovering temporizer:** i.e., wavering opportunist
369. **at once:** i.e., at the same time
371. **Infected:** i.e., as infected
372. **running . . . glass:** i.e., an hour (measured by an hourglass) See page 64.
374. **like her medal:** perhaps, as if he were wearing a medal with her figure on it
375–79. **Bohemia, who . . . doing:** The structure of Leontes' sentence is broken, with the subject **who** (i.e., **Bohemia**) shifting to **they** (i.e., **servants**) so that **who** is never given a predicate. **bare:** bore **alike . . . as:** i.e., my honor as well as **thrifts:** gains **undo:** cancel, destroy **doing:** action (perhaps, with wordplay on **doing** as sexual intercourse)
380–81. **from meaner . . . worship:** i.e., from humble condition have elevated to honor
383. **bespice:** i.e., season as with a spice
384. **lasting wink:** i.e., perpetual sleep
385. **draft:** drink
387. **rash potion:** i.e., quick-acting dose of poison (**Rash** may refer at the same time to the ill-considered hastiness of the perpetrator.)
389. **Maliciously:** violently
390. **crack:** flaw, failing
392. **Make . . . rot:** i.e., if you doubt the queen's misconduct, you can go rot
393. **muddy:** muddled, confused; **unsettled:** mentally affected
394. **appoint:** nominate (in a legal sense), assign, devote; **in:** i.e., to; **vexation:** distress, affliction

CAMILLO
  No, no, my lord.
LEONTES   It is. You lie, you lie.   365
  I say thou liest, Camillo, and I hate thee,
  Pronounce thee a gross lout, a mindless slave,
  Or else a hovering temporizer that
  Canst with thine eyes at once see good and evil,
  Inclining to them both. Were my wife's liver   370
  Infected as her life, she would not live
  The running of one glass.
CAMILLO   Who does infect her?
LEONTES
  Why, he that wears her like her medal, hanging
  About his neck—Bohemia, who, if I   375
  Had servants true about me, that bare eyes
  To see alike mine honor as their profits,
  Their own particular thrifts, they would do that
  Which should undo more doing. Ay, and thou,
  His cupbearer—whom I from meaner form   380
  Have benched and reared to worship, who mayst see
  Plainly as heaven sees earth and earth sees heaven
  How I am galled—mightst bespice a cup
  To give mine enemy a lasting wink,
  Which draft to me were cordial.   385
CAMILLO   Sir, my lord,
  I could do this, and that with no rash potion,
  But with a ling'ring dram that should not work
  Maliciously like poison. But I cannot
  Believe this crack to be in my dread mistress,   390
  So sovereignly being honorable. I have loved thee—
LEONTES   Make that thy question, and go rot!
  Dost think I am so muddy, so unsettled,
  To appoint myself in this vexation, sully
  The purity and whiteness of my sheets—   395
  Which to preserve is sleep, which being spotted

398. **Give . . . blood:** i.e., cast doubt on the legitimacy

400. **ripe moving to 't:** i.e., having been moved to do it by careful considerations

401. **blench:** swerve (as to embrace affliction groundlessly)

403. **fetch off:** kill

405. **at first:** i.e., when you first married her

406. **thereby:** in addition to that; **for sealing:** i.e., for the sake of silencing

407. **injury:** calumny

410. **set down:** resolved

413. **clear:** innocent

414. **keep with:** keep company with

423. **for:** i.e., as for

425. **to do 't:** i.e., for doing it

427. **with:** i.e., against

428. **To do:** i.e., if I do

Stinging nettles. (1.2.397)
From John Gerard, *The herball or generall historie of plantes* . . . (1597).

Is goads, thorns, nettles, tails of wasps—
Give scandal to the blood o' th' Prince, my son,
Who I do think is mine and love as mine,
Without ripe moving to 't? Would I do this?   400
Could man so blench?
CAMILLO   I must believe you, sir.
I do, and will fetch off Bohemia for 't—
Provided that, when he's removed, your Highness
Will take again your queen as yours at first,   405
Even for your son's sake, and thereby for sealing
The injury of tongues in courts and kingdoms
Known and allied to yours.
LEONTES   Thou dost advise me
Even so as I mine own course have set down.   410
I'll give no blemish to her honor, none.
CAMILLO   My lord,
Go then, and with a countenance as clear
As friendship wears at feasts, keep with Bohemia
And with your queen. I am his cupbearer.   415
If from me he have wholesome beverage,
Account me not your servant.
LEONTES   This is all.
Do 't and thou hast the one half of my heart;
Do 't not, thou splitt'st thine own.   420
CAMILLO   I'll do 't, my lord.
LEONTES
I will seem friendly, as thou hast advised me.
                                        He exits.
CAMILLO
O miserable lady! But, for me,
What case stand I in? I must be the poisoner
Of good Polixenes, and my ground to do 't   425
Is the obedience to a master, one
Who in rebellion with himself will have
All that are his so too. To do this deed,

432. **Nor:** i.e., neither; **not one:** i.e., a single one

434–35. **To . . . breakneck:** i.e., whether I poison Polixenes or not, I certainly face ruin **breakneck:** ruin, destruction

435. **Happy . . . now:** i.e., may a fortunate planet now be predominant

438. **warp:** shrink, shrivel

444. **As:** i.e., as if

447. **Wafting . . . contrary:** turning his eyes aside disdainfully

447–48. **falling . . . contempt:** expressing contempt by a movement of his lip

454. **intelligent:** communicative; intelligible; **'tis thereabouts:** i.e., the meaning of your statement that you **dare not know** is that **you know and dare not** tell me

455–56. **to yourself . . . dare not:** i.e., as far as you **yourself** are concerned, **you must** know **what you do know;** you **cannot say you dare not** know it

457. **complexions:** looks

A basilisk. (1.2.466)
From Edward Topsell, *The history of four-footed beasts and serpents* . . . (1658).

Promotion follows. If I could find example
Of thousands that had struck anointed kings   430
And flourished after, I'd not do 't. But since
Nor brass, nor stone, nor parchment bears not one,
Let villainy itself forswear 't. I must
Forsake the court. To do 't or no is certain
To me a breakneck. Happy star reign now!   435
Here comes Bohemia.

Enter Polixenes.

POLIXENES, ⌈*aside*⌉   This is strange. Methinks
My favor here begins to warp. Not speak?—
Good day, Camillo.
CAMILLO   Hail, most royal sir.   440
POLIXENES
What is the news i' th' court?
CAMILLO   None rare, my lord.
POLIXENES
The King hath on him such a countenance
As he had lost some province and a region
Loved as he loves himself. Even now I met him   445
With customary compliment, when he,
Wafting his eyes to th' contrary and falling
A lip of much contempt, speeds from me, and
So leaves me to consider what is breeding
That changes thus his manners.   450
CAMILLO   I dare not know, my
    lord.
POLIXENES
How, dare not? Do not? Do you know and dare not?
Be intelligent to me—'tis thereabouts;
For to yourself what you do know, you must,   455
And cannot say you dare not. Good Camillo,
Your changed complexions are to me a mirror
Which shows me mine changed too, for I must be

464. **Of:** i.e., from

466. **basilisk:** a mythical serpent whose look could kill (See page 36.)

467. **sped:** succeeded

469. **By:** as a result of

470–73. **As . . . gentle:** i.e., you as a gentleman are adorned by your learning as I am ennobled by my ancestry **thereto:** moreover, besides **Clerklike experienced:** experienced as a scholar **gentry:** class below the nobility; gentlemen **In whose . . . gentle:** i.e., as whose successors we are noble

474–76. **which . . . informed:** i.e., that I need to know **knowledge:** understanding

476–77. **imprison . . . concealment:** i.e., do not keep me in ignorance by concealing it **ignorant:** i.e., causing ignorance

481. **conjure:** solemnly appeal to, implore; **parts:** duties

482–83. **whereof . . . mine:** i.e., not the least of which is your duty to respond to my petition

484. **incidency:** circumstance, incident; **harm:** evil

486. **if to be:** i.e., if it is to be prevented

490. **mark:** pay attention to

491. **e'en as:** even as, just as

492–93. **both . . . goodnight:** i.e., we are both finished

A party in this alteration, finding
Myself thus altered with 't.   460
CAMILLO   There is a sickness
    Which puts some of us in distemper, but
    I cannot name the disease, and it is caught
    Of you that yet are well.
POLIXENES   How caught of me?   465
    Make me not sighted like the basilisk.
    I have looked on thousands who have sped the
        better
    By my regard, but killed none so. Camillo,
    As you are certainly a gentleman, thereto   470
    Clerklike experienced, which no less adorns
    Our gentry than our parents' noble names,
    In whose success we are gentle, I beseech you,
    If you know aught which does behoove my
        knowledge   475
    Thereof to be informed, imprison 't not
    In ignorant concealment.
CAMILLO   I may not answer.
POLIXENES
    A sickness caught of me, and yet I well?
    I must be answered. Dost thou hear, Camillo?   480
    I conjure thee by all the parts of man
    Which honor does acknowledge, whereof the least
    Is not this suit of mine, that thou declare
    What incidency thou dost guess of harm
    Is creeping toward me; how far off, how near;   485
    Which way to be prevented, if to be;
    If not, how best to bear it.
CAMILLO   Sir, I will tell you,
    Since I am charged in honor and by him
    That I think honorable. Therefore mark my counsel, 490
    Which must be e'en as swiftly followed as
    I mean to utter it, or both yourself and me
    Cry lost, and so goodnight.

495. **him:** perhaps, the one; or, perhaps, by him

500. **As:** i.e., as if

501. **vice:** force (with an echo of the word's meaning as a noun)

505. **his . . . the Best:** i.e., Judas Iscariot, the apostle in the New Testament who betrayed Jesus

506. **freshest:** absolutely untainted

507. **strike:** affect

510. **read:** i.e., read of

511–12. **Swear . . . By:** i.e., even if you outswear . . . by (See longer note, page 240.)

513. **their influences:** i.e., their astrological power

514. **for to:** i.e., to

515. **or . . . or:** i.e., either . . . or

516. **fabric:** edifice

517. **faith:** firm belief

518. **The standing . . . body:** as long as his body exists

519. **How should this grow:** i.e., how did this start

523. **trunk:** body (with wordplay on **trunk** as luggage)

524. **impawned:** i.e., as security, as a pledge or guarantee

POLIXENES   On, good Camillo.
CAMILLO
  I am appointed him to murder you.   495
POLIXENES
  By whom, Camillo?
CAMILLO   By the King.
POLIXENES   For what?
CAMILLO
  He thinks, nay with all confidence he swears,
  As he had seen 't or been an instrument   500
  To vice you to 't, that you have touched his queen
  Forbiddenly.
POLIXENES   O, then my best blood turn
  To an infected jelly, and my name
  Be yoked with his that did betray the Best!   505
  Turn then my freshest reputation to
  A savor that may strike the dullest nostril
  Where I arrive, and my approach be shunned,
  Nay, hated too, worse than the great'st infection
  That e'er was heard or read.   510
CAMILLO   Swear his thought over
  By each particular star in heaven and
  By all their influences, you may as well
  Forbid the sea for to obey the moon
  As or by oath remove or counsel shake   515
  The fabric of his folly, whose foundation
  Is piled upon his faith and will continue
  The standing of his body.
POLIXENES   How should this grow?
CAMILLO
  I know not. But I am sure 'tis safer to   520
  Avoid what's grown than question how 'tis born.
  If therefore you dare trust my honesty,
  That lies enclosèd in this trunk which you
  Shall bear along impawned, away tonight!

525. **whisper to:** i.e., secretly instruct them to assist in

527. **Clear them o':** i.e., get them out of; **For:** i.e., as for

528. **to:** i.e., at

529. **discovery:** disclosure

534–35. **thereon . . . sworn:** i.e., just after the king has imposed the death penalty

538. **places:** (1) dwellings; (2) positions in my court

539. **Still:** always

540. **hence departure:** i.e., departure hence

542. **As:** i.e., to the same extent as

544. **as:** i.e., since, inasmuch as

545. **which:** i.e., who

546. **Professed:** i.e., professed friendship

547. **In:** on account of; **o'ershades:** overshadows

548. **expedition:** (1) voyage; (2) haste, promptness

549–50. **nothing . . . suspicion:** i.e., who has done nothing to provoke his unreasonable suspicion

552. **avoid:** depart

554. **Please:** i.e., may it please

Your followers I will whisper to the business,   525
And will by twos and threes at several posterns
Clear them o' th' city. For myself, I'll put
My fortunes to your service, which are here
By this discovery lost. Be not uncertain,
For, by the honor of my parents, I   530
Have uttered truth—which if you seek to prove,
I dare not stand by; nor shall you be safer
Than one condemned by the King's own mouth,
     thereon
His execution sworn.   535
POLIXENES   I do believe thee.
I saw his heart in 's face. Give me thy hand.
Be pilot to me and thy places shall
Still neighbor mine. My ships are ready and
My people did expect my hence departure   540
Two days ago. This jealousy
Is for a precious creature. As she's rare,
Must it be great; and as his person's mighty,
Must it be violent; and as he does conceive
He is dishonored by a man which ever   545
Professed to him, why, his revenges must
In that be made more bitter. Fear o'ershades me.
Good expedition be my friend, and comfort
The gracious queen, part of his theme, but nothing
Of his ill-ta'en suspicion. Come, Camillo,   550
I will respect thee as a father if
Thou bear'st my life off hence. Let us avoid.
CAMILLO
It is in mine authority to command
The keys of all the posterns. Please your Highness
To take the urgent hour. Come, sir, away.   555
                              They exit.

THE
WINTER'S TALE

ACT 2

2.1 Leontes learns of the departure of Polixenes and Camillo and has Hermione arrested for adultery and treason. He announces that he has sent couriers to the shrine of Apollo to obtain the god's advice about what action he should take.

———————

5. **I'll none of:** i.e., I do not want
10. **for because:** i.e., because
11. **brows:** i.e., eyebrows
12. **Become some women best:** i.e., best suit some women; **so:** i.e., provided
15. **taught:** i.e., taught you

Woman with a distaff. (1.2.47)
From Johann Engel, *Astrolabium* . . . (1488).

ACT 2

Scene 1
Enter Hermione, Mamillius, ⌜and⌝ Ladies.

HERMIONE
Take the boy to you. He so troubles me
'Tis past enduring.

FIRST LADY   Come, my gracious lord,
Shall I be your playfellow?

MAMILLIUS
No, I'll none of you.   5

FIRST LADY   Why, my sweet lord?

MAMILLIUS
You'll kiss me hard and speak to me as if
I were a baby still.—I love you better.

SECOND LADY
And why so, my lord?

MAMILLIUS   Not for because   10
Your brows are blacker—yet black brows, they say,
Become some women best, so that there be not
Too much hair there, but in a semicircle,
Or a half-moon made with a pen.

SECOND LADY   Who taught this?   15

MAMILLIUS
I learned it out of women's faces.—Pray now,
What color are your eyebrows?

FIRST LADY   Blue, my lord.

47

19. **mock:** joke, jest
24. **wanton:** play
27. **Good . . . her:** i.e., good luck to her
30. **tell 's:** i.e., tell me
31. **sad:** calamitous, distressing
34. **sprites:** terrifying, hostile supernatural beings
41. **Yond crickets:** i.e., the ladies
42. **give . . . ear:** i.e., whisper it to me
43. **he:** i.e., Polixenes

A cuckold. (1.2.232–33, 239)
From *Bagford Ballads* (printed in 1878).

MAMILLIUS
  Nay, that's a mock. I have seen a lady's nose
  That has been blue, but not her eyebrows.   20
FIRST LADY   Hark ye,
  The Queen your mother rounds apace. We shall
  Present our services to a fine new prince
  One of these days, and then you'd wanton with us
  If we would have you.   25
SECOND LADY   She is spread of late
  Into a goodly bulk. Good time encounter her!
HERMIONE
  What wisdom stirs amongst you?—Come, sir, now
  I am for you again. Pray you sit by us,
  And tell 's a tale.   30
MAMILLIUS   Merry or sad shall 't be?
HERMIONE   As merry as you will.
MAMILLIUS
  A sad tale's best for winter. I have one
  Of sprites and goblins.
HERMIONE   Let's have that, good sir.   35
  Come on, sit down. Come on, and do your best
  To fright me with your sprites. You're powerful at it.
MAMILLIUS
  There was a man—
HERMIONE   Nay, come sit down, then on.
MAMILLIUS
  Dwelt by a churchyard. I will tell it softly,   40
  Yond crickets shall not hear it.
HERMIONE
  Come on then, and give 't me in mine ear.

                              ⌜*They talk privately.*⌝

      ⌜*Enter*⌝ *Leontes, Antigonus,* ⌜*and*⌝ *Lords.*

LEONTES
  Was he met there? His train? Camillo with him?

45. **scour so:** go in such haste

49. **Alack . . . knowledge:** i.e., I wish there had been less for me to know

50–56. **There . . . hefts:** This metaphor alludes to the belief that a spider placed in a drink made the drink poisonous. Leontes claims that the **venom** does not work unless one sees **the spider. hefts:** heavings (in an effort to vomit)

57. **his:** i.e., Polixenes'

59. **mistrusted:** suspected

60. **pre-employed:** i.e., already employed

61. **discovered my design:** i.e., disclosed my plan

62. **pinched:** (1) tortured; (2) diminished; **trick:** toy, trifle

65. **his:** i.e., Camillo's

66. **so:** i.e., in this case

74. **about:** i.e., in contact with

75. **sport:** amuse

"Opposed winds." (1.1.32–33)
From Giulio Cesare Capaccio, *Delle imprese trattato . . .* (1592).

LORD
  Behind the tuft of pines I met them. Never
  Saw I men scour so on their way. I eyed them   45
  Even to their ships.
LEONTES   How blest am I
  In my just censure, in my true opinion!
  Alack, for lesser knowledge! How accursed
  In being so blest! There may be in the cup   50
  A spider steeped, and one may drink, depart,
  And yet partake no venom, for his knowledge
  Is not infected; but if one present
  Th' abhorred ingredient to his eye, make known
  How he hath drunk, he cracks his gorge, his sides,   55
  With violent hefts. I have drunk, and seen the spider.
  Camillo was his help in this, his pander.
  There is a plot against my life, my crown.
  All's true that is mistrusted. That false villain
  Whom I employed was pre-employed by him.   60
  He has discovered my design, and I
  Remain a pinched thing, yea, a very trick
  For them to play at will. How came the posterns
  So easily open?
LORD   By his great authority,   65
  Which often hath no less prevailed than so
  On your command.
LEONTES   I know 't too well.
  ⌜*To Hermione.*⌝ Give me the boy. I am glad you did
    not nurse him.   70
  Though he does bear some signs of me, yet you
  Have too much blood in him.
HERMIONE   What is this? Sport?
LEONTES, ⌜*to the Ladies*⌝
  Bear the boy hence. He shall not come about her.
  Away with him, and let her sport herself   75

76. **that:** i.e., that which

79. **I'd say:** i.e., I would (simply) say

81. **Howe'er . . . nayward:** i.e., however much you are inclined toward disbelief

83. **mark her well:** i.e., observe her closely

83–95. **Be . . . honest:** In these lines, Leontes imagines his lords as unable to speak in praise of Hermione without also immediately expressing their doubts about her chastity. **honest:** chaste **but:** only **without-door:** outward **high speech:** i.e., praise in a lofty or exalted style **straight:** straightaway, immediately **hum, ha:** expressions of hesitation **brands:** (1) stigmas; (2) marks burned into flesh (See **sear** in line 92.) **out:** confused **come between:** i.e., intervene

96. **grieve . . . be:** i.e., **grieve** that it is true

99. **replenished:** perfect

100. **as much more villain:** i.e., that much more the villain for having said it

102. **mistook:** mistaken

104. **Which . . . place:** i.e., whom I'll not address by the title of your position (as queen)

105. **barbarism:** rude and unpolished language

106. **a like language:** i.e., the same terms; **degrees:** ranks

107. **distinguishment:** distinction (according to social rank)

111. **federary:** confederate, accomplice

With that she's big with, (⌐*to Hermione*⌐) for 'tis
  Polixenes
Has made thee swell thus.
             ⌐*A Lady exits with Mamillius.*⌐
HERMIONE   But I'd say he had not,
And I'll be sworn you would believe my saying,   80
Howe'er you lean to th' nayward.
LEONTES   You, my lords,
Look on her, mark her well. Be but about
To say "She is a goodly lady," and
The justice of your hearts will thereto add   85
" 'Tis pity she's not honest, honorable."
Praise her but for this her without-door form,
Which on my faith deserves high speech, and
  straight
The shrug, the "hum," or "ha," these petty brands   90
That calumny doth use—O, I am out,
That mercy does, for calumny will sear
Virtue itself—these shrugs, these "hum"'s and "ha"'s,
When you have said she's goodly, come between
Ere you can say she's honest. But be 't known,   95
From him that has most cause to grieve it should be,
She's an adult'ress.
HERMIONE   Should a villain say so,
The most replenished villain in the world,
He were as much more villain. You, my lord,   100
Do but mistake.
LEONTES   You have mistook, my lady,
Polixenes for Leontes. O thou thing,
Which I'll not call a creature of thy place
Lest barbarism, making me the precedent,   105
Should a like language use to all degrees,
And mannerly distinguishment leave out
Betwixt the prince and beggar.—I have said
She's an adult'ress; I have said with whom.
More, she's a traitor, and Camillo is   110
A federary with her, and one that knows

112. **shame:** i.e., be ashamed

113. **But:** except; **principal:** (1) person directly responsible for a crime; (2) prince

114. **bed-swerver:** i.e., adulteress

115. **vulgars:** common people

116. **late:** recent

120. **published:** proclaimed, denounced; **Gentle my lord:** i.e., my noble lord

121. **scarce:** i.e., scarcely; **right:** vindicate; **throughly:** thoroughly

124. **foundations:** (1) lowest parts of a building; (2) principles

125. **center:** (1) i.e., the earth (as the **center** of the Ptolemaic universe); (2) the support for an arch or dome under construction

127. **afar off guilty:** i.e., indirectly guilty

128. **But . . . speaks:** i.e., merely for speaking

129. **ill:** pernicious, dangerous; **reigns:** i.e., is exerting its influence or power

131. **aspect:** configuration of planets (pronounced aspéct)

133. **want:** lack

135. **here:** perhaps with a gesture toward her heart or bosom

137. **qualified:** moderated, mitigated; **charities:** dispositions to judge leniently

138. **measure:** judge

143. **My plight:** a reference to her advanced pregnancy; **fools:** a term of endearment

147. **As I come out:** i.e., when I am released from **prison; action . . . go on**: i.e., course I now embark on (The word **action** carries overtones of legal suits, military engagements, and theatrical roles.)

What she should shame to know herself
But with her most vile principal: that she's
A bed-swerver, even as bad as those
That vulgars give bold'st titles; ay, and privy   115
To this their late escape.
HERMIONE   No, by my life,
Privy to none of this. How will this grieve you,
When you shall come to clearer knowledge, that
You thus have published me! Gentle my lord,   120
You scarce can right me throughly then to say
You did mistake.
LEONTES   No. If I mistake
In those foundations which I build upon,
The center is not big enough to bear   125
A schoolboy's top.—Away with her to prison.
He who shall speak for her is afar off guilty
But that he speaks.
HERMIONE   There's some ill planet reigns.
I must be patient till the heavens look   130
With an aspect more favorable. Good my lords,
I am not prone to weeping, as our sex
Commonly are, the want of which vain dew
Perchance shall dry your pities. But I have
That honorable grief lodged here which burns   135
Worse than tears drown. Beseech you all, my lords,
With thoughts so qualified as your charities
Shall best instruct you, measure me; and so
The King's will be performed.
LEONTES   Shall I be heard?   140
HERMIONE
Who is 't that goes with me? Beseech your Highness
My women may be with me, for you see
My plight requires it.—Do not weep, good fools;
There is no cause. When you shall know your
          mistress   145
Has deserved prison, then abound in tears
As I come out. This action I now go on

148. **grace:** credit, honor (but with the strong sense of spiritual **grace** gained through suffering)

156. **For:** i.e., as for

158. **Please:** i.e., if it please

160. **which:** i.e., of which

161–63. **If . . . her:** i.e., if Hermione is unchaste, then I can no longer trust even **my wife** (See longer note, page 240.)

167. **she be:** i.e., Hermione is

170. **for you:** i.e., for your sake

171. **abused:** deceived; **putter-on:** instigator

174. **land-damn:** perhaps, curse energetically (The precise meaning is uncertain because the word is not recorded elsewhere.); **honor-flawed:** i.e., unchaste

176. **some:** about

178. **geld:** spay

178–79. **fourteen . . . generations:** i.e., they will be spayed by age fourteen so that they cannot produce illegitimate offspring

179. **co-heirs:** joint heirs

Is for my better grace.—Adieu, my lord.
I never wished to see you sorry; now
I trust I shall.—My women, come; you have leave.　150
LEONTES　Go, do our bidding. Hence!
　　⌜*Hermione exits, under guard, with her Ladies.*⌝
LORD
Beseech your Highness, call the Queen again.
ANTIGONUS
Be certain what you do, sir, lest your justice
Prove violence, in the which three great ones suffer:
Yourself, your queen, your son.　155
LORD　　　　　　　　　　For her, my lord,
I dare my life lay down—and will do 't, sir,
Please you t' accept it—that the Queen is spotless
I' th' eyes of heaven, and to you—I mean
In this which you accuse her.　160
ANTIGONUS　　　　　　　　If it prove
She's otherwise, I'll keep my stables where
I lodge my wife. I'll go in couples with her;
Than when I feel and see her, no farther trust her.
For every inch of woman in the world,　165
Ay, every dram of woman's flesh, is false,
If she be.
LEONTES　　Hold your peaces.
LORD　　　　　　　　　　Good my lord—
ANTIGONUS
It is for you we speak, not for ourselves.　170
You are abused, and by some putter-on
That will be damned for 't. Would I knew the
　villain!
I would land-damn him. Be she honor-flawed,
I have three daughters—the eldest is eleven;　175
The second and the third, nine and some five;
If this prove true, they'll pay for 't. By mine honor,
I'll geld 'em all; fourteen they shall not see
To bring false generations. They are co-heirs,

180. **glib:** castrate

181. **fair:** i.e., legitimate

185. **doing thus:** Leontes may here pull Antigonus' nose or hair or strike himself.   **withal:** in addition

188. **honesty:** chastity (When applied to women, the word "honest" in Shakespeare generally means "chaste.")

190. **dungy:** abounding in dung, and therefore vile

191. **credit:** i.e., credibility

193. **Upon this ground:** i.e., in this matter

195. **Be . . . might:** i.e., however you might **be blamed for** suspecting her unjustly

197. **Commune:** confer, consult; **but rather follow:** i.e., instead of following

198. **instigation:** incentive (to act)

199. **Calls not:** does not require

199–200. **our . . . this:** i.e., I tell you this out of my own **natural goodness**

200–201. **or . . . skill:** either stunned or pretending to be so   **in skill:** using discretion

202. **Relish:** appreciate; **like us:** i.e., as I do

204. **ord'ring on 't:** management or treatment of it

205. **Properly ours:** entirely mine

207. **tried:** examined, tested

208. **overture:** i.e., public disclosure

210. **by age:** i.e., as a consequence of old age

212. **their familiarity:** i.e., the intimacy between Hermione and Polixenes

213. **touched conjecture:** was apprehended by reason

214. **approbation:** proof, confirmation

And I had rather glib myself than they   180
Should not produce fair issue.
LEONTES   Cease. No more.
You smell this business with a sense as cold
As is a dead man's nose. But I do see 't and feel 't,
As you feel doing thus, and see withal   185
The instruments that feel.
ANTIGONUS   If it be so,
We need no grave to bury honesty.
There's not a grain of it the face to sweeten
Of the whole dungy earth.   190
LEONTES   What? Lack I credit?
LORD
I had rather you did lack than I, my lord,
Upon this ground. And more it would content me
To have her honor true than your suspicion,
Be blamed for 't how you might.   195
LEONTES   Why, what need we
Commune with you of this, but rather follow
Our forceful instigation? Our prerogative
Calls not your counsels, but our natural goodness
Imparts this, which if you—or stupefied   200
Or seeming so in skill—cannot or will not
Relish a truth like us, inform yourselves
We need no more of your advice. The matter,
The loss, the gain, the ord'ring on 't is all
Properly ours.   205
ANTIGONUS   And I wish, my liege,
You had only in your silent judgment tried it,
Without more overture.
LEONTES   How could that be?
Either thou art most ignorant by age,   210
Or thou wert born a fool. Camillo's flight,
Added to their familiarity—
Which was as gross as ever touched conjecture,
That lacked sight only, naught for approbation

216. **Made . . . deed:** approached or added up to the act (of adultery); **push on:** press forward, urge on

220. **piteous:** deplorable; **wild:** reckless; **in post:** in haste

221. **Delphos:** i.e., the island Delos (See longer note, page 240.) **Apollo's temple:** i.e., temple of the sun god of Greco-Roman mythology, one of whose functions was to prophesy through oracles

223. **Of stuffed sufficiency:** i.e., to be more than capable

224. **had:** i.e., once I have received it

230. **he:** i.e., anyone

232. **Come up to:** rise to the level of

234. **the treachery:** i.e., the **plot** against his **life** and **crown** (line 58)

237. **raise:** rouse

2.2 Paulina attempts to visit Hermione in prison. Learning that the queen has given birth to a baby girl, Paulina decides to take the baby to Leontes in the hope that the sight of his infant daughter will alter his state of mind.

———————

3. **Good lady:** Paulina addresses Hermione as if she were present.

But only seeing, all other circumstances   215
Made up to th' deed—doth push on this
    proceeding.
Yet, for a greater confirmation—
For in an act of this importance 'twere
Most piteous to be wild—I have dispatched in post   220
To sacred Delphos, to Apollo's temple,
Cleomenes and Dion, whom you know
Of stuffed sufficiency. Now from the oracle
They will bring all, whose spiritual counsel had
Shall stop or spur me. Have I done well?   225
LORD   Well done,
    my lord.
LEONTES
Though I am satisfied and need no more
Than what I know, yet shall the oracle
Give rest to th' minds of others, such as he   230
Whose ignorant credulity will not
Come up to th' truth. So have we thought it good
From our free person she should be confined,
Lest that the treachery of the two fled hence
Be left her to perform. Come, follow us.   235
We are to speak in public, for this business
Will raise us all.
ANTIGONUS, ⌜*aside*⌝ To laughter, as I take it,
If the good truth were known.
                                    They exit.

                        Scene 2
Enter Paulina, a Gentleman, ⌜*and Paulina's Attendants.*⌝

PAULINA, ⌜*to Gentleman*⌝
The keeper of the prison, call to him.
Let him have knowledge who I am.
                            ⌜*Gentleman exits.*⌝
                            Good lady,

9. **who:** i.e., whom
10. **Pray:** i.e., I pray
15. **access:** pronounced accéss; **gentle:** noble
18. **put apart:** send away
22. **conference:** conversation
24–25. **such . . . coloring:** i.e., so much effort to make innocence look like undeniable guilt **no stain:** i.e., innocence **a stain /As passes coloring:** i.e., a discoloration that surpasses the dyer's skill
29. **hold together:** i.e., maintain control of herself; **On:** as a consequence of
30. **Which:** i.e., than which
31. **something:** somewhat

A baby being delivered. (2.2.31)
From Jakob Rüff, *De conceptu et generatione hominis* . . . (1580).

No court in Europe is too good for thee.
What dost thou then in prison?   5

⌜*Enter*⌝ *Jailer,* ⌜*with the Gentleman.*⌝

                          Now, good sir,
You know me, do you not?
JAILER   For a worthy lady
And one who much I honor.
PAULINA   Pray you then,   10
Conduct me to the Queen.
JAILER   I may not, madam.
To the contrary I have express commandment.
PAULINA
Here's ado, to lock up honesty and honor from
Th' access of gentle visitors. Is 't lawful, pray you,   15
To see her women? Any of them? Emilia?
JAILER So please you, madam,
To put apart these your attendants, I
Shall bring Emilia forth.
PAULINA   I pray now, call her.—   20
Withdraw yourselves.
                    ⌜*Attendants and Gentleman exit.*⌝
JAILER
And, madam, I must be present at your conference.
PAULINA Well, be 't so, prithee.   ⌜*Jailer exits.*⌝
Here's such ado to make no stain a stain
As passes coloring.   25

⌜*Enter*⌝ *Emilia* ⌜*with Jailer.*⌝

                    Dear gentlewoman,
How fares our gracious lady?
EMILIA
As well as one so great and so forlorn
May hold together. On her frights and griefs,
Which never tender lady hath borne greater,   30
She is something before her time delivered.

34. **Lusty:** vigorous; **like:** i.e., likely
35. **in 't:** i.e., from the baby
38. **lunes:** fits of lunacy; **beshrew:** curse
40. **on 't:** i.e., of it; **office:** business, function
41. **Becomes:** suits
43. **red-looked:** i.e., red-faced
45. **Commend:** present
53. **is:** i.e., are
54. **free:** generous
55. **thriving issue:** successful outcome
56. **meet:** suitable
57. **presently:** immediately
59. **hammered of:** earnestly debated; **design:** scheme, plan
60. **tempt:** try; venture to solicit; **minister of honor:** high-ranking agent
63. **wit:** wisdom, good judgment
64. **bosom:** heart

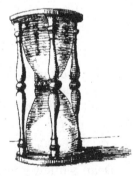

An hourglass. (1.2.372; 4.1.16)
From August Casimir Redel, *Apophtegmata symbolica* . . . [n.d.].

PAULINA
  A boy?
EMILIA   A daughter, and a goodly babe,
  Lusty and like to live. The Queen receives
  Much comfort in 't, says "My poor prisoner,   35
  I am innocent as you."
PAULINA   I dare be sworn.
  These dangerous unsafe lunes i' th' King, beshrew
    them!
  He must be told on 't, and he shall. The office   40
  Becomes a woman best. I'll take 't upon me.
  If I prove honey-mouthed, let my tongue blister
  And never to my red-looked anger be
  The trumpet anymore. Pray you, Emilia,
  Commend my best obedience to the Queen.   45
  If she dares trust me with her little babe,
  I'll show 't the King and undertake to be
  Her advocate to th' loud'st. We do not know
  How he may soften at the sight o' th' child.
  The silence often of pure innocence   50
  Persuades when speaking fails.
EMILIA   Most worthy madam,
  Your honor and your goodness is so evident
  That your free undertaking cannot miss
  A thriving issue. There is no lady living   55
  So meet for this great errand. Please your Ladyship
  To visit the next room, I'll presently
  Acquaint the Queen of your most noble offer,
  Who but today hammered of this design,
  But durst not tempt a minister of honor   60
  Lest she should be denied.
PAULINA   Tell her, Emilia,
  I'll use that tongue I have. If wit flow from 't
  As boldness from my bosom, let 't not be doubted
  I shall do good.   65

67. **I'll:** i.e., I'll go

67–68. **Please . . . nearer:** presumably a restatement of the invitation (lines 56–57) to Paulina to go into **the next room**

70. **pass:** allow

74. **process:** with wordplay on "legal proceeding," wordplay that begins earlier in the line with **law** and continues in the next line with **freed and enfranchised**—the doubling of synonymous words being a reflection of legal language (Possibly, **law and process** can be read to mean "legal process," an example of the figure of speech called *hendiadys*.)

2.3 Paulina brings the baby to the tormented Leontes, who first orders the baby burned, then orders Antigonus to take the baby to a deserted place and abandon it. News comes that the couriers have returned with the oracle from Apollo.

---

1. **Nor:** i.e., neither; **no rest:** i.e., any rest

2. **mere:** pure, sheer

3. **The cause:** i.e., those to blame; **in being:** i.e., alive

4. **harlot:** fornicator; villain

5. **arm:** power

5–6. **out . . . brain:** i.e., beyond the range of anything **my brain** can devise **blank:** in archery or gunnery, the target's white center **level:** aim

6. **plot-proof:** i.e., impervious to any plot against him

7. **hook:** grapple (as with a ship's grappling hook)

8. **Given . . . fire:** Burning was the punishment for women convicted of treason.

66

EMILIA   Now be you blest for it!
  I'll to the Queen. Please you come something
    nearer.
JAILER, ⌐*to Paulina*⌐
  Madam, if 't please the Queen to send the babe,
  I know not what I shall incur to pass it,   70
  Having no warrant.
PAULINA   You need not fear it, sir.
  This child was prisoner to the womb, and is
  By law and process of great nature thence
  Freed and enfranchised, not a party to   75
  The anger of the King, nor guilty of,
  If any be, the trespass of the Queen.
JAILER   I do believe it.
PAULINA
  Do not you fear. Upon mine honor, I
  Will stand betwixt you and danger.   80

They exit.

Scene 3
Enter Leontes.

LEONTES
  Nor night nor day no rest. It is but weakness
  To bear the matter thus, mere weakness. If
  The cause were not in being—part o' th' cause,
  She th' adult'ress, for the harlot king
  Is quite beyond mine arm, out of the blank   5
  And level of my brain, plot-proof. But she
  I can hook to me. Say that she were gone,
  Given to the fire, a moiety of my rest
  Might come to me again.—Who's there?

⌐*Enter a*⌐ *Servant.*

SERVANT   My lord.   10

11. **the boy:** i.e., Mamillius
12. **tonight:** i.e., last night
16. **straight:** immediately; **deeply:** profoundly
17. **on 't:** i.e., of it
19. **solely:** alone
21. **him:** i.e., Polixenes
24. **parties:** confederates; **alliance:** kindred, allies
25. **For:** i.e., as for; **present:** immediate
26. **Take:** i.e., let me take
27. **pastime:** amusement
31. **second:** helpful
32–33. **Fear . . . life?:** i.e., do you fear his tyrannous anger more than you fear for the queen's life?
34. **free:** noble; **he:** i.e., Leontes
35. **That's enough:** i.e., she is gracious, innocent, and noble enough
37. **come at:** approach
38. **hot:** zealous

Aiming at "the blank." (2.3.5)
From Gilles Corrozet, *Hecatongraphie* . . . (1543).

LEONTES   How does the boy?
SERVANT   He took good rest tonight. 'Tis hoped
  His sickness is discharged.
LEONTES   To see his nobleness,
  Conceiving the dishonor of his mother.   15
  He straight declined, drooped, took it deeply,
  Fastened and fixed the shame on 't in himself,
  Threw off his spirit, his appetite, his sleep,
  And downright languished. Leave me solely. Go,
  See how he fares.   ⌜*Servant exits.*⌝   20
                    Fie, fie, no thought of him.
  The very thought of my revenges that way
  Recoil upon me—in himself too mighty,
  And in his parties, his alliance. Let him be
  Until a time may serve. For present vengeance,   25
  Take it on her. Camillo and Polixenes
  Laugh at me, make their pastime at my sorrow.
  They should not laugh if I could reach them, nor
  Shall she within my power.

  Enter Paulina, ⌜*carrying the baby, with*⌝ *Servants,*
          Antigonus, and Lords.

LORD   You must not enter.   30
PAULINA
  Nay, rather, good my lords, be second to me.
  Fear you his tyrannous passion more, alas,
  Than the Queen's life? A gracious innocent soul,
  More free than he is jealous.
ANTIGONUS   That's enough.   35
SERVANT
  Madam, he hath not slept tonight, commanded
  None should come at him.
PAULINA   Not so hot, good sir.
  I come to bring him sleep. 'Tis such as you
  That creep like shadows by him and do sigh   40

41. **each:** i.e., each of; **heavings:** groans

44. **either:** i.e., either healing or truth; **purge** . . . **humor:** i.e., cleanse him of that mental state (Both **purge** and **humor** had specific medical meanings. The word *purge* referred to laxatives or bleedings; the word *humor* referred either to the fluids that were thought to determine one's mental states or to the mental states themselves.)

47. **conference:** conversation

48. **gossips** . . . **Highness:** godparents for your Highness (needed at your daughter's christening)

54. **On** . . . **mine:** i.e., that at risk of incurring your Highness' displeasure and mine

59. **Commit** . . . **committing:** i.e., send me to prison for perpetrating

61. **La you:** an exclamation for emphasis

62. **take the rein:** i.e., take the bit between her teeth (as if she were a horse freeing herself from her rider-husband's control)

65. **professes:** i.e., profess

67. **dares:** i.e., dare

69. **Than** . . . **yours:** i.e., than those who merely appear most loyal

At each his needless heavings, such as you
Nourish the cause of his awaking. I
Do come with words as medicinal as true,
Honest as either, to purge him of that humor
That presses him from sleep.   45
LEONTES   ⌜What⌝ noise there, ho?
PAULINA
No noise, my lord, but needful conference
About some gossips for your Highness.
LEONTES   How?—
Away with that audacious lady. Antigonus,   50
I charged thee that she should not come about me.
I knew she would.
ANTIGONUS   I told her so, my lord,
On your displeasure's peril and on mine,
She should not visit you.   55
LEONTES   What, canst not rule her?
PAULINA
From all dishonesty he can. In this,
Unless he take the course that you have done—
Commit me for committing honor—trust it,
He shall not rule me.   60
ANTIGONUS   La you now, you hear.
When she will take the rein I let her run,
But she'll not stumble.
PAULINA   Good my liege, I come—
And I beseech you hear me, who professes   65
Myself your loyal servant, your physician,
Your most obedient counselor, yet that dares
Less appear so in comforting your evils
Than such as most seem yours—I say I come
From your good queen.   70
LEONTES   Good queen?
PAULINA
Good queen, my lord, good queen, I say "good
     queen,"

74. **by . . . good:** i.e., prove her to be good through a trial by combat; **so were I:** i.e., if I were

75. **worst:** lowliest in rank

78. **hand:** lay hands on; **off:** i.e., leave

84. **mankind:** masculine, virago-like

85. **intelligencing bawd:** i.e., spy and go-between

94. **woman-tired:** hen-pecked

94–95. **unroosted . . . Partlet:** i.e., dislodged (from your perch) by your hen   **Dame Parlet:** Pertilote (or **Partlet**) is Chauntecleer's favorite (but nagging) hen in Chaucer's "Nun's Priest's Tale"

99. **forced baseness:** i.e., enforced bastardy

100. **put upon 't:** imposed on the princess

101. **dreads:** fears (Paulina's response plays on another sense of "dread" as "respect.")

105. **by . . . light:** a conventional oath

A combat in a list. (2.3.74)
From [Sir William Segar,] *The booke of honor and armes . . .* (1590).

And would by combat make her good, so were I
A man, the worst about you.   75
LEONTES   Force her hence.
PAULINA
  Let him that makes but trifles of his eyes
  First hand me. On mine own accord I'll off,
  But first I'll do my errand.—The good queen,
  For she is good, hath brought you forth a   80
    daughter—
  Here 'tis—commends it to your blessing.
                            ⌜*She lays down the baby.*⌝
LEONTES   Out!
  A mankind witch! Hence with her, out o' door.
  A most intelligencing bawd.   85
PAULINA   Not so.
  I am as ignorant in that as you
  In so entitling me, and no less honest
  Than you are mad—which is enough, I'll warrant,
  As this world goes, to pass for honest.   90
LEONTES   Traitors,
  Will you not push her out? ⌜*To Antigonus.*⌝ Give her
    the bastard,
  Thou dotard; thou art woman-tired, unroosted
  By thy Dame Partlet here. Take up the bastard,   95
  Take 't up, I say. Give 't to thy crone.
PAULINA, ⌜*to Antigonus*⌝   Forever
  Unvenerable be thy hands if thou
  Tak'st up the Princess by that forced baseness
  Which he has put upon 't.   100
LEONTES   He dreads his wife.
PAULINA
  So I would you did. Then 'twere past all doubt
  You'd call your children yours.
LEONTES   A nest of traitors!
ANTIGONUS
  I am none, by this good light.   105

112. **as . . . stands:** See longer note, page 240.

113. **to 't:** i.e., to change his opinion

116. **callet:** (1) lewd woman; (2) scold

117. **late:** i.e., lately, recently

121. **dam:** mother (usually only in reference to animals)

124. **might . . . charge:** i.e., if we may accuse you with **th' old proverb**

125. **So . . . worse:** Proverbial: "They are so like that they are the worse for it."

125–31. **Behold . . . finger:** Paulina compares the biological reproduction of Leontes in his child to the reproduction of a text through the art of printing. **print:** image **matter:** subject matter, contents

132. **which:** i.e., who; **it:** i.e., the baby

133. **got:** begot, fathered

135. **No . . . in 't:** i.e., don't include the color **yellow,** which is the color of jealousy

135–36. **she . . . husband's:** This suggestion that the female baby when grown into a woman could have doubts about the legitimacy of her children is, of course, absurd—just as absurd, Paulina may be saying, as Leontes' suspicions of his baby's legitimacy.

137. **gross:** rude

138. **losel:** worthless fellow

139. **stay her tongue:** i.e., prevent her talking

140. **Hang:** i.e., if you hang

PAULINA   Nor I, nor any
  But one that's here, and that's himself. For he
  The sacred honor of himself, his queen's,
  His hopeful son's, his babe's, betrays to slander,
  Whose sting is sharper than the sword's; and will   110
    not—
  For, as the case now stands, it is a curse
  He cannot be compelled to 't—once remove
  The root of his opinion, which is rotten
  As ever oak or stone was sound.   115
LEONTES   A callet
  Of boundless tongue, who late hath beat her
    husband
  And now baits me! This brat is none of mine.
  It is the issue of Polixenes.   120
  Hence with it, and together with the dam
  Commit them to the fire.
PAULINA   It is yours,
  And, might we lay th' old proverb to your charge,
  So like you 'tis the worse.—Behold, my lords,   125
  Although the print be little, the whole matter
  And copy of the father—eye, nose, lip,
  The trick of 's frown, his forehead, nay, the valley,
  The pretty dimples of his chin and cheek, his
    smiles,   130
  The very mold and frame of hand, nail, finger.
  And thou, good goddess Nature, which hast made it
  So like to him that got it, if thou hast
  The ordering of the mind too, 'mongst all colors
  No yellow in 't, lest she suspect, as he does,   135
  Her children not her husband's.
LEONTES   A gross hag!—
  And, losel, thou art worthy to be hanged
  That wilt not stay her tongue.
ANTIGONUS   Hang all the husbands 140
  That cannot do that feat, you'll leave yourself
  Hardly one subject.

148. **heretic . . . fire:** Heretics were punished by being burned at the stake.
151. **Not able:** i.e., you being unable; **more accusation:** i.e., more evidence for your accusation
152. **weak-hinged fancy:** i.e., unfounded imagining (**Weak-hinged,** a word whose only recorded use is in this play, probably refers to the hook-and-eye hinge then in use and indicates that Leontes' imagining is not firmly hooked or attached to any event.); **something:** somewhat
161. **Look to:** attend to, take care of; **Jove:** king of the Greco-Roman gods
162. **better guiding spirit:** perhaps, a better temper or disposition than yours; **these hands:** i.e., the hands of those who, following Leontes' command, are trying to push her out
163. **tender o'er:** considerate of; **follies:** weaknesses or derangements of mind
166. **set:** urged
170. **straight:** straightaway, immediately
173. **what . . . thine:** i.e., whatever else you call yours

LEONTES   Once more, take her hence.
PAULINA
  A most unworthy and unnatural lord
  Can do no more.   145
LEONTES   I'll ha' thee burnt.
PAULINA   I care not.
  It is an heretic that makes the fire,
  Not she which burns in 't. I'll not call you tyrant;
  But this most cruel usage of your queen,   150
  Not able to produce more accusation
  Than your own weak-hinged fancy, something
    savors
  Of tyranny, and will ignoble make you,
  Yea, scandalous to the world.   155
LEONTES, ⌐to Antigonus⌐   On your allegiance,
  Out of the chamber with her! Were I a tyrant,
  Where were her life? She durst not call me so
  If she did know me one. Away with her!
PAULINA, ⌐to Lords⌐
  I pray you do not push me; I'll be gone.—   160
  Look to your babe, my lord; 'tis yours. Jove send her
  A better guiding spirit.—What needs these hands?
  You that are thus so tender o'er his follies
  Will never do him good, not one of you.
  So, so. Farewell, we are gone.   *She exits.* 165
LEONTES, ⌐to Antigonus⌐
  Thou, traitor, hast set on thy wife to this.
  My child? Away with 't! Even thou, that hast
  A heart so tender o'er it, take it hence,
  And see it instantly consumed with fire.
  Even thou, and none but thou. Take it up straight. 170
  Within this hour bring me word 'tis done,
  And by good testimony, or I'll seize thy life,
  With what thou else call'st thine. If thou refuse
  And wilt encounter with my wrath, say so.

175. **proper:** own

185. **beseech:** i.e., beseech you

186. **So . . . us:** i.e., to have the opinion of us that we thereby deserve

187. **dear:** (1) loving; (2) valuable

190. **issue:** outcome; **We all kneel:** The stage action is clear in these words. It is not so clear when the courtiers again stand.

191. **I . . . blows:** Proverbial: "As wavering as feathers in the wind."

194. **be it:** perhaps, so be it

198. **Margery:** a margery-prater was a slang term for a hen (See note to lines 94–95.); **midwife:** perhaps because she brought the baby to him, as a **midwife** would do after a birth (But see longer note, page 241.)

200. **So:** i.e., as

204. **my . . . undergo:** i.e., I am capable of performing **undergo:** undertake

A kite. (2.3.227)
From Konrad Gesner, . . . *Historiae animalium* . . . (1585–1604).

The bastard brains with these my proper hands   175
Shall I dash out. Go, take it to the fire,
For thou sett'st on thy wife.
ANTIGONUS   I did not, sir.
These lords, my noble fellows, if they please,
Can clear me in 't.   180
LORDS   We can, my royal liege.
He is not guilty of her coming hither.
LEONTES   You're liars all.
LORD
Beseech your Highness, give us better credit.
We have always truly served you, and beseech   185
So to esteem of us. And on our knees we beg,
As recompense of our dear services
Past and to come, that you do change this purpose,
Which being so horrible, so bloody, must
Lead on to some foul issue. We all kneel.   190
LEONTES
I am a feather for each wind that blows.
Shall I live on to see this bastard kneel
And call me father? Better burn it now
Than curse it then. But be it; let it live.
It shall not neither. ⌜*To Antigonus.*⌝ You, sir, come 195
    you hither,
You that have been so tenderly officious
With Lady Margery, your midwife there,
To save this bastard's life—for 'tis a bastard,
So sure as this beard's gray. What will you   200
    adventure
To save this brat's life?
ANTIGONUS   Anything, my lord,
That my ability may undergo
And nobleness impose. At least thus much: 205
I'll pawn the little blood which I have left
To save the innocent. Anything possible.

211. **Mark:** pay attention; **seest thou:** perhaps, "see to it"

211–12. **the fail / Of:** i.e., your failure to perform **fail:** failure

213. **lewd-:** vulgar-, wicked-, foolish-

214. **this time:** i.e., the time being

217. **desert:** uninhabited; **out:** outside

219. **it own:** i.e., its own

222. **On . . . torture:** i.e., if you are to avoid the destruction of your soul and the torture of your body

223. **strangely:** perhaps, as a stranger; perhaps, coldly

225. **a present:** an immediate

227. **kites:** birds of prey, hawks (See page 78.)

230. **Like:** similar; **offices of pity:** compassionate duties (The allusion may be to the familiar story of the mythical Romulus and Remus, raised by a she-wolf. See picture on page 82.)

231. **In more:** perhaps, to a greater extent; perhaps, in more ways; **this deed does require:** i.e., your cruelty calls for or deserves

233. **loss:** destruction

236. **Please:** i.e., if it please; **posts:** couriers

LEONTES
It shall be possible. Swear by this sword
Thou wilt perform my bidding.
ANTIGONUS, ⌜*his hand on the hilt*⌝ I will, my lord.   210
LEONTES
Mark, and perform it, seest thou; for the fail
Of any point in 't shall not only be
Death to thyself but to thy lewd-tongued wife,
Whom for this time we pardon. We enjoin thee,
As thou art liegeman to us, that thou carry   215
This female bastard hence, and that thou bear it
To some remote and desert place quite out
Of our dominions, and that there thou leave it,
Without more mercy, to it own protection
And favor of the climate. As by strange fortune   220
It came to us, I do in justice charge thee,
On thy soul's peril and thy body's torture,
That thou commend it strangely to some place
Where chance may nurse or end it. Take it up.
ANTIGONUS
I swear to do this, though a present death   225
Had been more merciful.—Come on, poor babe.
                    ⌜*He picks up the baby.*⌝
Some powerful spirit instruct the kites and ravens
To be thy nurses! Wolves and bears, they say,
Casting their savageness aside, have done
Like offices of pity. ⌜*To Leontes.*⌝ Sir, be prosperous   230
In more than this deed does require.—And blessing
Against this cruelty fight on thy side,
Poor thing, condemned to loss.
                    He exits, ⌜*carrying the baby.*⌝
LEONTES   No, I'll not rear
Another's issue.   235

                    Enter a Servant.

SERVANT   Please your Highness, posts

238. **since:** ago
239. **well:** successfully, without harm or accident
241. **So please you:** i.e., if it please (a deferential phrase of address)
242. **account:** explanation
245. **suddenly:** immediately
247. **session:** sitting of a court

Wolf nursing Romulus and Remus. (2.3.227–30)
From Guillaume Du Choul, *Los discursos de la religion* . . . (1579).

From those you sent to th' oracle are come
An hour since. Cleomenes and Dion,
Being well arrived from Delphos, are both landed,
Hasting to th' court.   240
LORD, ⌜*to Leontes*⌝   So please you, sir, their speed
Hath been beyond account.
LEONTES   Twenty-three days
They have been absent. 'Tis good speed, foretells
The great Apollo suddenly will have   245
The truth of this appear. Prepare you, lords.
Summon a session, that we may arraign
Our most disloyal lady; for, as she hath
Been publicly accused, so shall she have
A just and open trial. While she lives,   250
My heart will be a burden to me. Leave me,
And think upon my bidding.   *They exit.*

THE
WINTER'S TALE

ACT 3

3.1 The couriers, en route from Delphos with the oracle's response, discuss the ceremony they observed and express their hopes for Hermione's good fortune.

---

2. **the isle:** Delphos (See longer note to 2.1.221, page 240.)

3. **common:** usual

5. **caught:** captivated, charmed; **habits:** garments

6. **Methinks:** it seems to me

7. **grave:** dignified, respected

12. **Jove's thunder:** Jove was the mythological god of **thunder.** (See page 92.) **my sense:** i.e., all my senses

14. **event:** result

17. **is . . . on 't:** i.e., was well spent

18–19. **Great . . . best:** Proverbial: "God turn all to good."

22. **violent carriage:** rapid, impetuous management

23–25. **the oracle . . . discover:** i.e., the oracle, sealed up by Apollo's eminent priest, will reveal its own contents by being opened **divine:** priest **discover:** reveal

ACT 3

Scene 1
Enter Cleomenes and Dion.

CLEOMENES
The climate's delicate, the air most sweet,
Fertile the isle, the temple much surpassing
The common praise it bears.

DION   I shall report,
For most it caught me, the celestial habits—   5
Methinks I so should term them—and the reverence
Of the grave wearers. O, the sacrifice,
How ceremonious, solemn, and unearthly
It was i' th' off'ring!

CLEOMENES   But of all, the burst   10
And the ear-deaf'ning voice o' th' oracle,
Kin to Jove's thunder, so surprised my sense
That I was nothing.

DION   If th' event o' th' journey
Prove as successful to the Queen—O, be 't so!—   15
As it hath been to us rare, pleasant, speedy,
The time is worth the use on 't.

CLEOMENES   Great Apollo
Turn all to th' best! These proclamations,
So forcing faults upon Hermione,   20
I little like.

DION   The violent carriage of it
Will clear or end the business when the oracle,

87

26. **Go . . . horses:** If this is a command to provide fresh horses, it may be delivered to onstage or
offstage attendants. It may, though, be shorthand for
"let's go; let's get fresh horses."

27. **gracious:** prosperous, fortunate, happy; **issue:**
outcome

3.2 As Hermione tries to defend herself in open
court, the oracle is read and she is declared chaste
and Polixenes innocent. Leontes pronounces the
oracle false, and a messenger rushes in with news
that Mamillius has died. Hermione swoons and is
carried off by Paulina and others, while, at the same
time, Leontes repents. Paulina enters with news that
Hermione is dead. Leontes vows to spend the rest of
his life grieving for the deaths of his wife and son.

----

1. **sessions:** i.e., session, sitting of a court
4. **Of us:** i.e., by me
7. **purgation:** i.e., acquittal
11. **Silence:** See longer note, page 241.
18–19. **pretense:** design, scheme, plot; **circumstances:** i.e., circumstantial evidence
19. **laid open:** revealed

Thus by Apollo's great divine sealed up,
Shall the contents discover. Something rare   25
Even then will rush to knowledge. Go. Fresh horses;
And gracious be the issue.
                                             They exit.

                         Scene 2
         Enter Leontes, Lords, ⌜and⌝ Officers.

LEONTES
This sessions, to our great grief we pronounce,
Even pushes 'gainst our heart: the party tried
The daughter of a king, our wife, and one
Of us too much beloved. Let us be cleared
Of being tyrannous, since we so openly   5
Proceed in justice, which shall have due course
Even to the guilt or the purgation.
Produce the prisoner.
OFFICER
It is his Highness' pleasure that the Queen
Appear in person here in court.   10

⌜Enter⌝ *Hermione, as to her trial, ⌜Paulina, and⌝ Ladies.*

                                        Silence!
LEONTES   Read the indictment.
OFFICER ⌜reads⌝ *Hermione, queen to the worthy Leontes,*
     King of Sicilia, thou art here accused and arraigned
     of high treason, in committing adultery with Polix-   15
     enes, King of Bohemia, and conspiring with Camillo
     to take away the life of our sovereign lord the King, thy
     royal husband; the pretense whereof being by circum-
     stances partly laid open, thou, Hermione, contrary to
     the faith and allegiance of a true subject, didst coun-   20
     sel and aid them, for their better safety, to fly away by
     night.

23. **but:** only
25. **on my part:** i.e., in my support
26. **scarce boot:** hardly help
28. **counted:** accounted, considered
31. **but:** i.e., that
33. **patience:** suffering endured with calmness
34. **Whom:** i.e., who
35. **continent:** marked by self-restraint
36. **unhappy:** unfortunate; **which is more:** i.e., which misfortune is greater
37. **history:** narrative or drama; **pattern:** equal
38. **take:** captivate, charm
39. **which owe:** i.e., who owns, possesses
41. **hopeful:** promising
42. **fore:** in the presence of
43. **Who please:** i.e., whoever chooses; **For:** i.e., as for
44. **weigh:** value; **spare:** avoid
44–46. **For honor . . . stand for:** i.e., as for (my) **honor,** I defend it only because it is a thing flowing from me to my children **derivative:** thing flowing or originating **stand for:** defend, uphold
48. **grace:** favor
49. **merited:** i.e., I merited, deserved
50–51. **With . . . thus:** This obscure and much-debated passage may mean "with what unacceptable behavior I have so transgressed that I must stand here." **encounter:** behavior **uncurrent:** unacceptable **strained:** perhaps, transgressed (though the usual meaning was "endeavored, tried my hardest")
52. **or . . . or:** either . . . or

HERMIONE
   Since what I am to say must be but that
   Which contradicts my accusation, and
   The testimony on my part no other   25
   But what comes from myself, it shall scarce boot me
   To say "Not guilty." Mine integrity,
   Being counted falsehood, shall, as I express it,
   Be so received. But thus: if powers divine
   Behold our human actions, as they do,   30
   I doubt not then but innocence shall make
   False accusation blush and tyranny
   Tremble at patience. You, my lord, best know,
   Whom least will seem to do so, my past life
   Hath been as continent, as chaste, as true,   35
   As I am now unhappy; which is more
   Than history can pattern, though devised
   And played to take spectators. For behold me,
   A fellow of the royal bed, which owe
   A moiety of the throne, a great king's daughter,   40
   The mother to a hopeful prince, here standing
   To prate and talk for life and honor fore
   Who please to come and hear. For life, I prize it
   As I weigh grief, which I would spare. For honor,
   'Tis a derivative from me to mine,   45
   And only that I stand for. I appeal
   To your own conscience, sir, before Polixenes
   Came to your court, how I was in your grace,
   How merited to be so; since he came,
   With what encounter so uncurrent I   50
   Have strained t' appear thus; if one jot beyond
   The bound of honor, or in act or will
   That way inclining, hardened be the hearts
   Of all that hear me, and my near'st of kin
   Cry fie upon my grave.   55

57–58. **wanted / Less impudence:** i.e., lacked any less shameless effrontery or insolence

61. **due:** appropriate (Leontes' reply in the next line plays on the sense of **due** as payable.)

62. **own:** admit to, acknowledge (with wordplay on the sense of **own** as "possess" something paid one)

63–65. **More . . . acknowledge:** i.e., I must not admit to any faults that are not mine   **mistress of:** in my possession

65. **For:** i.e., as for

67. **he required:** was his right

68. **become:** be appropriate to

74. **spoke:** i.e., spoken

81. **Wotting:** knowing

83. **in 's:** i.e., in his

86. **level:** line of fire

87. **Which:** i.e., **my life**; **lay down:** sacrifice; or, wager

Jove throwing a thunderbolt. (3.1.12)
From Vincenzo Cartari, *Le vere e noue imagini de gli dei delli antichi . . .* (1615).

LEONTES   I ne'er heard yet
That any of these bolder vices wanted
Less impudence to gainsay what they did
Than to perform it first.
HERMIONE   That's true enough,   60
Though 'tis a saying, sir, not due to me.
LEONTES
You will not own it.
HERMIONE   More than mistress of
Which comes to me in name of fault, I must not
At all acknowledge. For Polixenes,   65
With whom I am accused, I do confess
I loved him as in honor he required,
With such a kind of love as might become
A lady like me, with a love even such,
So and no other, as yourself commanded,   70
Which not to have done, I think, had been in me
Both disobedience and ingratitude
To you and toward your friend, whose love had
    spoke,
Even since it could speak, from an infant, freely   75
That it was yours. Now, for conspiracy,
I know not how it tastes, though it be dished
For me to try how. All I know of it
Is that Camillo was an honest man;
And why he left your court, the gods themselves,   80
Wotting no more than I, are ignorant.
LEONTES
You knew of his departure, as you know
What you have underta'en to do in 's absence.
HERMIONE   Sir,
You speak a language that I understand not.   85
My life stands in the level of your dreams,
Which I'll lay down.
LEONTES   Your actions are my dreams.

91. **of your fact:** guilty of your crime

92. **to deny:** i.e., for you **to deny; concerns . . . avails:** i.e., is of more concern than of help to you

93. **like to itself:** i.e., as is appropriate to it

94. **owning:** i.e., acknowledging as his own

96. **easiest passage:** least painful proceeding

99. **bug:** bugbear

100. **commodity:** benefit

102. **give:** i.e., give up as

106. **Starred most unluckily:** born under a most unlucky star

107. **it:** i.e., its

108. **Haled . . . murder:** dragged out to be murdered; **post:** It was the custom to fix proclamations to posts in front of sheriffs' offices.

109. **immodest:** excessive, arrogant

110. **childbed privilege:** i.e., the privilege of bed rest after childbirth; **longs:** i.e., belongs

111. **fashion:** sorts

113. **of limit:** perhaps, through the prescribed period of repose after child-bearing (a much-debated passage, since the phrase does not appear elsewhere)

116. **no life:** i.e., it is not to preserve my **life** that I speak

118. **free:** clear from blame or stain

119. **all . . . else:** i.e., all other **proofs** left **sleeping**

122. **refer me:** submit myself

You had a bastard by Polixenes,
And I but dreamed it. As you were past all shame—   90
Those of your fact are so—so past all truth,
Which to deny concerns more than avails; for as
Thy brat hath been cast out, like to itself,
No father owning it—which is indeed
More criminal in thee than it—so thou   95
Shalt feel our justice, in whose easiest passage
Look for no less than death.
HERMIONE   Sir, spare your threats.
The bug which you would fright me with I seek.
To me can life be no commodity.   100
The crown and comfort of my life, your favor,
I do give lost, for I do feel it gone,
But know not how it went. My second joy
And first fruits of my body, from his presence
I am barred like one infectious. My third comfort,   105
Starred most unluckily, is from my breast,
The innocent milk in it most innocent mouth,
Haled out to murder; myself on every post
Proclaimed a strumpet; with immodest hatred
The childbed privilege denied, which longs   110
To women of all fashion; lastly, hurried
Here to this place, i' th' open air, before
I have got strength of limit. Now, my liege,
Tell me what blessings I have here alive,
That I should fear to die? Therefore proceed.   115
But yet hear this (mistake me not: no life,
I prize it not a straw, but for mine honor,
Which I would free), if I shall be condemned
Upon surmises, all proofs sleeping else
But what your jealousies awake, I tell you   120
'Tis rigor, and not law. Your Honors all,
I do refer me to the oracle.
Apollo be my judge.
LORD   This your request

130. **flatness:** absoluteness
144. **truly:** legitimately
152. **mere:** sheer, absolute

Justice. (3.2.132)
From Thomas Peyton, *The glasse of time . . .* (1620).

Is altogether just. Therefore bring forth,   125
And in Apollo's name, his oracle.   ⌐*Officers exit.*⌐

HERMIONE
The Emperor of Russia was my father.
O, that he were alive and here beholding
His daughter's trial, that he did but see
The flatness of my misery, yet with eyes   130
Of pity, not revenge.

          ⌐*Enter*⌐ *Cleomenes, Dion,* ⌐*with Officers.*⌐

OFFICER, ⌐*presenting a sword*⌐
You here shall swear upon this sword of justice
That you, Cleomenes and Dion, have
Been both at Delphos, and from thence have
          brought   135
This sealed-up oracle, by the hand delivered
Of great Apollo's priest, and that since then
You have not dared to break the holy seal
Nor read the secrets in 't.

CLEOMENES, DION   All this we swear.   140

LEONTES   Break up the seals and read.

OFFICER ⌐*reads*⌐ *Hermione is chaste, Polixenes blame-*
     less, Camillo a true subject, Leontes a jealous tyrant,
     his innocent babe truly begotten; and the King shall
     live without an heir if that which is lost be not 145
     found.

LORDS
Now blessèd be the great Apollo!

HERMIONE   Praised!

LEONTES   Hast thou read truth?

OFFICER
Ay, my lord, even so as it is here set down.   150

LEONTES
There is no truth at all i' th' oracle.
The sessions shall proceed. This is mere falsehood.

154. **business:** errand on which you come
155. **to report:** i.e., for reporting
156. **conceit:** thought, imaginings
157. **Of:** concerning; **speed:** success
166. **but o'ercharged:** i.e., simply overburdened
172. **me:** i.e., myself
173. **New:** i.e., newly
177. **minister:** agent

"The innocent milk in it most innocent
mouth." (3.2.107)
From Desiderius Erasmus, *Morias enkomion* [transl.]
Stultitiae laus . . . (1676).

⌜*Enter a Servant.*⌝

SERVANT
My lord the King, the King!

LEONTES   What is the business?

SERVANT
O sir, I shall be hated to report it.   155
The Prince your son, with mere conceit and fear
Of the Queen's speed, is gone.

LEONTES   How? Gone?

SERVANT   Is dead.

LEONTES
Apollo's angry, and the heavens themselves   160
Do strike at my injustice.
                         ⌜*Hermione falls.*⌝
                    How now there?

PAULINA
This news is mortal to the Queen. Look down
And see what death is doing.

LEONTES   Take her hence.   165
Her heart is but o'ercharged. She will recover.
I have too much believed mine own suspicion.
Beseech you, tenderly apply to her
Some remedies for life.

        ⌜*Paulina exits with Officers carrying Hermione.*⌝

                    Apollo, pardon   170
My great profaneness 'gainst thine oracle.
I'll reconcile me to Polixenes,
New woo my queen, recall the good Camillo,
Whom I proclaim a man of truth, of mercy;
For, being transported by my jealousies   175
To bloody thoughts and to revenge, I chose
Camillo for the minister to poison

179. **tardied:** delayed (in carrying out)

180. **swift command:** i.e., order that Polixenes be immediately killed

180–82. **though . . . done:** i.e., though I threatened him with death if he did not do it, and encouraged him with reward if he did it

184. **Unclasped:** opened up, displayed; **practice:** scheming, treachery; **fortunes:** success, wealth, position

185. **you knew great:** i.e., you know were great

186. **incertainties:** uncertainties

187. **No richer . . . honor:** i.e., with his integrity as his only wealth

188. **rust:** moral corrosion, corruption

191. **lace:** cord that draws closed the bodice of her dress; **cracking:** splitting, breaking

195. **wheels, racks:** instruments of torture (See page 186.)

196. **old:** long-used

200. **green:** simple-minded; **idle:** silly

203. **spices of it:** i.e., traces or slight touches of what you have now done

205. **of a fool:** i.e., a fool

206. **damnable ingrateful:** i.e., damnably ungrateful

207. **Thou:** i.e., that thou

My friend Polixenes, which had been done
But that the good mind of Camillo tardied
My swift command, though I with death and with   180
Reward did threaten and encourage him,
Not doing it and being done. He, most humane
And filled with honor, to my kingly guest
Unclasped my practice, quit his fortunes here,
Which you knew great, and to the hazard   185
Of all incertainties himself commended,
No richer than his honor. How he glisters
Through my rust, and how his piety
Does my deeds make the blacker!

                    ⌜*Enter Paulina.*⌝

PAULINA   Woe the while!   190
  O, cut my lace, lest my heart, cracking it,
  Break too!
LORD   What fit is this, good lady?
PAULINA, ⌜*to Leontes*⌝
  What studied torments, tyrant, hast for me?
  What wheels, racks, fires? What flaying? Boiling   195
  In leads or oils? What old or newer torture
  Must I receive, whose every word deserves
  To taste of thy most worst? Thy tyranny,
  Together working with thy jealousies,
  Fancies too weak for boys, too green and idle   200
  For girls of nine, O, think what they have done,
  And then run mad indeed, stark mad, for all
  Thy bygone fooleries were but spices of it.
  That thou betrayedst Polixenes, 'twas nothing;
  That did but show thee of a fool, inconstant   205
  And damnable ingrateful. Nor was 't much
  Thou wouldst have poisoned good Camillo's honor,
  To have him kill a king: poor trespasses,
  More monstrous standing by, whereof I reckon

211. **or . . . or:** i.e., either . . . or

212. **water:** i.e., tears of pity; **done 't:** i.e., he had done it

213. **Nor . . . death:** i.e., neither are you entirely (or immediately) at fault in the **death**

215. **high:** noble

216. **conceive:** imagine or understand that; **gross and foolish:** perhaps, grossly foolish

217. **Blemished:** i.e., stained the reputation of

218. **Laid . . . answer:** brought as a charge against which you must defend yourself

224–25. **If . . . / Prevail:** i.e., if neither my **word** nor my **oath** persuades you

226. **Tincture . . . eye:** i.e., color to **her lip** or brightness to **her eye**

227. **Heat outwardly:** external heat

229. **heavier:** (1) weightier; (2) more oppressive

230. **woes can stir:** lamentations can move; **betake thee:** i.e., deliver yourself

231. **knees:** i.e., supplicants offering prayers on their **knees**

232. **together:** without intermission

233. **still:** always

234. **move:** persuade

240. **business:** matter; **made fault:** done wrong

The casting forth to crows thy baby daughter 210
To be or none or little, though a devil
Would have shed water out of fire ere done 't.
Nor is 't directly laid to thee the death
Of the young prince, whose honorable thoughts,
Thoughts high for one so tender, cleft the heart 215
That could conceive a gross and foolish sire
Blemished his gracious dam. This is not, no,
Laid to thy answer. But the last—O lords,
When I have said, cry woe!—the Queen, the Queen,
The sweet'st, dear'st creature's dead, and vengeance 220
for 't
Not dropped down yet.
LORD   The higher powers forbid!
PAULINA
I say she's dead. I'll swear 't. If word nor oath
Prevail not, go and see. If you can bring 225
Tincture or luster in her lip, her eye,
Heat outwardly or breath within, I'll serve you
As I would do the gods.—But, O thou tyrant,
Do not repent these things, for they are heavier
Than all thy woes can stir. Therefore betake thee 230
To nothing but despair. A thousand knees
Ten thousand years together, naked, fasting,
Upon a barren mountain, and still winter
In storm perpetual, could not move the gods
To look that way thou wert. 235
LEONTES   Go on, go on.
Thou canst not speak too much. I have deserved
All tongues to talk their bitt'rest.
LORD, ⌜*to Paulina*⌝   Say no more.
Howe'er the business goes, you have made fault 240
I' th' boldness of your speech.
PAULINA   I am sorry for 't.
All faults I make, when I shall come to know them,

245. **touched:** moved or stirred (emotionally)

246–48. **What's gone . . . grief:** Proverbial: "Past cure past care."

248–49. **Do . . . petition:** At lines 230–31 Paulina had committed Leontes to perpetual **affliction:** "Therefore betake thee / To . . . despair."

250. **that have minded:** i.e., who have reminded

253. **fool:** addressed to herself in (real or feigned) anger at having mentioned Hermione

255. **remember:** remind

256. **patience:** capacity to bear suffering

258. **but:** only

262. **them:** i.e., their gravestones

266. **nature:** i.e., my physical strength

267. **bear up with:** withstand; **exercise:** spiritual exercise, act of devotion

268. **daily . . . it:** i.e., **vow** to observe or perform it **daily**

3.3 Antigonus leaves the baby in Bohemia, where Polixenes is king. In a sudden storm, the ship sinks and Antigonus is chased by a bear, who then eats him. The baby, along with the gold left with her, is found by a shepherd and his son.

––––––––––––

1. **perfect, then:** i.e., certain then that

2. **deserts:** wilderness; **Bohemia:** The fact that Shakespeare gives his Bohemia a seacoast has occasioned much comment. Some think it an error; others think it a deliberate strategy to make the setting clearly fictional.

I do repent. Alas, I have showed too much
The rashness of a woman. He is touched   245
To th' noble heart.—What's gone and what's past
    help
Should be past grief. Do not receive affliction
At my petition. I beseech you, rather
Let me be punished, that have minded you   250
Of what you should forget. Now, good my liege,
Sir, royal sir, forgive a foolish woman.
The love I bore your queen—lo, fool again!—
I'll speak of her no more, nor of your children.
I'll not remember you of my own lord,   255
Who is lost too. Take your patience to you,
And I'll say nothing.
LEONTES   Thou didst speak but well
When most the truth, which I receive much better
Than to be pitied of thee. Prithee, bring me   260
To the dead bodies of my queen and son.
One grave shall be for both. Upon them shall
The causes of their death appear, unto
Our shame perpetual. Once a day I'll visit
The chapel where they lie, and tears shed there   265
Shall be my recreation. So long as nature
Will bear up with this exercise, so long
I daily vow to use it. Come, and lead me
To these sorrows.
                                                            They exit.

                         Scene 3
Enter Antigonus ⌐carrying the⌐ babe, ⌐and⌐ a Mariner.

ANTIGONUS
    Thou art perfect, then, our ship hath touched upon
    The deserts of Bohemia?

4. **grimly:** forbidding
5. **present:** immediate; **blusters:** stormy blasts; **In my conscience:** i.e., truly
6. **that . . . hand:** what we are doing
9. **bark:** ship
12. **i' th' land:** i.e., inland; **like:** likely
14. **keep:** dwell
23. **waking:** i.e., waking experience
24. **some another:** i.e., sometimes on the other
26. **So . . . becoming:** i.e., so full of becoming sorrow
27. **very sanctity:** holiness itself
28. **cabin:** berth
30. **fury:** fierce passion; **anon:** soon
33. **for:** i.e., to be
36. **for:** because
37. **counted:** accounted, considered; **Perdita:** she who is lost (Latin)

"The storm begins." (3.3.53)
From Lodovico Dolce, *Imprese nobili* . . . (1583).

MARINER   Ay, my lord, and fear
We have landed in ill time. The skies look grimly
And threaten present blusters. In my conscience,   5
The heavens with that we have in hand are angry
And frown upon 's.
ANTIGONUS
Their sacred wills be done. Go, get aboard.
Look to thy bark. I'll not be long before
I call upon thee.   10
MARINER   Make your best haste, and go not
Too far i' th' land. 'Tis like to be loud weather.
Besides, this place is famous for the creatures
Of prey that keep upon 't.
ANTIGONUS   Go thou away.   15
I'll follow instantly.
MARINER   I am glad at heart
To be so rid o' th' business.   *He exits.*
ANTIGONUS   Come, poor babe.
I have heard, but not believed, the spirits o' th' dead   20
May walk again. If such thing be, thy mother
Appeared to me last night, for ne'er was dream
So like a waking. To me comes a creature,
Sometimes her head on one side, some another.
I never saw a vessel of like sorrow,   25
So filled and so becoming. In pure white robes,
Like very sanctity, she did approach
My cabin where I lay, thrice bowed before me,
And, gasping to begin some speech, her eyes
Became two spouts. The fury spent, anon   30
Did this break from her: "Good Antigonus,
Since fate, against thy better disposition,
Hath made thy person for the thrower-out
Of my poor babe, according to thine oath,
Places remote enough are in Bohemia.   35
There weep, and leave it crying. And, for the babe
Is counted lost forever, Perdita

38. **For:** because of; **ungentle:** violent, harsh

39. **Put:** imposed

43. **was so:** i.e., was real; **toys:** trifles

45. **squared:** directed

47. **would:** wishes; **issue:** offspring

49. **for . . . death:** i.e., either to live or to die; **earth:** land

50. **right:** true; **speed:** prosper

51. **thy character:** i.e., letters containing, among other things, her name (Literally, **character** means simply "writing.")

52. **breed thee:** i.e., pay for upbringing and/or education

53. **rest thine:** remain yours (The gold and treasure left with her will, he hopes, exceed the costs of her rearing.)

56. **loss:** ruin and separation from family

63. **the chase:** the hunt; or, perhaps, the hunted animal (here, the bear)

65. **would:** wish

67. **rest:** i.e., years between

68. **ancientry:** elders, old people

I prithee call 't. For this ungentle business
Put on thee by my lord, thou ne'er shalt see
Thy wife Paulina more." And so, with shrieks,   40
She melted into air. Affrighted much,
I did in time collect myself and thought
This was so and no slumber. Dreams are toys,
Yet for this once, yea, superstitiously,
I will be squared by this. I do believe   45
Hermione hath suffered death, and that
Apollo would, this being indeed the issue
Of King Polixenes, it should here be laid,
Either for life or death, upon the earth
Of its right father.—Blossom, speed thee well.   50
There lie, and there thy character; there these,
        ⌜*He lays down the baby, a bundle, and a box.*⌝
Which may, if fortune please, both breed thee, pretty,
And still rest thine. ⌜*Thunder.*⌝ The storm begins.
    Poor wretch,
That for thy mother's fault art thus exposed   55
To loss and what may follow. Weep I cannot,
But my heart bleeds, and most accurst am I
To be by oath enjoined to this. Farewell.
The day frowns more and more. Thou'rt like to have
A lullaby too rough. I never saw   60
The heavens so dim by day.
            ⌜*Thunder, and sounds of hunting.*⌝
                A savage clamor!
Well may I get aboard! This is the chase.
I am gone forever!   *He exits, pursued by a bear.*
        ⌜*Enter*⌝ Shepherd.

SHEPHERD   I would there were no age between ten and   65
    three-and-twenty, or that youth would sleep out the
    rest, for there is nothing in the between but getting
    wenches with child, wronging the ancientry, steal-

74. **ivy:** perhaps, sea holly or seaweed
76. **child:** baby girl
77. **scape:** sexual transgression
78–79. **waiting-gentlewoman:** a **gentlewoman** who serves a lady of higher rank
79–80. **stair-work . . . behind-door work:** perhaps, furtive lovemaking in stairwells, on trunks, behind doors
81. **got:** begot, conceived
90. **and it:** i.e., and the sea
93. **chafes:** frets, fumes
94. **takes up:** begins to occupy
98. **anon:** immediately; **yeast:** foam
99. **thrust . . . hogshead:** i.e., drive a **cork** stopper into a large cask (in order to draw out the beer)
99–100. **land service:** i.e., action on land (**Service** could be either military action or the serving of food.)

Bears "are never curst but when they
are hungry." (3.3.136–37)
From Henry Peacham, *Minerua Britanna* . . . (1612).

110

ing, fighting—Hark you now. Would any but these
boiled brains of nineteen and two-and-twenty hunt   70
this weather? They have scared away two of my best
sheep, which I fear the wolf will sooner find than
the master. If anywhere I have them, 'tis by the
seaside, browsing of ivy. Good luck, an 't be thy will,
what have we here? Mercy on 's, a bairn! A very   75
pretty bairn. A boy or a child, I wonder? A pretty
one, a very pretty one. Sure some scape. Though I
am not bookish, yet I can read waiting-gentlewoman in the scape. This has been some stair-work,
some trunk-work, some behind-door work. They   80
were warmer that got this than the poor thing is
here. I'll take it up for pity. Yet I'll tarry till my son
come. He halloed but even now.—Whoa-ho-ho!

Enter ⌐Shepherd's Son.⌐

SHEPHERD'S SON   Hilloa, loa!
SHEPHERD   What, art so near? If thou'lt see a thing to   85
talk on when thou art dead and rotten, come hither.
What ail'st thou, man?
SHEPHERD'S SON   I have seen two such sights, by sea
and by land—but I am not to say it is a sea, for it is
now the sky; betwixt the firmament and it, you   90
cannot thrust a bodkin's point.
SHEPHERD   Why, boy, how is it?
SHEPHERD'S SON   I would you did but see how it chafes,
how it rages, how it takes up the shore. But that's
not to the point. O, the most piteous cry of the poor   95
souls! Sometimes to see 'em, and not to see 'em.
Now the ship boring the moon with her mainmast,
and anon swallowed with yeast and froth, as you'd
thrust a cork into a hogshead. And then for the land
service, to see how the bear tore out his shoulder-   100
bone, how he cried to me for help, and said his

102–3. **to make an end:** to finish the story (with wordplay on "to destroy")

103. **flap-dragoned it:** i.e., swallowed it the way revelers would catch raisins out of flaming brandy and swallow them

105. **mocked:** i.e., by imitating

109. **winked:** blinked

113. **by:** i.e., nearby

115. **ship:** i.e., ship's

117. **footing:** a secure place to stand (with wordplay on charitable "foundation")

118. **Heavy:** sad

121. **bearing cloth:** (ornamental) christening robe; **squire's:** A squire was the rank just below knight and perhaps the highest rank with which the shepherd is familiar.

124. **changeling:** child left by the fairies

126–27. **made old man:** an **old man** whose fortune has been **made**

128. **you're . . . live:** perhaps, you'll live well; or, you're well-to-do

129. **fairy gold:** gold given by fairies (Folklore about **fairy gold** includes the belief that to tell about the **gold** brings bad luck.)

130. **close:** secret; **next:** nearest (i.e., fastest)

131. **to be so still:** i.e., to continue to be so

name was Antigonus, a nobleman. But to make an
end of the ship: to see how the sea flap-dragoned it.
But, first, how the poor souls roared and the sea
mocked them, and how the poor gentleman roared 105
and the bear mocked him, both roaring louder than
the sea or weather.

SHEPHERD Name of mercy, when was this, boy?

SHEPHERD'S SON Now, now. I have not winked since I
saw these sights. The men are not yet cold under 110
water, nor the bear half dined on the gentleman.
He's at it now.

SHEPHERD Would I had been by to have helped the old
man.

SHEPHERD'S SON I would you had been by the ship side, 115
to have helped her. There your charity would have
lacked footing.

SHEPHERD Heavy matters, heavy matters. But look
thee here, boy. Now bless thyself. Thou met'st with
things dying, I with things newborn. Here's a sight 120
for thee. Look thee, a bearing cloth for a squire's
child. Look thee here. Take up, take up, boy. Open
't. So, let's see. It was told me I should be rich by
the fairies. This is some changeling. Open 't. What's
within, boy? 125

SHEPHERD'S SON, ⌜*opening the box*⌝ You're a made old
man. If the sins of your youth are forgiven you,
you're well to live. Gold, all gold.

SHEPHERD This is fairy gold, boy, and 'twill prove so.
Up with 't, keep it close. Home, home, the next way. 130
We are lucky, boy, and to be so still requires
nothing but secrecy. Let my sheep go. Come, good
boy, the next way home.

SHEPHERD'S SON Go you the next way with your
findings. I'll go see if the bear be gone from the 135
gentleman and how much he hath eaten. They are

137. **curst:** savage

142. **Marry:** i.e., indeed (formerly an oath on the name of the Virgin Mary)

"Thou met'st with things dying, I with things newborn." (3.3.119–20)
From Andrea Alciati, . . . *Emblemata* . . . (1661).

never curst but when they are hungry. If there be
any of him left, I'll bury it.

SHEPHERD That's a good deed. If thou mayest discern
by that which is left of him what he is, fetch me to   140
th' sight of him.

SHEPHERD'S SON Marry, will I, and you shall help to
put him i' th' ground.

SHEPHERD 'Tis a lucky day, boy, and we'll do good
deeds on 't.   145

They exit.

THE
WINTER'S TALE

ACT 4

4.1 Father Time appears and bridges the sixteen-year gap following the abandonment of Perdita in Bohemia.

———————

0 SD. **Time, the Chorus:** This character, probably appearing as an old man, carries an hourglass and wears wings (proverbially, "Time has wings"). As **Chorus,** he comments on the action. See longer note, page 241, and picture, page xix.

   1. **that:** i.e., who; **try all:** i.e., test everyone

   2. **unfolds:** reveals; **error:** mistaken idea

   6. **growth untried:** i.e., developments unexamined

   8–9. **law . . . custom:** See longer note, page 242. **one self-born hour:** one and the same hour

   9. **pass:** (1) proceed; (2) elapse; (3) be allowed to go uncensured

   10. **The . . . was:** i.e., as I was before laws and customs were established

   11. **received:** generally accepted

   14–15. **as my tale . . . it:** i.e., just as my tale (the play you are viewing) seems stale in comparison to the shining (**glistering**) present

   16. **glass:** hourglass (See page 64.)

   16–17. **give . . . between:** i.e., advance the action of the play as if you had slept between acts   **scene:** play   **growing:** advance, progress

   17. **Leontes leaving:** i.e., as we now leave Leontes

   18. **fond:** foolish

   22. **th' King's:** Polixenes'; **which:** whom (See longer note, page 242.)

   23. **pace:** proceed or advance

ACT 4

Scene 1
Enter Time, the Chorus.

TIME
I, that please some, try all—both joy and terror
Of good and bad, that makes and unfolds error—
Now take upon me, in the name of Time,
To use my wings. Impute it not a crime
To me or my swift passage that I slide   5
O'er sixteen years, and leave the growth untried
Of that wide gap, since it is in my power
To o'erthrow law and in one self-born hour
To plant and o'erwhelm custom. Let me pass
The same I am ere ancient'st order was   10
Or what is now received. I witness to
The times that brought them in. So shall I do
To th' freshest things now reigning, and make stale
The glistering of this present, as my tale
Now seems to it. Your patience this allowing,   15
I turn my glass and give my scene such growing
As you had slept between. Leontes leaving,
Th' effects of his fond jealousies so grieving
That he shuts up himself, imagine me,
Gentle spectators, that I now may be   20
In fair Bohemia. And remember well
I mentioned a son o' th' King's, which Florizell
I now name to you, and with speed so pace

119

25. **wond'ring:** i.e., the wonder she inspires in others

26. **list not:** choose not to

30. **argument:** subject, theme; **Of this allow:** accept this

4.2 Camillo asks permission to return to Sicilia. Polixenes refuses his request and asks Camillo instead to go with him in disguise to the shepherd's home where Polixenes' son is spending his time.

---

5. **been aired:** i.e., lived (literally, exposed to the open air)

7. **feeling:** deeply felt, heartfelt

8. **be some allay:** i.e., provide some relief; **o'erween:** i.e., am presumptuous enough

13. **want:** lack

14. **made me businesses:** i.e., created projects for me

18. **considered:** recompensed

19. **study:** pursuit, concern

20. **the heaping friendships:** perhaps, an increase in your friendly services (But see longer note, page 242.)

To speak of Perdita, now grown in grace
Equal with wond'ring. What of her ensues   25
I list not prophesy; but let Time's news
Be known when 'tis brought forth. A shepherd's
    daughter
And what to her adheres, which follows after,
Is th' argument of Time. Of this allow,   30
If ever you have spent time worse ere now.
If never, yet that Time himself doth say
He wishes earnestly you never may.

                                        He exits.

                    Scene 2
            Enter Polixenes and Camillo.

POLIXENES I pray thee, good Camillo, be no more
    importunate. 'Tis a sickness denying thee anything,
    a death to grant this.
CAMILLO It is fifteen years since I saw my country.
    Though I have for the most part been aired abroad,   5
    I desire to lay my bones there. Besides, the penitent
    king, my master, hath sent for me, to whose feeling
    sorrows I might be some allay—or I o'erween to
    think so—which is another spur to my departure.
POLIXENES As thou lov'st me, Camillo, wipe not out the   10
    rest of thy services by leaving me now. The need I
    have of thee thine own goodness hath made. Better
    not to have had thee than thus to want thee. Thou,
    having made me businesses which none without
    thee can sufficiently manage, must either stay to   15
    execute them thyself or take away with thee the very
    services thou hast done, which if I have not enough
    considered, as too much I cannot, to be more
    thankful to thee shall be my study, and my profit
    therein the heaping friendships. Of that fatal coun- 20

23. **reconciled:** alluding presumably to a restoration of good, if distant, relations between Leontes and Polixenes

25. **are:** i.e., is

29. **approved:** proved

31. **are:** i.e., is

32. **missingly noted:** i.e., observed with a sense of loss that

33. **retired:** withdrawn, removed; **frequent to:** frequently at

34. **princely exercises:** aristocratic activities, e.g., athletics, hunting, military training

35. **considered so much:** i.e., noticed the same thing

36–37. **so far . . . service:** i.e., so much so that I have spies

37. **his removedness:** i.e., him in his absence

39. **homely:** simple

40–41. **the imagination . . . neighbors:** i.e., what his neighbors could have imagined

41–42. **an unspeakable estate:** a fortune beyond description

44. **note:** distinction

44–46. **The report . . . cottage:** i.e., her reputation is more widely known than one would expect from her low social condition   **cottage:** small, humble dwelling

48. **angle:** fishhook; **our son:** Polixenes here shifts to the "royal we," which he uses through line 50.

49–50. **not appearing what we are:** i.e., in disguise

50. **question:** talk

52. **uneasy:** difficult

try Sicilia, prithee speak no more, whose very
naming punishes me with the remembrance of that
penitent, as thou call'st him, and reconciled king
my brother, whose loss of his most precious queen
and children are even now to be afresh lamented.   25
Say to me, when sawst thou the Prince Florizell, my
son? Kings are no less unhappy, their issue not
being gracious, than they are in losing them when
they have approved their virtues.

CAMILLO   Sir, it is three days since I saw the Prince.   30
What his happier affairs may be are to me un-
known, but I have missingly noted he is of late
much retired from court and is less frequent to his
princely exercises than formerly he hath appeared.

POLIXENES   I have considered so much, Camillo, and   35
with some care, so far that I have eyes under my
service which look upon his removedness, from
whom I have this intelligence: that he is seldom
from the house of a most homely shepherd, a man,
they say, that from very nothing, and beyond the   40
imagination of his neighbors, is grown into an
unspeakable estate.

CAMILLO   I have heard, sir, of such a man, who hath a
daughter of most rare note. The report of her is
extended more than can be thought to begin from   45
such a cottage.

POLIXENES   That's likewise part of my intelligence, but,
I fear, the angle that plucks our son thither. Thou
shalt accompany us to the place, where we will, not
appearing what we are, have some question with   50
the shepherd, from whose simplicity I think it not
uneasy to get the cause of my son's resort thither.
Prithee be my present partner in this business, and
lay aside the thoughts of Sicilia.

CAMILLO   I willingly obey your command.   55

4.3 Autolycus, a con man, steals the shepherd's son's money and decides to use the upcoming sheep-shearing feast as an occasion for yet more thievery.

---

1. **peer:** (1) peep out; (2) appear
2. **doxy:** beggar's woman
3. **sweet:** pleasant part
4. **winter's pale:** Winter is being pictured as an enclosed area (a **pale**); there is also wordplay on paleness of skin occasioned by winter.
7. **pugging:** perhaps, thieving (a word not recorded elsewhere) "To set the tooth on edge" was proverbial for "to whet the appetite." **an:** i.e., on
11. **aunts:** i.e., whores
14. **three-pile:** i.e., rich velvet with a deep pile
20. **sow-skin budget:** bag made of pigskin
21. **account:** explanation for one's behavior
22. **in the stocks:** i.e., for vagrancy

A man in the stocks. (4.3.22)
From August Casimir Redel, *Apophtegmata symbolica* . . . [n.d.].

POLIXENES My best Camillo. We must disguise ourselves.

⌜*They*⌝ *exit.*

Scene 3
Enter Autolycus singing.

⌜AUTOLYCUS⌝
When daffodils begin to peer,
  With heigh, the doxy over the dale,
Why, then comes in the sweet o' the year,
  For the red blood reigns in the winter's pale.

The white sheet bleaching on the hedge,   5
  With heigh, the sweet birds, O how they sing!
Doth set my pugging tooth an edge,
  For a quart of ale is a dish for a king.

The lark, that tirralirra chants,
  With heigh, ⌜with heigh,⌝ the thrush and the jay,   10
Are summer songs for me and my aunts,
  While we lie tumbling in the hay.

I have served Prince Florizell and in my time wore
three-pile, but now I am out of service.

But shall I go mourn for that, my dear?   15
  The pale moon shines by night,
And when I wander here and there,
  I then do most go right.

If tinkers may have leave to live,
  And bear the sow-skin budget,   20
Then my account I well may give,
  And in the stocks avouch it.

23. **traffic:** goods or merchandise

23–24. **When . . . linen:** i.e., when the hawk is nest-building, protect your small linens (The **kite** steals **lesser linen,** while the **white sheet bleaching on the hedge** [line 5] is Autolycus' prey.)

24. **Autolycus:** See longer note, page 243.

25. **littered under Mercury:** born when the planet Mercury was in the ascendant **Mercury:** in classical mythology, the winged messenger god who sometimes stole from the other gods (See longer note to **Autolycus,** line 24, page 243.)

26. **snapper-up:** thief

26–27. **With . . . caparison:** i.e., through gambling and whoring I acquired this outfit (namely, the rags he is wearing) **die:** one of a pair of dice **drab:** slut, prostitute

28. **the silly cheat:** petty theft

28–29. **Gallows . . . highway:** perhaps, fear of the gallows and of being beaten deter me from committing highway robbery

30. **For:** i.e., as for

31. **prize:** booty (or someone from whom it may be taken)

31 SD. **Shepherd's Son:** See longer note, page 243.

32–33. **every . . . shilling:** i.e., the fleeces from eleven wethers (gelded sheep) weigh a **tod** (twenty-eight pounds); **every tod** of wool will bring in a **pound** and one **shilling**

33–34. **fifteen hundred:** i.e., sheep

34. **what . . . to:** i.e., what is the total value of **the wool**?

(continued)

My traffic is sheets. When the kite builds, look to
lesser linen. My father named me Autolycus, who,
being, as I am, littered under Mercury, was likewise   25
a snapper-up of unconsidered trifles. With die and
drab I purchased this caparison, and my revenue is
the silly cheat. Gallows and knock are too powerful
on the highway. Beating and hanging are terrors to
me. For the life to come, I sleep out the thought of   30
it. A prize, a prize!

Enter ⌜Shepherd's Son.⌝

SHEPHERD'S SON   Let me see, every 'leven wether tods,
   every tod yields pound and odd shilling; fifteen
   hundred shorn, what comes the wool to?
AUTOLYCUS, ⌜*aside*⌝   If the springe hold, the cock's   35
   mine.   ⌜*He lies down.*⌝
SHEPHERD'S SON   I cannot do 't without counters. Let
   me see, what am I to buy for our sheep-shearing
   feast? (⌜*He reads a paper.*⌝) Three pound of sugar,
   five pound of currants, rice—what will this sister of   40
   mine do with rice? But my father hath made her
   mistress of the feast, and she lays it on. She hath
   made me four-and-twenty nosegays for the shearers, three-man song men all, and very good ones;
   but they are most of them means and basses, but   45
   one Puritan amongst them, and he sings psalms to
   hornpipes. I must have saffron to color the warden
   pies; mace; dates, none, that's out of my note;
   nutmegs, seven; a race or two of ginger, but that I
   may beg; four pound of prunes, and as many of   50
   raisins o' th' sun.
AUTOLYCUS, ⌜*writhing as if in pain*⌝   O, that ever I was
   born!
SHEPHERD'S SON   I' th' name of me!

35. **springe:** snare (to catch woodcocks, proverbially stupid birds) See longer note to 4.3.36 SD, page 243, and picture, page 190.

37. **counters:** round pieces of metal (or some other substance) used to do arithmetic

42. **lays it on:** is lavish in expense

43. **made me:** i.e., made

44. **three-man song men:** singers of songs written for three voices (countertenor or alto, tenor, and bass)

45. **means:** i.e., tenors

45–47. **but . . . hornpipes:** i.e., except for **one Puritan**, who **sings psalms** even to dance tunes

47. **warden:** i.e., warden pear

48. **out of my note:** i.e., not on my list; or, not something I need to take note of (See longer note, page 244.)

49. **race:** root

51. **o' th' sun:** i.e., sun-dried

67. **footman:** i.e., a man on foot

68. **footman:** attendant (as Autolycus once was)

69–71. **should . . . service:** The shepherd's son here plays with yet another meaning of **footman**— i.e., a foot soldier, whose clothing would be inferior to that of a **horseman**—i.e., a mounted soldier— unless the **horseman** had been in furious combat.

76. **softly:** gently

77. **out:** dislocated

80–81. **charitable office:** i.e., act of kindness

85. **past:** more than

89. **manner:** kind

AUTOLYCUS O, help me, help me! Pluck but off these   55
rags, and then death, death.

SHEPHERD'S SON Alack, poor soul, thou hast need of
more rags to lay on thee rather than have these off.

AUTOLYCUS O sir, the loathsomeness of them ⌜offends⌝
me more than the stripes I have received, which are   60
mighty ones and millions.

SHEPHERD'S SON Alas, poor man, a million of beating
may come to a great matter.

AUTOLYCUS I am robbed, sir, and beaten, my money
and apparel ta'en from me, and these detestable   65
things put upon me.

SHEPHERD'S SON What, by a horseman, or a footman?

AUTOLYCUS A footman, sweet sir, a footman.

SHEPHERD'S SON Indeed, he should be a footman by
the garments he has left with thee. If this be a   70
horseman's coat, it hath seen very hot service. Lend
me thy hand; I'll help thee. Come, lend me thy
hand.

AUTOLYCUS O, good sir, tenderly, O!

SHEPHERD'S SON Alas, poor soul.   75

AUTOLYCUS O, good sir, softly, good sir. I fear, sir, my
shoulder blade is out.

SHEPHERD'S SON How now? Canst stand?

AUTOLYCUS, ⌜*stealing the Shepherd's Son's purse*⌝ Softly,
dear sir, good sir, softly. You ha' done me a chari-   80
table office.

SHEPHERD'S SON Dost lack any money? I have a little
money for thee.

AUTOLYCUS No, good sweet sir, no, I beseech you, sir. I
have a kinsman not past three-quarters of a mile   85
hence, unto whom I was going. I shall there have
money or anything I want. Offer me no money, I
pray you; that kills my heart.

SHEPHERD'S SON What manner of fellow was he that
robbed you?   90

92. **troll-my-dames:** i.e., troll-madams, literally a board game, but here probably meaning whores ("Troll" could mean "pass around"; it was also sometimes spelled "trull," which, as a noun, meant "strumpet."); **once:** i.e., to have once been

96. **would:** i.e., should

98. **no . . . abide:** i.e., only pause before going away

100. **ape-bearer:** an itinerant entertainer with a trained monkey

101. **process-server:** sheriff's officer who serves summonses; **compassed:** obtained; devised

101–2. **motion:** puppet show

102. **Prodigal Son:** For the parable of the Prodigal Son, see Luke 15.11–32; **wife:** perhaps, woman; or, perhaps, widow

103. **living:** property

105. **in rogue:** i.e., on **rogue** (See longer note, page 244.)

106. **Out upon him:** an expression of abhorrence; **Prig:** thief

107. **wakes:** rural feasts

111. **big:** haughty, pretentious

119. **softly:** i.e., slowly

120. **bring:** accompany

124. **Prosper you:** i.e., may you prosper

125. **not hot enough:** i.e., too cold because it is empty (with wordplay on the **hot** flavor of spices)

AUTOLYCUS   A fellow, sir, that I have known to go about
with troll-my-dames. I knew him once a servant of
the Prince. I cannot tell, good sir, for which of his
virtues it was, but he was certainly whipped out of
the court.   95
SHEPHERD'S SON   His vices, you would say. There's no
virtue whipped out of the court. They cherish it to
make it stay there, and yet it will no more but abide.
AUTOLYCUS   Vices, I would say, sir. I know this man
well. He hath been since an ape-bearer, then a   100
process-server, a bailiff. Then he compassed a motion of the Prodigal Son, and married a tinker's wife
within a mile where my land and living lies, and,
having flown over many knavish professions, he
settled only in rogue. Some call him Autolycus.   105
SHEPHERD'S SON   Out upon him! Prig, for my life, prig!
He haunts wakes, fairs, and bearbaitings.
AUTOLYCUS   Very true, sir: he, sir, he. That's the rogue
that put me into this apparel.
SHEPHERD'S SON   Not a more cowardly rogue in all   110
Bohemia. If you had but looked big and spit at him,
he'd have run.
AUTOLYCUS   I must confess to you, sir, I am no fighter. I
am false of heart that way, and that he knew, I
warrant him.   115
SHEPHERD'S SON   How do you now?
AUTOLYCUS   Sweet sir, much better than I was. I can
stand and walk. I will even take my leave of you and
pace softly towards my kinsman's.
SHEPHERD'S SON   Shall I bring thee on the way?   120
AUTOLYCUS   No, good-faced sir, no, sweet sir.
SHEPHERD'S SON   Then fare thee well. I must go buy
spices for our sheep-shearing.
AUTOLYCUS   Prosper you, sweet sir.
                    ⌜*Shepherd's Son*⌝ *exits.*
Your purse is not hot enough to purchase your   125

127. **cheat:** theft; **bring out:** produce
128. **sheep:** i.e., to be fleeced or robbed; **let . . . unrolled:** i.e., let my name be deleted (presumably, from the roll of thieves)
130. **Jog on:** trudge
131. **hent:** lay hold of; **stile-a:** A **stile** is a set of steps for crossing a fence. The suffix **-a** merely adds a syllable needed for the song's rhythm.
133. **Your sad:** i.e., any **sad** (heart)

4.4   At the sheepshearing feast, Florizell and Perdita declare their love before the disguised Polixenes and Camillo. When Polixenes orders Florizell never to see Perdita again, the two decide to flee. Camillo, for his own ends, advises them to go to Sicilia. The shepherd and his son, seeking the king to protest their innocence, are steered by Autolycus to Florizell's ship.

---

1. **weeds:** garments
2. **a life:** an animation, vitality; **no . . . Flora:** i.e., you are **no shepherdess,** but instead the Roman goddess of flowers and spring
3. **Peering . . . front:** showing herself in the beginning of April   **front:** literally, brow or forehead
4. **petty gods:** lesser deities of classical mythology
5. **on 't:** i.e., of it
7. **extremes:** extravagances (in praise); **not becomes:** is not appropriate for
9. **mark . . . land:** object of attention throughout the country

(continued)

spice. I'll be with you at your sheep-shearing too. If
I make not this cheat bring out another, and the
shearers prove sheep, let me be unrolled and my
name put in the book of virtue.

⌜*Sings.*⌝   *Jog on, jog on, the footpath way,*   130
And merrily hent the stile-a.
A merry heart goes all the day,
Your sad tires in a mile-a.

He exits.

Scene 4
Enter Florizell ⌜and⌝ Perdita.

FLORIZELL
These your unusual weeds to each part of you
Does give a life—no shepherdess, but Flora
Peering in April's front. This your sheep-shearing
Is as a meeting of the petty gods,
And you the queen on 't.   5
PERDITA   Sir, my gracious lord,
To chide at your extremes it not becomes me;
O, pardon that I name them! Your high self,
The gracious mark o' th' land, you have obscured
With a swain's wearing, and me, poor lowly maid,   10
Most goddesslike pranked up. But that our feasts
In every mess have folly, and the feeders
Digest ⌜it⌝ with a custom, I should blush
To see you so attired, ⌜swoon,⌝ I think,
To show myself a glass.   15
FLORIZELL   I bless the time
When my good falcon made her flight across
Thy father's ground.
PERDITA   Now Jove afford you cause.
To me the difference forges dread. Your greatness   20

10. **swain's wearing:** garments of a country youth

12. **In . . . folly:** i.e., in every group of diners there are some who act foolishly; **feeders:** i.e., those who feed on folly

13. **with a custom:** i.e., because they are used to it

15. **show . . . glass:** i.e., see myself in a mirror

17. **her:** i.e., its (Shakespeare uses **her** because the **falcon** is female; the male of the species is called a "tercel.")

19. **afford you cause:** give you reason (to **bless the time**)

20. **difference:** i.e., in rank

23. **Fates:** In Greek mythology, the three Fates wove one's life and brought about one's death by cutting life's thread.

24. **work:** i.e., son

26. **flaunts:** finery

28. **Apprehend:** anticipate; fear, dread

31–34. **Jupiter . . . swain:** In classical mythology, **Jupiter** (or Jove) assumed the shape of a **bull** in order to carry off Europa; **Neptune,** god of the sea, became a **ram** to carry off Theophane; **Apollo,** the sun god, became a shepherd in an effort to seduce Issa. (See longer note, page 245, and picture, page 202.)

36. **piece:** masterpiece

37. **way:** (1) manner; (2) course of action

38. **honor:** sense of what is right

39. **faith:** duty to fulfill your trust in me

43. **necessities:** i.e., unavoidable

46. **Or I my life:** i.e., I must change my life (a line much debated by editors and critics, many of whom suggest that it means "I must exchange my life for death")

(continued)

134

Hath not been used to fear. Even now I tremble
To think your father by some accident
Should pass this way as you did. O the Fates,
How would he look to see his work, so noble,
Vilely bound up? What would he say? Or how   25
Should I, in these my borrowed flaunts, behold
The sternness of his presence?
FLORIZELL   Apprehend
Nothing but jollity. The gods themselves,
Humbling their deities to love, have taken   30
The shapes of beasts upon them. Jupiter
Became a bull, and bellowed; the green Neptune
A ram, and bleated; and the fire-robed god,
Golden Apollo, a poor humble swain,
As I seem now. Their transformations   35
Were never for a piece of beauty rarer,
Nor in a way so chaste, since my desires
Run not before mine honor, nor my lusts
Burn hotter than my faith.
PERDITA   O, but sir,   40
Your resolution cannot hold when 'tis
Opposed, as it must be, by th' power of the King.
One of these two must be necessities,
Which then will speak: that you must change this
     purpose   45
Or I my life.
FLORIZELL   Thou dear'st Perdita,
With these forced thoughts I prithee darken not
The mirth o' th' feast. Or I'll be thine, my fair,
Or not my father's. For I cannot be   50
Mine own, nor anything to any, if
I be not thine. To this I am most constant,
Though destiny say no. Be merry, gentle.
Strangle such thoughts as these with anything
That you behold the while. Your guests are coming. 55

48. **forced:** strained, distorted (See longer note, page 245.)

49. **Or:** i.e., either; **fair:** beautiful one

51. **any:** i.e., anyone

54–55. **anything . . . while:** i.e., whatever you see around you in the meantime

56. **Lift . . . countenance:** look up; **as:** i.e., as if

59. **Lady Fortune:** i.e., the goddess Fortuna, who distributes one's good and bad luck as she chooses (See page 210.)

63. **red:** i.e., red-faced, flushed

65. **pantler, butler:** servants who supplied bread (the **pantler**) and liquor (the **butler**)

69. **On:** i.e., at

71. **She . . . sip:** i.e., she would offer as a toast to each guest in turn; **retired:** withdrawn into yourself

72. **a feasted one:** i.e., one of the guests being entertained

73. **meeting:** party

74. **unknown . . . welcome:** i.e., **welcome** these **friends** yet **unknown** to us

75. **more known:** better acquainted

76. **yourself:** i.e., yourself as

79. **As:** i.e., so (that)

80 SD. **to Polixenes:** See longer note, page 245.

Lift up your countenance as it were the day
Of celebration of that nuptial which
We two have sworn shall come.
PERDITA   O Lady Fortune,
Stand you auspicious!   60
FLORIZELL   See, your guests approach.
Address yourself to entertain them sprightly,
And let's be red with mirth.

⌈*Enter*⌉ *Shepherd,* ⌈*Shepherd's Son,*⌉ *Mopsa, Dorcas,*
⌈*Shepherds and Shepherdesses,*⌉ *Servants,* ⌈*Musicians,*
and⌉ *Polixenes* ⌈*and*⌉ *Camillo* ⌈*in disguise.*⌉

SHEPHERD
Fie, daughter, when my old wife lived, upon
This day she was both pantler, butler, cook,   65
Both dame and servant; welcomed all; served all;
Would sing her song and dance her turn, now here
At upper end o' th' table, now i' th' middle;
On his shoulder, and his; her face afire
With labor, and the thing she took to quench it   70
She would to each one sip. You are retired
As if you were a feasted one and not
The hostess of the meeting. Pray you bid
These unknown friends to 's welcome, for it is
A way to make us better friends, more known.   75
Come, quench your blushes and present yourself
That which you are, mistress o' th' feast. Come on,
And bid us welcome to your sheep-shearing,
As your good flock shall prosper.
PERDITA, ⌈*to Polixenes*⌉   Sir, welcome.   80
It is my father's will I should take on me
The hostess-ship o' th' day. ⌈*To Camillo.*⌉ You're
    welcome, sir.—
Give me those flowers there, Dorcas.—Reverend
    sirs,   85

86–88. **rosemary . . . both:** Compare Ophelia's speeches in *Hamlet* 4.5.199–206: "There's **rosemary**, that's for **remembrance**. . . . There's **rue** for you, and here's some for me; we may call it herb of **grace** o' Sundays." **Seeming:** appearance **savor:** fragrance **Grace and remembrance:** i.e., God's grace and remembrance (after your deaths) See page 198.

93. **the year growing ancient:** perhaps, "when fall arrives" (with the suggestion that autumn rather than winter flowers would suit the men's age)

96. **gillyvors:** i.e., gillyflowers

97. **bastards:** a word used to refer to hybrids and to things spurious or counterfeit (See longer note, page 246.)

103. **art:** human skill (here, horticultural skill in altering flowers' colors); **piedness:** variegation

106. **mean:** i.e., means (to effect a purpose)

107. **But:** unless; **over that art:** i.e., above the human skill

108–9. **an art . . . makes:** perhaps a reference to the idea that human skills are themselves a product of nature

109–12. **we marry . . . race:** i.e., we graft a twig (**scion**) from a cultivated plant onto a wild **stock** to produce, from this "base **bark**," a **nobler** flower **marry:** permanently join **gentler:** i.e., more cultivated, domesticated

For you there's rosemary and rue. These keep
Seeming and savor all the winter long.
Grace and remembrance be to you both,
And welcome to our shearing.
POLIXENES   Shepherdess—   90
A fair one are you—well you fit our ages
With flowers of winter.
PERDITA   Sir, the year growing ancient,
Not yet on summer's death nor on the birth
Of trembling winter, the fairest flowers o' th' season   95
Are our carnations and streaked gillyvors,
Which some call nature's bastards. Of that kind
Our rustic garden's barren, and I care not
To get slips of them.
POLIXENES   Wherefore, gentle maiden,   100
Do you neglect them?
PERDITA   For I have heard it said
There is an art which in their piedness shares
With great creating nature.
POLIXENES   Say there be;   105
Yet nature is made better by no mean
But nature makes that mean. So, over that art
Which you say adds to nature is an art
That nature makes. You see, sweet maid, we marry
A gentler scion to the wildest stock,   110
And make conceive a bark of baser kind
By bud of nobler race. This is an art
Which does mend nature, change it rather, but
The art itself is nature.
PERDITA   So it is.   115
POLIXENES
Then make ⌜your⌝ garden rich in gillyvors,
And do not call them bastards.
PERDITA   I'll not put
The dibble in earth to set one slip of them,

120. **painted:** i.e., wearing cosmetics

122. **therefore:** i.e., because of my artificial beauty

125–26. **marigold . . . weeping:** The **marigold** was called "the spouse of the sun" because it closes its petals at the end of the day and opens them at dawn. **weeping:** i.e., wet with dew

127. **given:** i.e., customarily given

131. **Out:** an exclamation expressing reproach

135. **would:** wish

136. **Become:** suit; **day:** i.e., life

139–41. **O Proserpina . . . wagon:** According to Ovid's *Metamorphoses* (5.391–99), when the maid Proserpina, daughter of Ceres, was gathering flowers in a grove, the king of the underworld, Dis or Pluto, carried her off in his **wagon** (i.e., chariot). See picture on page 270.

142. **take:** captivate, charm

144. **Juno's eyes:** the **eyes** of the mythological queen of the gods

145. **Cytherea's breath:** the breath of Venus, goddess of love (born from the waves near the island of Cythera)

147. **Phoebus:** i.e., the sun (literally, Phoebus Apollo, the sun god of mythology)

147–48. **a malady . . . maids:** a reference to the parallel perceived between the pale-green primrose, which dies before spring fully arrives, and the disease of "green-sickness" (perhaps, anemia) that was fatal to young girls

149. **crown imperial:** a showy plant whose flowers (according to Gerard's *Herbal* [1597]) encompass the stalk "in form of an imperial crown"

150. **flower-de-luce:** i.e., fleur-de-lis, or iris

153. **corse:** i.e., corpse

No more than, were I painted, I would wish   120
This youth should say 'twere well, and only
   therefore
Desire to breed by me. Here's flowers for you:
Hot lavender, mints, savory, marjoram,
The marigold, that goes to bed wi' th' sun   125
And with him rises weeping. These are flowers
Of middle summer, and I think they are given
To men of middle age. You're very welcome.

CAMILLO
I should leave grazing, were I of your flock,
And only live by gazing.   130

PERDITA   Out, alas!
You'd be so lean that blasts of January
Would blow you through and through. (⌐*To
   Florizell.*¬) Now, my fair'st friend,
I would I had some flowers o' th' spring, that might   135
Become your time of day, (⌐*to the Shepherdesses*¬)
   and yours, and yours,
That wear upon your virgin branches yet
Your maidenheads growing. O Proserpina,
For the flowers now that, frighted, thou let'st fall   140
From Dis's wagon! Daffodils,
That come before the swallow dares, and take
The winds of March with beauty; violets dim,
But sweeter than the lids of Juno's eyes
Or Cytherea's breath; pale primroses,   145
That die unmarried ere they can behold
Bright Phoebus in his strength—a malady
Most incident to maids; bold oxlips and
The crown imperial; lilies of all kinds,
The flower-de-luce being one—O, these I lack   150
To make you garlands of, and my sweet friend,
   To strew him o'er and o'er.

FLORIZELL   What, like a corse?

154. **bank:** i.e., bank of flowers

155. **or if:** i.e., or if you are a body (the more general meaning of **corse**)

156. **quick:** alive

158. **Methinks:** i.e., it seems to me

159. **Whitsun pastorals:** i.e., May games and morris dances associated with the late spring feast of Pentecost (see page 230); **Sure:** i.e., surely

162. **Still . . . done:** i.e., always raises in value the thing you are doing

165. **for:** i.e., as for; **ord'ring:** giving orders about

168. **still:** always (but with wordplay on the stillness of the wave as it crests)

169. **own . . . function:** i.e., have nothing else to do; **Each your doing:** i.e., your performance of **each** thing you do

171. **what . . . deeds:** i.e., whatever you are doing at the moment

172. **That:** i.e., so that

173. **Doricles:** the name Florizell has assumed in disguise

174. **large:** extravagant; **But that:** i.e., if it were not that

175. **blood:** disposition; **peeps:** shows itself

176. **give you out:** proclaim you; **unstained:** pure, morally unsullied

180. **skill:** reason

181. **put:** i.e., force

182. **turtles:** turtledoves; **pair:** mate

184. **I'll . . . 'em:** a general term of agreement

187. **greater:** of higher social rank

PERDITA
No, like a bank for love to lie and play on,
Not like a corse; or if, not to be buried,   155
But quick and in mine arms. Come, take your
   flowers.
Methinks I play as I have seen them do
In Whitsun pastorals. Sure this robe of mine
Does change my disposition.   160
FLORIZELL   What you do
Still betters what is done. When you speak, sweet,
I'd have you do it ever. When you sing,
I'd have you buy and sell so, so give alms,
Pray so; and for the ord'ring your affairs,   165
To sing them too. When you do dance, I wish you
A wave o' th' sea, that you might ever do
Nothing but that, move still, still so,
And own no other function. Each your doing,
So singular in each particular,   170
Crowns what you are doing in the present deeds,
That all your acts are queens.
PERDITA   O Doricles,
Your praises are too large. But that your youth
And the true blood which peeps fairly through 't   175
Do plainly give you out an unstained shepherd,
With wisdom I might fear, my Doricles,
You wooed me the false way.
FLORIZELL   I think you have
As little skill to fear as I have purpose   180
To put you to 't. But come, our dance, I pray.
Your hand, my Perdita. So turtles pair
That never mean to part.
PERDITA   I'll swear for 'em.
POLIXENES, ⌈*to Camillo*⌉
This is the prettiest lowborn lass that ever   185
Ran on the greensward. Nothing she does or seems
But smacks of something greater than herself,
Too noble for this place.

190. **look out:** appear; **Good sooth:** a mild oath

193. **mistress:** sweetheart; **garlic:** i.e., give her some garlic

195. **in good time:** i.e., indeed!

196. **stand upon:** i.e., must mind

200–201. **boasts . . . feeding:** i.e., (they say he) brags about owning good pasture land

203. **like sooth:** i.e., truthful

208. **another:** i.e., the other

209. **featly:** nimbly, gracefully

211. **That:** i.e., who

215. **after a tabor:** i.e., to the music of a drum (See page 220.)

A peddler with his wares. (4.4.214–66)
From Hartmann Schopper, *Panoplia omnium illiberalium . . .* (1568).

CAMILLO   He tells her something
  That makes her blood look ⌐out.⌐ Good sooth, she is   190
  The queen of curds and cream.
SHEPHERD'S SON, ⌐*to Musicians*⌐ Come on, strike up.
DORCAS
  Mopsa must be your mistress? Marry, garlic
  To mend her kissing with.
MOPSA   Now, in good time!   195
SHEPHERD'S SON
  Not a word, a word. We stand upon our manners.—
  Come, strike up. ⌐*Music begins.*⌐
       Here a Dance of Shepherds and Shepherdesses.
POLIXENES
  Pray, good shepherd, what fair swain is this
  Which dances with your daughter?
SHEPHERD
  They call him Doricles, and boasts himself   200
  To have a worthy feeding. But I have it
  Upon his own report, and I believe it.
  He looks like sooth. He says he loves my daughter.
  I think so too, for never gazed the moon
  Upon the water as he'll stand and read,   205
  As 'twere, my daughter's eyes. And, to be plain,
  I think there is not half a kiss to choose
  Who loves another best.
POLIXENES   She dances featly.
SHEPHERD
  So she does anything, though I report it   210
  That should be silent. If young Doricles
  Do light upon her, she shall bring him that
  Which he not dreams of.

       Enter ⌐a⌐ Servant.

SERVANT O, master, if you did but hear the peddler at
  the door, you would never dance again after a tabor   215
  and pipe; no, the bagpipe could not move you. He

217. **several:** different; **you'll tell:** i.e., you can count

218. **as:** i.e., as if; **ballads:** See longer note, page 246.

220. **come better:** i.e., be more welcome

222. **pleasant:** amusing

223. **lamentably:** mournfully (the word can also mean "deplorably")

225. **milliner:** seller of ribbons, **gloves,** and other fancy apparel

227. **bawdry:** indecency (The servant's claim seems contradicted by his examples in lines 227–29.)

227–28. **delicate burdens:** fastidious refrains

228. **dildos and fadings:** nonsense words used in ballad refrains (but the word "dildo" means an artificial phallus, and the refrain "With a fading" occurred in an indecent popular song)

230–31. **break . . . matter:** perhaps, insert indecent words or gestures into the song

232. **puts:** i.e., she puts

235. **brave:** excellent

236–37. **admirable conceited:** i.e., admirably ingenious or amusing

237. **unbraided:** perhaps, untarnished or undamaged

240. **points:** tagged laces used instead of buttons to fasten clothing (with wordplay on "items or clauses in legal documents")

241–42. **by th' gross:** in great numbers (literally twelve dozen at a time)

242. **inkles:** linen tapes; **caddises:** i.e., caddis ribbon (worsted tape or binding, used for garters)

243. **sings 'em over:** describes them in song

(continued)

sings several tunes faster than you'll tell money. He
utters them as he had eaten ballads and all men's
ears grew to his tunes.

SHEPHERD'S SON   He could never come better. He shall   220
come in. I love a ballad but even too well if it be
doleful matter merrily set down, or a very pleasant
thing indeed and sung lamentably.

SERVANT   He hath songs for man or woman, of all sizes.
No milliner can so fit his customers with gloves. He   225
has the prettiest love songs for maids, so without
bawdry, which is strange, with such delicate burdens of dildos and fadings, "Jump her and thump
her." And where some stretch-mouthed rascal
would, as it were, mean mischief and break a foul   230
gap into the matter, he makes the maid to answer
"Whoop, do me no harm, good man"; puts him off,
slights him, with "Whoop, do me no harm, good
man."

POLIXENES   This is a brave fellow.   235

SHEPHERD'S SON   Believe me, thou talkest of an admirable conceited fellow. Has he any unbraided
wares?

SERVANT   He hath ribbons of all the colors i' th' rain-
bow; points more than all the lawyers in Bohemia   240
can learnedly handle, though they come to him by
th' gross; inkles, caddises, cambrics, lawns—why,
he sings 'em over as they were gods or goddesses.
You would think a smock were a she-angel, he so
chants to the sleeve-hand and the work about the   245
square on 't.

SHEPHERD'S SON   Prithee bring him in, and let him
approach singing.

PERDITA   Forewarn him that he use no scurrilous words
in 's tunes.   ⌜*Servant exits.*⌝   250

SHEPHERD'S SON   You have of these peddlers that have
more in them than you'd think, sister.

244. **smock:** woman's shirtlike undergarment

245. **chants to:** i.e., sings the praises of; **sleeve-hand:** sleeve's cuff

245–46. **work . . . on 't:** embroidery around the smock's breast-piece

250. **in 's:** i.e., in his

251. **You have of:** i.e., there are some

253. **go about:** i.e., have any desire

255. **Cypress:** a light transparent fabric (often used for mourning)

256. **sweet:** scented, perfumed

257. **Masks . . . noses:** worn by upper-class women to protect themselves from the sun or to conceal their identity

258. **Bugle bracelet:** a **bracelet** of glass beads

260. **coifs:** tight-fitting caps

262. **poking-sticks:** rods used to stiffen the pleats of ruffs

263. **lack:** need

268. **enthralled:** captivated (with wordplay on "enslaved," "put into bondage")

269. **it:** i.e., my love for Mopsa (and my enslavement)

271. **against:** in time for

277. **again:** i.e., back again

279–80. **Will . . . faces:** i.e., will they announce what they should keep hidden?   **plackets:** openings in petticoats or in skirts (and, by extension, women's private parts)

281. **kiln-hole:** i.e., fireplace (literally, fire-hole of a kiln); **whistle:** whisper

284. **Clamor:** perhaps, silence (though the word usually means just the opposite)

PERDITA   Ay, good brother, or go about to think.

Enter Autolycus, ⌜*wearing a false beard,*⌝ *singing.*

⌜AUTOLYCUS⌝
    Lawn as white as driven snow,
    Cypress black as e'er was crow,   255
    Gloves as sweet as damask roses,
    Masks for faces and for noses,
    Bugle bracelet, necklace amber,
    Perfume for a lady's chamber,
    Golden coifs and stomachers   260
    For my lads to give their dears,
    Pins and poking-sticks of steel,
    What maids lack from head to heel,
    Come buy of me, come. Come buy, come buy.
    Buy, lads, or else your lasses cry.   265
    Come buy.

SHEPHERD'S SON   If I were not in love with Mopsa, thou
shouldst take no money of me; but being enthralled
as I am, it will also be the bondage of certain
ribbons and gloves.   270

MOPSA   I was promised them against the feast, but they
come not too late now.

DORCAS   He hath promised you more than that, or there
be liars.

MOPSA   He hath paid you all he promised you. Maybe   275
he has paid you more, which will shame you to give
him again.

SHEPHERD'S SON   Is there no manners left among
maids? Will they wear their plackets where they
should bear their faces? Is there not milking time,   280
when you are going to bed, or kiln-hole, to whistle
of these secrets, but you must be tittle-tattling
before all our guests? 'Tis well they are whisp'ring.
Clamor your tongues, and not a word more.

285–86. **tawdry lace:** silk neckerchief
291. **Fear not thou:** don't be afraid
294. **parcels of charge:** i.e., expensive items
296. **ballad in print:** See longer note to 4.4.218.
297. **alife:** dearly
299. **brought to bed:** delivered
300. **at a burden:** at a single birth
305. **to 't:** i.e., as a witness to it
306. **Taleporter:** The name means "tale bearer" or "gossip." **wives:** women
311. **anon:** soon
313–14. **the fourscore of April:** i.e., the 80th of April
317. **for:** because; **exchange flesh:** i.e., have sexual intercourse

Shearing sheep. (4.4)
From Pietro de Crescenzi, [Ruralia commoda, 1561].

MOPSA I have done. Come, you promised me a tawdry 285
lace and a pair of sweet gloves.
SHEPHERD'S SON Have I not told thee how I was coz-
ened by the way and lost all my money?
AUTOLYCUS And indeed, sir, there are cozeners abroad;
therefore it behooves men to be wary. 290
SHEPHERD'S SON Fear not thou, man. Thou shalt lose
nothing here.
AUTOLYCUS I hope so, sir, for I have about me many
parcels of charge.
SHEPHERD'S SON What hast here? Ballads? 295
MOPSA Pray now, buy some. I love a ballad in print
alife, for then we are sure they are true.
AUTOLYCUS Here's one to a very doleful tune, how a
usurer's wife was brought to bed of twenty money-
bags at a burden, and how she longed to eat adders' 300
heads and toads carbonadoed.
MOPSA Is it true, think you?
AUTOLYCUS Very true, and but a month old.
DORCAS Bless me from marrying a usurer!
AUTOLYCUS Here's the midwife's name to 't, one Mis- 305
tress Taleporter, and five or six honest wives that
were present. Why should I carry lies abroad?
MOPSA, ⌈to Shepherd's Son⌉ Pray you now, buy it.
SHEPHERD'S SON, ⌈to Autolycus⌉ Come on, lay it by, and
let's first see more ballads. We'll buy the other 310
things anon.
AUTOLYCUS Here's another ballad, of a fish that appeared upon the coast on Wednesday the fourscore
of April, forty thousand fathom above water, and
sung this ballad against the hard hearts of maids. It 315
was thought she was a woman, and was turned into
a cold fish for she would not exchange flesh with
one that loved her. The ballad is very pitiful, and as
true.
DORCAS Is it true too, think you? 320

321. **Five . . . at it:** i.e., its truth is attested by the signatures of five justices; **witnesses:** testimony

327. **passing:** exceedingly

327–28. **goes to:** i.e., is set to

329. **westward:** i.e., in the west country

333. **on 't:** i.e., of it

337. **fits not:** is not fitting for

344. **Or thou goest:** i.e., you are going either; **grange:** barn

345. **ill:** evil

352. **have this song out:** finish this song

353. **sad:** serious

A sheepcote. (4.4.911)
From August Casimir Redel, *Annus symbolicus* . . . [c. 1695].

AUTOLYCUS Five justices' hands at it, and witnesses
    more than my pack will hold.
SHEPHERD'S SON Lay it by too. Another.
AUTOLYCUS This is a merry ballad, but a very pretty
    one.   325
MOPSA Let's have some merry ones.
AUTOLYCUS Why, this is a passing merry one and goes
    to the tune of "Two Maids Wooing a Man." There's
    scarce a maid westward but she sings it. 'Tis in
    request, I can tell you.   330
MOPSA We can both sing it. If thou'lt bear a part, thou
    shalt hear; 'tis in three parts.
DORCAS We had the tune on 't a month ago.
AUTOLYCUS I can bear my part. You must know 'tis my
    occupation. Have at it with you.   335

Song.

AUTOLYCUS	*Get you hence, for I must go*
	Where it fits not you to know.
DORCAS	*Whither?*
MOPSA	*O, whither?*
DORCAS	*Whither?* 340
MOPSA	*It becomes thy oath full well*
	Thou to me thy secrets tell.
DORCAS	*Me too. Let me go thither.*
MOPSA	*Or thou goest to th' grange or mill.*
DORCAS	*If to either, thou dost ill.* 345
AUTOLYCUS	*Neither.*
DORCAS	*What, neither?*
AUTOLYCUS	*Neither.*
DORCAS	*Thou hast sworn my love to be.*
MOPSA	*Thou hast sworn it more to me.* 350
	Then whither goest? Say whither.

SHEPHERD'S SON We'll have this song out anon by
    ourselves. My father and the gentlemen are in sad

361. **duck:** a term of endearment; **dear-a:** i.e., dear

363. **toys:** trifles, knickknacks

367. **utter:** put on the market, put into circulation

370. **made . . . hair:** i.e., dressed up in animal skins

371. **saultiers:** leapers, dancers (The Servant may be confusing the word with **Satyrs**—mythological woodland gods with animal forms and covered all in hair. See 388 SD, which uses the word **Satyrs** to describe them.)

372–73. **gallimaufry of gambols:** confused jumble of leaps

377. **on 't:** i.e., of it

381. **threes of:** i.e., groups of three

A satyr. (4.4.388 SD)
From Vincenzo Cartari, *Le vere e noue imagini* . . . (1615).

talk, and we'll not trouble them. Come, bring away
thy pack after me.—Wenches, I'll buy for you   355
both.—Peddler, let's have the first choice.—Follow
me, girls.
⌐*He exits with Mopsa, Dorcas, Shepherds and*
Shepherdesses.⌐

AUTOLYCUS   And you shall pay well for 'em.

Song.

Will you buy any tape,
  Or lace for your cape,   360
My dainty duck, my dear-a?
  Any silk, any thread,
  Any toys for your head,
Of the new'st and fin'st, fin'st wear-a?
  Come to the peddler.   365
  Money's a meddler
That doth utter all men's ware-a.
                                He exits.

⌐*Enter a Servant.*⌐

SERVANT, ⌐*to Shepherd*⌐   Master, there is three carters,
three shepherds, three neatherds, three swine-
herds, that have made themselves all men of hair.   370
They call themselves saultiers, and they have a
dance which the wenches say is a gallimaufry of
gambols, because they are not in 't, but they themselves are o' th' mind, if it be not too rough for
some that know little but bowling, it will please   375
plentifully.

SHEPHERD   Away! We'll none on 't. Here has been too
much homely foolery already.—I know, sir, we
weary you.

POLIXENES   You weary those that refresh us. Pray, let's   380
see these four threes of herdsmen.

384–85. **by th' square:** exactly, precisely

388. **door:** i.e., the door

389. **O father ... hereafter:** Polixenes is presented as answering some question put to him by the shepherd. **father:** term of address to an old man

391. **them:** i.e., Florizell and Perdita

392. **simple:** honest and straightforward (referring to the Shepherd)

395. **Sooth:** i.e., in truth

396. **handed:** dealt with; **wont:** accustomed

397. **she:** ladylove; **knacks:** trinkets

400. **nothing marted with:** i.e., bought nothing from

401. **Interpretation should abuse:** i.e., should misunderstand, interpret wrongly

402. **were straited:** would be at a loss

403–4. **make a care / Of:** i.e., are seriously concerned with

404. **happy holding her:** (1) keeping her happy; (2) happily keeping her

407. **looks:** i.e., looks for

409. **delivered:** (1) uttered, spoken; (2) formally transferred into her possession (legal term)

SERVANT   One three of them, by their own report, sir,
   hath danced before the King, and not the worst of
   the three but jumps twelve foot and a half by th'
   square.   385
SHEPHERD   Leave your prating. Since these good men
   are pleased, let them come in—but quickly now.
SERVANT   Why, they stay at door, sir.

⌐He admits the herdsmen.⌐

Here a Dance of twelve ⌐herdsmen, dressed as⌐ Satyrs.
                ⌐*Herdsmen, Musicians, and Servants exit.*⌐
POLIXENES, ⌐*to Shepherd*⌐
   O father, you'll know more of that hereafter.
⌐*Aside to Camillo.*⌐ Is it not too far gone? 'Tis time to   390
   part them.
   He's simple, and tells much. ⌐*To Florizell.*⌐ How now,
   fair shepherd?
   Your heart is full of something that does take
   Your mind from feasting. Sooth, when I was young   395
   And handed love, as you do, I was wont
   To load my she with knacks. I would have ransacked
   The peddler's silken treasury and have poured it
   To her acceptance. You have let him go
   And nothing marted with him. If your lass   400
   Interpretation should abuse and call this
   Your lack of love or bounty, you were straited
   For a reply, at least if you make a care
   Of happy holding her.
FLORIZELL   Old sir, I know   405
   She prizes not such trifles as these are.
   The gifts she looks from me are packed and locked
   Up in my heart, which I have given already,
   But not delivered. ⌐*To Perdita.*⌐ O, hear me breathe
   my life   410
   Before this ancient sir, ⌐who,⌐ it should seem,

417. **What follows this:** i.e., what is this speech leading to

418. **swain:** here perhaps meaning "lover" as well as "shepherd"

418–19. **to . . . before:** i.e., to make whiter (through his words) **the hand** that was already **fair**

419. **put you out:** disconcerted you, confused you

427. **most imperial:** supreme, most exalted

428. **Thereof most worthy:** i.e., and most deserving of being so

429. **force:** power

432–33. **Commend . . . perdition:** i.e., either **commend them . . . to her service** or **condemn them** to destruction

442. **Take . . . bargain:** proverbial (See longer note, page 246, and picture, page 208.)

445. **portion:** dowry

A carnation. (4.4.96)
From John Gerard, *The herball or generall historie
of plantes . . .* (1597).

158

Hath sometime loved. I take thy hand, this hand
As soft as dove's down and as white as it,
Or Ethiopian's tooth, or the fanned snow that's
    bolted 415
By th' northern blasts twice o'er.
POLIXENES   What follows this?—
How prettily th' young swain seems to wash
The hand was fair before.—I have put you out.
But to your protestation. Let me hear 420
What you profess.
FLORIZELL   Do, and be witness to 't.
POLIXENES
And this my neighbor too?
FLORIZELL   And he, and more
Than he, and men—the earth, the heavens, and 425
    all—
That were I crowned the most imperial monarch,
Thereof most worthy, were I the fairest youth
That ever made eye swerve, had force and knowledge
More than was ever man's, I would not prize them 430
Without her love; for her employ them all,
Commend them and condemn them to her service
Or to their own perdition.
POLIXENES   Fairly offered.
CAMILLO
This shows a sound affection. 435
SHEPHERD   But my daughter,
Say you the like to him?
PERDITA   I cannot speak
So well, nothing so well, no, nor mean better.
By th' pattern of mine own thoughts I cut out 440
The purity of his.
SHEPHERD   Take hands, a bargain.—
And, friends unknown, you shall bear witness to 't:
I give my daughter to him and will make
Her portion equal his. 445

450. **Contract us:** i.e., bind us, perhaps, in a contract of marriage, or, perhaps, to a promise to marry (betrothal); **fore:** i.e., before

453. **Soft:** an exclamation meaning "wait"; **beseech:** i.e., I beseech

459. **Methinks:** i.e., it seems to me

461. **That best becomes:** i.e., who is most appropriate to be present at

462–63. **incapable . . . affairs:** i.e., unable to attend to concerns requiring the use of reason

463. **stupid:** in a stupor

464. **alt'ring rheums:** perhaps, abnormal or diseased secretions; or perhaps, inflammations of the nose or throat that have altered his health

465. **Know man from man:** i.e., distinguish one man from another; **Dispute . . . estate:** i.e., reason concerning his own condition

467. **being childish:** i.e., when he was a child

473. **Something:** somewhat; **unfilial:** i.e., unbecoming to a dutiful son; **Reason my son:** i.e., it is reasonable that the **son**

474. **as good reason:** i.e., equally reasonable that

475. **all whose:** i.e., all of whose

476. **fair posterity:** i.e., descendants who give promise of success, who are reputable

478. **yield:** grant

FLORIZELL   O, that must be
I' th' virtue of your daughter. One being dead,
I shall have more than you can dream of yet,
Enough then for your wonder. But come on,
Contract us fore these witnesses.   450
SHEPHERD   Come, your hand—
And daughter, yours.
POLIXENES, ⌐to Florizell⌐ Soft, swain, awhile, beseech
    you.
Have you a father?   455
FLORIZELL   I have, but what of him?
POLIXENES
Knows he of this?
FLORIZELL   He neither does nor shall.
POLIXENES Methinks a father
Is at the nuptial of his son a guest   460
That best becomes the table. Pray you once more,
Is not your father grown incapable
Of reasonable affairs? Is he not stupid
With age and alt'ring rheums? Can he speak? Hear?
Know man from man? Dispute his own estate?   465
Lies he not bedrid, and again does nothing
But what he did being childish?
FLORIZELL   No, good sir.
He has his health and ampler strength indeed
Than most have of his age.   470
POLIXENES   By my white beard,
You offer him, if this be so, a wrong
Something unfilial. Reason my son
Should choose himself a wife, but as good reason
The father, all whose joy is nothing else   475
But fair posterity, should hold some counsel
In such a business.
FLORIZELL   I yield all this;
But for some other reasons, my grave sir,

480. **I not:** i.e., I cannot or will not

489. **Mark:** observe, attend to; **contract:** probably accented on the second syllable

494. **That:** who; **affects:** i.e., desires, aspires to (**Sheep-hook** is set in opposition to royal **scepter** and may signify Perdita, the shepherd's life, or an actual shepherd's crook.)

496. **fresh:** young, vigorous

497. **piece:** masterpiece

498. **whom of force:** i.e., who necessarily, unavoidably

499. **thou cop'st:** you have to do

502. **homely:** ugly (but with the meaning "lacking refinement" in reference to her **state,** or social condition); **fond:** (1) foolish; (2) immoderately affectionate

503. **may:** should

504. **knack:** trifle; choice dish; crafty device

505. **we'll:** Polixenes here uses the royal "we."

506. **hold thee:** i.e., regard you as

507. **Far'r . . . off:** i.e., further removed from any relation to me than **Deucalion** (a Noah-like figure who, in mythology, was the only man to survive when Zeus flooded the earth, and who repeopled the earth by casting stones over his shoulder; see page 164); **Mark thou:** pay attention to

511. **dead:** deadly

512. **yea, him too:** i.e., and worthy to marry Florizell

Which 'tis not fit you know, I not acquaint   480
My father of this business.
POLIXENES   Let him know 't.
FLORIZELL
He shall not.
POLIXENES   Prithee let him.
FLORIZELL   No, he must not.   485
SHEPHERD
Let him, my son. He shall not need to grieve
At knowing of thy choice.
FLORIZELL   Come, come, he must not.
Mark our contract.
POLIXENES, ⌐*removing his disguise*⌐ Mark your divorce, 490
    young sir,
Whom son I dare not call. Thou art too base
To be ⌐acknowledged.⌐ Thou a scepter's heir
That thus affects a sheep-hook!—Thou, old traitor,
I am sorry that by hanging thee I can   495
But shorten thy life one week.—And thou, fresh
    piece
Of excellent witchcraft, whom of force must know
The royal fool thou cop'st with—
SHEPHERD   O, my heart!   500
POLIXENES
I'll have thy beauty scratched with briers and made
More homely than thy state.—For thee, fond boy,
If I may ever know thou dost but sigh
That thou no more shalt see this knack—as never
I mean thou shalt—we'll bar thee from succession, 505
Not hold thee of our blood, no, not our kin,
⌐Far'r⌐ than Deucalion off. Mark thou my words.
Follow us to the court. ⌐*To Shepherd.*⌐ Thou, churl,
    for this time,
Though full of our displeasure, yet we free thee   510
From the dead blow of it.—And you, enchantment,
Worthy enough a herdsman—yea, him too,

513–14. **That . . . thee:** i.e., who, were it not for his royal blood, has made himself **unworthy** of you

518. **tender to 't:** i.e., vulnerable to such cruelty (The word **tender** could refer to her youth, her fragility, or perhaps her sensitivity to pain.)

519. **undone:** ruined

522–24. **The selfsame . . . alike:** Proverbial: "The sun shines upon all alike."

527. **state:** (1) rank (as heir to the throne); (2) condition; **This:** i.e., as for this

535. **fourscore three:** eighty-three

536. **thought:** expected

537. **bed:** i.e., bed on which

540. **Where . . . dust:** i.e., in unconsecrated ground, because he is a felon (See longer note, page 246.)

543. **adventure:** dare

544. **mingle faith:** exchange vows

Deucalion and Pyrrha repopulating the earth. (4.4.507)
From Lodovico Dolce, *Le trasformationi* . . . (1570).

That makes himself, but for our honor therein,
Unworthy thee—if ever henceforth thou
These rural latches to his entrance open,   515
Or ⌐hoop⌐ his body more with thy embraces,
I will devise a death as cruel for thee
As thou art tender to 't.   *He exits.*
PERDITA   Even here undone.
I was not much afeard, for once or twice   520
I was about to speak and tell him plainly
The selfsame sun that shines upon his court
Hides not his visage from our cottage but
Looks on alike. ⌐*To Florizell.*⌐ Will't please you, sir,
      be gone?   525
I told you what would come of this. Beseech you,
Of your own state take care. This dream of mine—
Being now awake, I'll queen it no inch farther,
But milk my ewes and weep.
CAMILLO, ⌐*to Shepherd*⌐   Why, how now, father?   530
Speak ere thou diest.
SHEPHERD   I cannot speak, nor think,
Nor dare to know that which I know. ⌐*To Florizell.*⌐
      O sir,
You have undone a man of fourscore three,   535
That thought to fill his grave in quiet, yea,
To die upon the bed my father died,
To lie close by his honest bones; but now
Some hangman must put on my shroud and lay me
Where no priest shovels in dust. ⌐*To Perdita.*⌐ O   540
      cursèd wretch,
That knew'st this was the Prince, and wouldst
      adventure
To mingle faith with him!—Undone, undone!
If I might die within this hour, I have lived   545
To die when I desire.   *He exits.*
FLORIZELL, ⌐*to Perdita*⌐ Why look you so upon me?
I am but sorry, not afeard; delayed,

550–51. **More . . . unwillingly:** Florizell pictures himself as a hunting dog straining at its leash to move forward, not being dragged unwillingly along by its leash.   **plucking:** i.e., being plucked

552. **Gracious my lord:** i.e., my gracious lord

555. **purpose:** i.e., intend to offer; **as hardly:** i.e., with as great difficulty, as painfully

560. **think:** i.e., think you are

563. **dignity:** high position (as the prince's beloved)

565. **but by:** except through

566. **faith:** vow (of love); **then:** i.e., when that happens

568. **seeds:** i.e., sources of all life and growth; **Lift . . . looks:** look up

571. **advised:** cautious (Florizell replies as if **advised** had its meaning "counseled.")

572. **fancy:** (1) imagination; (2) love

573. **thereto:** i.e., to **my fancy**

578. **needs must:** i.e., am obliged to

580. **thereat gleaned:** i.e., got by ruling **Bohemia**

581. **close:** closed, shut; **wombs:** encloses as if in a womb

But <u>nothing altered</u>. What I <u>was</u>, I am,
More straining on for plucking back, not following   550
My leash unwillingly.
CAMILLO   Gracious my lord,
You know ⌐your¬ father's temper. At this time
He will allow no speech, which I do guess
You do not purpose to him; and as hardly   555
Will he endure your sight as yet, I fear.
Then, till the fury of his Highness settle,
Come not before him.
FLORIZELL   I not purpose it.
I think Camillo?   560
CAMILLO, ⌐*removing his disguise*¬ Even he, my lord.
PERDITA, ⌐*to Florizell*¬
How often have I told you 'twould be thus?
How often said my dignity would last
But till 'twere known?
FLORIZELL   It cannot fail but by   565
The violation of my faith; and then
Let nature crush the sides o' th' earth together
And mar the seeds within. Lift up thy looks.
From my succession wipe me, father. I
Am heir to my affection.   570
CAMILLO   Be advised.
FLORIZELL
I am, and by my fancy. If my reason
Will thereto be obedient, I have reason.
If not, my senses, better pleased with madness,
Do bid it welcome.   575
CAMILLO   This is desperate, sir.
FLORIZELL
So call it; but it does fulfill my vow.
I needs must think it honesty. Camillo,
Not for Bohemia nor the pomp that may
Be thereat gleaned, for all the sun sees or   580
The close earth wombs or the profound seas hides

587–88. **Let . . . come:** i.e., let me contend with fortune to determine my own future

589. **deliver:** report, communicate

590. **who:** i.e., whom

591. **opportune:** accent on second syllable

592. **rides:** lies at anchor; **fast by:** nearby

593. **this design:** i.e., my present plan to depart

594. **benefit:** improve

595. **Concern . . . reporting:** i.e., am I interested in telling you

597. **would:** wish; **easier for:** i.e., readier to take

598. **for:** i.e., considering

601. **irremovable:** immovable, inflexible

603. **serve my turn:** i.e., serve my purpose

604. **do:** i.e., show

605. **Purchase:** obtain; win

606. **unhappy:** unfortunate

609. **curious business:** i.e., matters that cause me anxiety and care

610. **leave out ceremony:** i.e., neglect the courtesy (I owe you)

615. **music:** i.e., delight

In unknown fathoms, will I break my oath
To this my fair beloved. Therefore, I pray you,
As you have ever been my father's honored friend,
When he shall miss me, as in faith I mean not   585
To see him anymore, cast your good counsels
Upon his passion. Let myself and fortune
Tug for the time to come. This you may know
And so deliver: I am put to sea
With her who here I cannot hold on shore.   590
And most opportune to ⌜our⌝ need I have
A vessel rides fast by, but not prepared
For this design. What course I mean to hold
Shall nothing benefit your knowledge, nor
Concern me the reporting.   595
CAMILLO   O my lord,
I would your spirit were easier for advice
Or stronger for your need.
FLORIZELL   Hark, Perdita.—
I'll hear you by and by.   600
                    ⌜*Florizell and Perdita walk aside.*⌝
CAMILLO   He's irremovable,
Resolved for flight. Now were I happy if
His going I could frame to serve my turn,
Save him from danger, do him love and honor,
Purchase the sight again of dear Sicilia   605
And that unhappy king, my master, whom
I so much thirst to see.
FLORIZELL, ⌜*coming forward*⌝ Now, good Camillo,
I am so fraught with curious business that
I leave out ceremony.   610
CAMILLO   Sir, I think
You have heard of my poor services i' th' love
That I have borne your father?
FLORIZELL   Very nobly
Have you deserved. It is my father's music   615

617. **as thought on:** i.e., as he thinks of them

620. **If . . . think:** a courteous way of saying "if you think"

623. **more ponderous:** weightier, more serious; **settled:** fixed, firmly embraced

624. **suffer:** allow, permit

625. **receiving:** reception, welcome

626. **shall become:** is appropriate to

627. **the whom:** i.e., whom

629. **As . . . forfend:** i.e., may heaven forbid

631. **discontenting:** discontented; **strive:** i.e., I will strive; **qualify:** pacify, moderate

632. **bring . . . liking:** i.e., raise (his opinion) to the point of approval

640. **unthought-on accident:** i.e., unexpected discovery (of us by Polixenes)

640–41. **guilty / To:** responsible for

641. **wildly:** in confusion

644. **list:** listen

646. **undergo:** undertake

648. **'fore:** i.e., before

649. **habited:** dressed

To speak your deeds, not little of his care
To have them recompensed as thought on.
CAMILLO   Well, my
   lord,
   If you may please to think I love the King   620
   And, through him, what's nearest to him, which is
   Your gracious self, embrace but my direction,
   If your more ponderous and settled project
   May suffer alteration. On mine honor,
   I'll point you where you shall have such receiving   625
   As shall become your Highness, where you may
   Enjoy your mistress—from the whom I see
   There's no disjunction to be made but by,
   As heavens forfend, your ruin—marry her,
   And with my best endeavors in your absence,   630
   Your discontenting father strive to qualify
   And bring him up to liking.
FLORIZELL   How, Camillo,
   May this, almost a miracle, be done,
   That I may call thee something more than man,   635
   And after that trust to thee?
CAMILLO   Have you thought on
   A place whereto you'll go?
FLORIZELL   Not any yet.
   But as th' unthought-on accident is guilty   640
   To what we wildly do, so we profess
   Ourselves to be the slaves of chance, and flies
   Of every wind that blows.
CAMILLO   Then list to me.
   This follows: if you will not change your purpose   645
   But undergo this flight, make for Sicilia,
   And there present yourself and your fair princess,
   For so I see she must be, 'fore Leontes.
   She shall be habited as it becomes
   The partner of your bed. Methinks I see   650

651. **free:** noble, magnanimous

653. **As 'twere . . . person:** i.e., as though he were asking **forgiveness** of your father

654. **him:** i.e., himself

659. **color:** pretext

660. **Hold up before:** present to

661. **Sent:** i.e., say that you were **sent**

664. **as:** i.e., as if; **deliver:** speak

665. **betwixt us three:** i.e., only among Polixenes, Leontes, and Camillo

666. **point you forth:** i.e., guide; **sitting:** conference

668. **bosom:** thoughts, counsel, secrets

671. **sap:** life, vitality

673. **wild dedication:** rash giving-up

674. **unpathed:** pathless, trackless; **undreamed:** unimagined

675. **certain:** i.e., certainly

677. **one:** i.e., one misery; **take:** contract (as if a disease)

678. **Nothing:** i.e., in no way; **your anchors, who:** i.e., anchors (in general), which (The anchor is the traditional symbol of **hope**.)

679. **Do . . . can:** i.e., at best

679–80. **but . . . be:** i.e., merely hold you where you hate to be

681. **bond:** cementing force

682. **fresh:** blooming and youthful; **together:** simultaneously

686. **take in:** conquer

Leontes opening his free arms and weeping
His welcomes forth, asks thee, ⌐the¬ son, forgiveness,
As 'twere i' th' father's person; kisses the hands
Of your fresh princess; o'er and o'er divides him
'Twixt his unkindness and his kindness. Th' one   655
He chides to hell and bids the other grow
Faster than thought or time.
FLORIZELL   Worthy Camillo,
What color for my visitation shall I
Hold up before him?   660
CAMILLO   Sent by the King your father
To greet him and to give him comforts. Sir,
The manner of your bearing towards him, with
What you, as from your father, shall deliver,
Things known betwixt us three, I'll write you down,   665
The which shall point you forth at every sitting
What you must say, that he shall not perceive
But that you have your father's bosom there
And speak his very heart.
FLORIZELL   I am bound to you.   670
There is some sap in this.
CAMILLO   A course more promising
Than a wild dedication of yourselves
To unpathed waters, undreamed shores, most
     certain   675
To miseries enough; no hope to help you,
But as you shake off one to take another;
Nothing so certain as your anchors, who
Do their best office if they can but stay you
Where you'll be loath to be. Besides, you know   680
Prosperity's the very bond of love,
Whose fresh complexion and whose heart together
Affliction alters.
PERDITA   One of these is true.
I think affliction may subdue the cheek   685
But not take in the mind.

688–89. **these seven years:** i.e., in a long time

690. **another such:** i.e., such a one (as Perdita)

692–93. **as forward . . . birth:** i.e., as far ahead of her (lowly) upbringing as she lags behind my (royal) birth

695. **instructions:** schooling; **mistress:** woman of mastery (in learning)

696. **To:** i.e., in comparison to

700. **the thorns . . . upon:** "To sit or **stand** on **thorns**" was proverbial for "to be impatient."

704. **appear:** i.e., appear as such

708. **royally appointed:** furnished like a prince

710. **want:** lack (anything)

712. **simple:** (1) innocent; (2) stupid

714. **glass:** looking glass, mirror; **table book:** memorandum book, pocket notebook

715. **shoe tie:** shoelace; **horn ring:** cheap ring made of animals' horn

719. **best in picture:** perhaps, best looking

A pomander. (4.4.714)
From Walther Hermann Ryff, *Confect Bûch* . . . [1563].

CAMILLO   Yea, say you so?
  There shall not at your father's house these seven
    years
  Be born another such.   690
FLORIZELL   My good Camillo,
  She's as forward of her breeding as she is
  I' th' rear our birth.
CAMILLO   I cannot say 'tis pity
  She lacks instructions, for she seems a mistress   695
  To most that teach.
PERDITA   Your pardon, sir. For this
  I'll blush you thanks.
FLORIZELL   My prettiest Perdita.
  But O, the thorns we stand upon!—Camillo,   700
  Preserver of my father, now of me,
  The medicine of our house, how shall we do?
  We are not furnished like Bohemia's son,
  Nor shall appear in Sicilia.
CAMILLO   My lord,   705
  Fear none of this. I think you know my fortunes
  Do all lie there. It shall be so my care
  To have you royally appointed as if
  The scene you play were mine. For instance, sir,
  That you may know you shall not want, one word.   710
         ⌜*They step aside and talk.*⌝

Enter Autolycus.

AUTOLYCUS Ha, ha, what a fool honesty is! And trust,
  his sworn brother, a very simple gentleman! I have
  sold all my trumpery. Not a counterfeit stone, not a
  ribbon, glass, pomander, brooch, table book, ballad, knife, tape, glove, shoe tie, bracelet, horn ring,   715
  to keep my pack from fasting. They throng who
  should buy first, as if my trinkets had been hallowed
  and brought a benediction to the buyer; by which
  means I saw whose purse was best in picture, and

720–21. **My clown:** i.e., the Shepherd's Son (The word **clown** here has its meaning of "rustic simpleton." See longer note to 4.3.31 SD, page 243.)

723. **pettitoes:** i.e., feet (literally, pig's feet, usually as an article of food); **had:** i.e., had mastered

725. **all . . . ears:** i.e., they became all ears

726. **placket:** See note to 4.4.279–80. **senseless:** without sense or feeling

727. **geld . . . purse:** i.e., cut **a purse** from **a codpiece** (See longer note, page 246.)

729. **my sir's:** i.e., the Shepherd's Son's; **nothing:** (1) nothingness; (2) noting

730. **lethargy:** i.e., unconsciousness of all senses but hearing

733. **choughs:** (1) easily captured birds; (2) chuffs or rustics

735. **letters:** i.e., letter (Latin *litterae*)

736. **So:** i.e., as

739. **Happy be you:** i.e., may you have good fortune

740. **shows fair:** seems plausible, gives promise of success

744. **hanging:** the punishment for all felonies, except thefts of goods valued at less than twelve pence

748. **that:** i.e., your poverty

749. **outside . . . poverty:** i.e., your clothes

what I saw, to my good use I remembered. My 720
clown, who wants but something to be a reasonable
man, grew so in love with the wenches' song that he
would not stir his pettitoes till he had both tune and
words, which so drew the rest of the herd to me that
all their other senses stuck in ears. You might have 725
pinched a placket, it was senseless; 'twas nothing to
geld a codpiece of a purse. I ⌐could⌐ have ⌐filed⌐
keys off that hung in chains. No hearing, no feeling,
but my sir's song and admiring the nothing of it. So
that in this time of lethargy I picked and cut most of 730
their festival purses. And had not the old man come
in with a hubbub against his daughter and the
King's son, and scared my choughs from the chaff, I
had not left a purse alive in the whole army.
　　　⌐*Camillo, Florizell, and Perdita come forward.*⌐
CAMILLO, ⌐*to Florizell*⌐
Nay, but my letters, by this means being there 735
So soon as you arrive, shall clear that doubt.
FLORIZELL
And those that you'll procure from King Leontes—
CAMILLO
Shall satisfy your father.
PERDITA　　　　　　　　Happy be you!
All that you speak shows fair. 740
CAMILLO, ⌐*noticing Autolycus*⌐　Who have we here?
We'll make an instrument of this, omit
Nothing may give us aid.
AUTOLYCUS, ⌐*aside*⌐
If they have overheard me now, why, hanging.
CAMILLO　How now, good fellow? Why shak'st thou so? 745
　　Fear not, man. Here's no harm intended to thee.
AUTOLYCUS　I am a poor fellow, sir.
CAMILLO　Why, be so still. Here's nobody will steal that
　　from thee. Yet for the outside of thy poverty we

750. **discase thee:** undress
751. **think:** realize
752. **change garments:** exchange clothes (See longer note, page 247.)
753. **pennyworth:** bargain
754. **some boot:** something in addition
755–56. **I know . . . enough:** proverbial for "I see your villainy"
757. **dispatch:** be quick
758. **flayed:** stripped
760. **on 't:** i.e., of it
762. **earnest:** a small payment to seal a bargain (i.e., the money given him by Camillo)
765–66. **let . . . to you:** i.e., may you indeed be **fortunate**
766. **retire yourself:** withdraw
767. **covert:** thicket
769. **Dismantle:** remove your mantle or cloak; **disliken:** disguise
770. **The truth of your own seeming:** i.e., how you actually look (See longer note, page 247.)
771. **eyes over:** possibly, spies
772. **Get undescried:** i.e., arrive undiscovered

must make an exchange. Therefore discase thee   750
instantly—thou must think there's a necessity in
't—and change garments with this gentleman.
Though the pennyworth on his side be the worst,
yet hold thee, there's some boot.
                    ⌐*He hands Autolycus money.*⌐
AUTOLYCUS I am a poor fellow, sir. ⌐*Aside.*⌐ I know you   755
well enough.
CAMILLO Nay, prithee, dispatch. The gentleman is half
flayed already.
AUTOLYCUS Are you in earnest, sir? ⌐*Aside.*⌐ I smell the
trick on 't.   760
FLORIZELL Dispatch, I prithee.
AUTOLYCUS Indeed, I have had earnest, but I cannot
with conscience take it.
CAMILLO Unbuckle, unbuckle.
                ⌐*Florizell and Autolycus exchange garments.*⌐
Fortunate mistress—let my prophecy   765
Come home to you!—you must retire yourself
Into some covert. Take your sweetheart's hat
And pluck it o'er your brows, muffle your face,
Dismantle you, and, as you can, disliken
The truth of your own seeming, that you may—   770
For I do fear eyes over—to shipboard
Get undescried.
PERDITA   I see the play so lies
That I must bear a part.
CAMILLO   No remedy.—   775
Have you done there?
FLORIZELL   Should I now meet my father,
He would not call me son.
CAMILLO   Nay, you shall have no hat.
                ⌐*He gives Florizell's hat to Perdita.*⌐
Come, lady, come.—Farewell, my friend.   780
AUTOLYCUS   Adieu, sir.

789. **a . . . longing:** proverbial for an intense **longing**

790. **speed:** bring success to

798. **without boot:** i.e., without the money thrown in; **a boot:** a profit

800. **connive:** shut their eyes

801. **about:** engaged in

802. **clog:** hindrance, impediment (a reference to Perdita, but literally a block of wood attached to the leg or neck of a man to prevent escape)

804. **withal:** with this information

807. **matter:** business; **hot:** eager; keen

808. **session:** i.e., of a court

809. **careful:** attentive, watchful

A courtier and a countryman. (4.4.841–963)
From [Robert Greene,] *A quip for an vpstart courtier* . . . (1592).

FLORIZELL
O Perdita, what have we twain forgot?
Pray you, a word. 「*They talk aside.*」
CAMILLO, 「*aside*」
What I do next shall be to tell the King
Of this escape, and whither they are bound; 785
Wherein my hope is I shall so prevail
To force him after, in whose company
I shall re-view Sicilia, for whose sight
I have a woman's longing.
FLORIZELL Fortune speed us!— 790
Thus we set on, Camillo, to th' seaside.
CAMILLO The swifter speed the better.
「*Camillo, Florizell, and Perdita*」 *exit.*
AUTOLYCUS I understand the business; I hear it. To have
an open ear, a quick eye, and a nimble hand is
necessary for a cutpurse; a good nose is requisite 795
also, to smell out work for th' other senses. I see this
is the time that the unjust man doth thrive. What an
exchange had this been without boot! What a boot
is here with this exchange! Sure the gods do this
year connive at us, and we may do anything extem- 800
pore. The Prince himself is about a piece of iniqui-
ty, stealing away from his father with his clog at his
heels. If I thought it were a piece of honesty to
acquaint the King withal, I would not do 't. I hold it
the more knavery to conceal it, and therein am I 805
constant to my profession.

Enter 「*Shepherd's Son*」 *and Shepherd,* 「*carrying the
bundle and the box.*」

Aside, aside! Here is more matter for a hot brain.
Every lane's end, every shop, church, session, hanging, yields a careful man work. 「*He moves aside.*」

812. **changeling:** child left by the fairies

812–13. **none . . . blood:** i.e., not your child (By line 819, the phrase **your flesh and blood** has acquired its more literal sense as well.)

816. **Go to:** i.e., go on

822. **let . . . go whistle:** an expression of contemptuous dismissal

826. **go about:** set to work

827. **the King's brother-in-law:** a humorous misuse of **brother-in-law** to mean the father of the king's daughter-in-law

830. **dearer:** more valuable; **I know how much:** The usual expression is "I know *not* how much."

834. **fardel:** bundle

836. **my master:** i.e., Florizell, his former **master**

837. **at' palace:** i.e., at the palace

840. **excrement:** (false) beard

842. **an it like:** i.e., if it please

843. **Your affairs:** In addressing the shepherd and his son, Autolycus affects a grand style of speech that might have been almost as difficult for the ordinary person to understand then as it is now.

844. **condition:** nature

SHEPHERD'S SON, ⌜*to Shepherd*⌝ See, see, what a man 810
you are now! There is no other way but to tell the
King she's a changeling and none of your flesh and
blood.

SHEPHERD Nay, but hear me.

SHEPHERD'S SON Nay, but hear me! 815

SHEPHERD Go to, then.

SHEPHERD'S SON She being none of your flesh and
blood, your flesh and blood has not offended the
King, and so your flesh and blood is not to be
punished by him. Show those things you found 820
about her, those secret things, all but what she has
with her. This being done, let the law go whistle, I
warrant you.

SHEPHERD I will tell the King all, every word, yea, and
his son's pranks too; who, I may say, is no honest 825
man, neither to his father nor to me, to go about to
make me the King's brother-in-law.

SHEPHERD'S SON Indeed, brother-in-law was the far-
thest off you could have been to him, and then your
blood had been the dearer by I know how much an 830
ounce.

AUTOLYCUS, ⌜*aside*⌝ Very wisely, puppies.

SHEPHERD Well, let us to the King. There is that in this
fardel will make him scratch his beard.

AUTOLYCUS, ⌜*aside*⌝ I know not what impediment this 835
complaint may be to the flight of my master.

SHEPHERD'S SON Pray heartily he be at' palace.

AUTOLYCUS, ⌜*aside*⌝ Though I am not naturally honest,
I am so sometimes by chance. Let me pocket up my
peddler's excrement. (⌜*He removes his false beard.*⌝) 840
How now, rustics, whither are you bound?

SHEPHERD To th' palace, an it like your Worship.

AUTOLYCUS Your affairs there? What, with whom, the
condition of that fardel, the place of your dwelling,

845. **having:** property; **breeding:** perhaps, descent; perhaps, upbringing

846. **fitting:** appropriate; **discover:** reveal

847. **plain:** ordinary (but Autolycus plays on **plain** in the sense of "smooth")

849. **becomes:** is appropriate to

850. **give . . . the lie:** i.e., cheat us soldiers with inferior goods ("To give [someone] the lie" usually meant "to accuse [someone] of lying," an insult to which a soldier's response would be **stabbing steel** [line 851].)

852. **they . . . lie:** i.e., **they do not give** it; instead, they are paid **for it** (line 850)

853–55. **Your . . . manner:** i.e., you were likely to have lied to us if you had not caught yourself in the act

858. **air:** (1) style; (2) odor

858–59. **enfoldings:** garments

859–60. **measure of the court:** the grave and stately step of a court dance called the **measure**

861. **baseness:** low social status

862. **for that:** because; **insinuate and toze:** cajole and tease

864. **cap-a-pie:** from head to toe

865. **Whereupon:** on which account

866. **open thy affair:** disclose your business

871. **pheasant:** perhaps, a satiric allusion to the use of game to pay country lawyers' fees

874. **simple:** ignorant, uneducated

your names, your ages, of what having, breeding,   845
and anything that is fitting to be known, discover!
SHEPHERD'S SON   We are but plain fellows, sir.
AUTOLYCUS   A lie; you are rough and hairy. Let me have
no lying. It becomes none but tradesmen, and they
often give us soldiers the lie, but we pay them for it   850
with stamped coin, not stabbing steel; therefore
they do not give us the lie.
SHEPHERD'S SON   Your Worship had like to have given
us one, if you had not taken yourself with the
manner.   855
SHEPHERD   Are you a courtier, an 't like you, sir?
AUTOLYCUS   Whether it like me or no, I am a courtier.
Seest thou not the air of the court in these enfoldings? Hath not my gait in it the measure of the
court? Receives not thy nose court odor from me?   860
Reflect I not on thy baseness court contempt?
Think'st thou, for that I insinuate ⌐and⌐ toze from
thee thy business, I am therefore no courtier? I am
courtier cap-a-pie; and one that will either push on
or pluck back thy business there. Whereupon I   865
command thee to open thy affair.
SHEPHERD   My business, sir, is to the King.
AUTOLYCUS   What advocate hast thou to him?
SHEPHERD   I know not, an 't like you.
SHEPHERD'S SON, ⌐*aside to Shepherd*⌐   Advocate's the   870
court word for a pheasant. Say you have none.
SHEPHERD, ⌐*to Autolycus*⌐   None, sir. I have no pheas-
ant, cock nor hen.
AUTOLYCUS
How blest are we that are not simple men!
Yet Nature might have made me as these are.   875
Therefore I will not disdain.
SHEPHERD'S SON, ⌐*to Shepherd*⌐   This cannot be but a
great courtier.

882. **fantastical:** extraordinarily odd in behavior; or, eccentric in clothing

883. **the . . . teeth:** i.e., the fact that he picks his teeth (Toothpicks were then a new fashion imported from the Continent.)

885. **Wherefore:** i.e., for what purpose is

889. **to th' speech of:** i.e., where I may speak to

894. **beest capable of:** i.e., can comprehend

898. **in handfast:** i.e., imprisoned

903. **wit:** ingenuity

904. **heavy:** hard to endure, grievous

905. **germane:** related, akin

908. **offer:** attempt

909. **grace:** favor (by marrying Prince Florizell)

911. **sheepcote:** a shelter for sheep (See page 152.)

911–12. **sharpest:** severest

913. **e'er a son:** i.e., by any chance a son

Victims tortured on a rack. (3.2.195)
From Girolamo Maggi, . . . *De tintinnabulis liber* . . . (1689).

SHEPHERD   His garments are rich, but he wears them
   not handsomely.   880
SHEPHERD'S SON   He seems to be the more noble in
   being fantastical. A great man, I'll warrant. I know
   by the picking on 's teeth.
AUTOLYCUS   The fardel there. What's i' th' fardel?
   Wherefore that box?   885
SHEPHERD   Sir, there lies such secrets in this fardel and
   box which none must know but the King, and
   which he shall know within this hour if I may come
   to th' speech of him.
AUTOLYCUS   Age, thou hast lost thy labor.   890
SHEPHERD   Why, sir?
AUTOLYCUS   The King is not at the palace. He is gone
   aboard a new ship to purge melancholy and air
   himself, for, if thou beest capable of things serious,
   thou must know the King is full of grief.   895
SHEPHERD   So 'tis said, sir—about his son, that should
   have married a shepherd's daughter.
AUTOLYCUS   If that shepherd be not in handfast, let him
   fly. The curses he shall have, the tortures he shall
   feel, will break the back of man, the heart of   900
   monster.
SHEPHERD'S SON   Think you so, sir?
AUTOLYCUS   Not he alone shall suffer what wit can
   make heavy and vengeance bitter; but those that are
   germane to him, though removed fifty times, shall   905
   all come under the hangman—which, though it be
   great pity, yet it is necessary. An old sheep-whistling
   rogue, a ram tender, to offer to have his daughter
   come into grace! Some say he shall be stoned, but
   that death is too soft for him, say I. Draw our throne 910
   into a sheepcote? All deaths are too few, the sharpest too easy.
SHEPHERD'S SON   Has the old man e'er a son, sir, do you
   hear, an 't like you, sir?

916. **'nointed:** anointed; **head:** top

917. **stand:** i.e., made to stand

918. **a dram:** a bit more; **aqua vitae:** strong drink, usually brandy

920. **prognostication:** i.e., the almanac

921–22. **with . . . eye:** i.e., from the south

922. **he:** perhaps, the sun; perhaps, his father

923. **with flies blown:** i.e., infected and swollen with the eggs of flies; **what:** i.e., for what, why

924. **traitorly:** treacherous

925. **capital:** serious (with wordplay on "punishable by death")

926. **what:** i.e., what business

927. **Being . . . considered:** i.e., given a somewhat gentlemanly consideration (a bribe) **something:** somewhat

928–29. **tender . . . presence:** i.e., present you to him

929. **whisper him:** i.e., speak secretly to him

930. **in man:** i.e., in any man's power; **effect your suits:** i.e., achieve success for your petitions

931. **man:** i.e., the man who

933. **Close:** come to terms

934–35. **authority . . . nose:** i.e., **authority** can be made a fool of (Tame bears were literally **led by the nose.**)

938. **An 't:** i.e., if it

941. **in pawn:** as your hostage

944. **the moiety:** half

946. **In some sort:** i.e., in a way; **case:** (1) situation; (2) hide

950. **Comfort:** i.e., take comfort

AUTOLYCUS   He has a son, who shall be flayed alive; then   915
'nointed over with honey, set on the head of a
wasps'-nest; then stand till he be three-quarters and
a dram dead, then recovered again with aqua vitae
or some other hot infusion; then, raw as he is, and
in the hottest day prognostication proclaims, shall   920
he be set against a brick wall, the sun looking with a
southward eye upon him, where he is to behold him
with flies blown to death. But what talk we of these
traitorly rascals, whose miseries are to be smiled at,
their offenses being so capital? Tell me—for you   925
seem to be honest plain men—what you have to the
King. Being something gently considered, I'll bring
you where he is aboard, tender your persons to his
presence, whisper him in your behalfs; and if it be
in man besides the King to effect your suits, here is   930
man shall do it.
SHEPHERD'S SON, ⌜to Shepherd⌝ He seems to be of
great authority. Close with him, give him gold; and
though authority be a stubborn bear, yet he is oft
led by the nose with gold. Show the inside of your   935
purse to the outside of his hand, and no more ado.
Remember: "stoned," and "flayed alive."
SHEPHERD, ⌜to Autolycus⌝ An 't please you, sir, to
undertake the business for us, here is that gold I
have. I'll make it as much more, and leave this   940
young man in pawn till I bring it you.
AUTOLYCUS   After I have done what I promised?
SHEPHERD   Ay, sir.
AUTOLYCUS   Well, give me the moiety. ⌜Shepherd hands
him money.⌝ Are you a party in this business?   945
SHEPHERD'S SON   In some sort, sir; but though my case
be a pitiful one, I hope I shall not be flayed out of it.
AUTOLYCUS   O, that's the case of the shepherd's son!
Hang him, he'll be made an example.
SHEPHERD'S SON, ⌜to Shepherd⌝ Comfort, good com-   950

951. **must:** i.e., must go
952. **'tis none of:** i.e., Perdita is not
953. **gone:** undone, lost, ruined; **else:** otherwise
957. **before:** ahead of me
958. **look upon:** i.e., urinate by
962. **Let's before:** i.e., let's go on ahead
965. **suffer:** allow; **booties:** spoils, gains
966. **courted:** enticed; **occasion:** opportunity
968. **that:** i.e., doing Florizell a good turn; **turn back:** return, recoil
970. **blind:** Proverbial: "As **blind** as a mole." **aboard him:** i.e., on board Florizell's ship; **fit:** appropriate
970–71. **shore them:** put them ashore
972. **concerns him nothing:** i.e., is of no concern to him
973. **proof against:** impervious to
975. **matter in it:** i.e., some importance to it

Woodcocks caught in a springe. (4.3.35–36)
From Henry Parrot, *Laquei ridiculosi* . . . (1613).

fort. We must to the King, and show our strange
sights. He must know 'tis none of your daughter nor
my sister. We are gone else.—Sir, I will give you as
much as this old man does when the business is
performed, and remain, as he says, your pawn till it   955
be brought you.

AUTOLYCUS   I will trust you. Walk before toward the
seaside. Go on the right hand. I will but look upon
the hedge, and follow you.

SHEPHERD'S SON, ⌜*to Shepherd*⌝   We are blessed in this   960
man, as I may say, even blessed.

SHEPHERD   Let's before, as he bids us. He was provided
to do us good.   ⌜*Shepherd and his son exit.*⌝

AUTOLYCUS   If I had a mind to be honest, I see Fortune
would not suffer me. She drops booties in my   965
mouth. I am courted now with a double occasion:
gold, and a means to do the Prince my master good;
which who knows how that may turn back to my
advancement? I will bring these two moles, these
blind ones, aboard him. If he think it fit to shore   970
them again and that the complaint they have to the
King concerns him nothing, let him call me rogue
for being so far officious, for I am proof against that
title and what shame else belongs to 't. To him will I
present them. There may be matter in it.   975

⌜*He exits.*⌝

THE
WINTER'S TALE

ACT 5

5.1 Paulina insists that Leontes must not remarry, despite the urgings of his courtiers. Florizell and Perdita arrive, and are greeted warmly. Then news comes that Polixenes and Camillo are in Sicilia. Leontes agrees to speak to Polixenes on the young couple's behalf.

———————

2. **No . . . make:** i.e., there is no offence that you might have committed

3. **redeemed:** (1) made up for; (2) paid off

4. **At the last:** i.e., now at last

6. **them:** i.e., the gods

8. **Her:** i.e., Hermione

9. **still:** always

16. **from . . . good:** i.e., from each woman took one good quality

17. **To make:** i.e., and combined them to **make**

21. **Sorely:** severely

A penitent at prayer. (5.1.2–6)
From August Casimir Redel, *Apophtegmata symbolica* . . . [n.d.].

ACT 5

Scene 1

Enter Leontes, Cleomenes, Dion, Paulina, ⌐and⌐
Servants.

CLEOMENES
Sir, you have done enough, and have performed
A saintlike sorrow. No fault could you make
Which you have not redeemed—indeed, paid down
More penitence than done trespass. At the last,
Do as the heavens have done: forget your evil;   5
With them forgive yourself.

LEONTES   Whilst I remember
Her and her virtues, I cannot forget
My blemishes in them, and so still think of
The wrong I did myself, which was so much   10
That heirless it hath made my kingdom and
Destroyed the sweet'st companion that e'er man
Bred his hopes out of.

PAULINA   True, too true, my lord.
If one by one you wedded all the world,   15
Or from the all that are took something good
To make a perfect woman, she you killed
Would be unparalleled.

LEONTES   I think so. Killed?
She I killed? I did so, but thou strik'st me   20
Sorely to say I did. It is as bitter

195

22. **good now:** an expression of entreaty

30. **Would have him:** i.e., want him to

32. **remembrance:** i.e., the future memory

34. **fail of issue:** lack of an heir

36. **Incertain:** uncertain

37. **well:** dead ("She is well" was a phrase used for one who had died.)

38. **royalty's repair:** i.e., the restoration of the royal dynasty

43. **Respecting:** i.e., in comparison to

44. **Will have fulfilled:** i.e., demand the fulfillment of

48. **Which:** i.e., and

49. **all as monstrous to:** altogether as unnatural from the point of view of

50. **As:** i.e., as for

54. **Care not for:** do not worry about

55–56. **Great Alexander . . . worthiest:** According to classical historians, **Alexander** the Great, the Macedonian conqueror of Asia, on his deathbed named as his heir **"the worthiest."**

57. **like:** i.e., likely

"Great Alexander." (5.1.55)
From Valentin Thilo, *Icones heroum* . . . (1589).

Upon thy tongue as in my thought. Now, good now,
Say so but seldom.
CLEOMENES   Not at all, good lady.
You might have spoken a thousand things that   25
   would
Have done the time more benefit and graced
Your kindness better.
PAULINA   You are one of those
Would have him wed again.   30
DION   If you would not so,
You pity not the state nor the remembrance
Of his most sovereign name, consider little
What dangers by his Highness' fail of issue
May drop upon his kingdom and devour   35
Incertain lookers-on. What were more holy
Than to rejoice the former queen is well?
What holier than, for royalty's repair,
For present comfort, and for future good,
To bless the bed of majesty again   40
With a sweet fellow to 't?
PAULINA   There is none worthy,
Respecting her that's gone. Besides, the gods
Will have fulfilled their secret purposes.
For has not the divine Apollo said,   45
Is 't not the tenor of his oracle,
That King Leontes shall not have an heir
Till his lost child be found? Which that it shall
Is all as monstrous to our human reason
As my Antigonus to break his grave   50
And come again to me—who, on my life,
Did perish with the infant. 'Tis your counsel
My lord should to the heavens be contrary,
Oppose against their wills. Care not for issue.
The crown will find an heir. Great Alexander   55
Left his to th' worthiest; so his successor
Was like to be the best.

61. **squared me to:** i.e., governed myself according to

62. **full:** large

69–70. **and on . . . soul-vexed:** See longer note, page 248, for a variety of editorial attempts to cope with these difficult lines. If one follows the Folio (as we do), it is helpful to read **"on this stage"** as meaning "appear on this stage."

71. **Why to me:** presumably, an expression of remonstrance against Leontes for remarrying

74. **incense:** incite

77. **mark:** observe

80. **rift:** split

83. **eyes else:** i.e., other eyes

86. **but by . . . leave:** i.e., unless I freely give you permission

Rosemary. (4.4.86)
From *The grete herball . . .* (1529).

LEONTES   Good Paulina,
Who hast the memory of Hermione,
I know, in honor, O, that ever I   60
Had squared me to thy counsel! Then even now
I might have looked upon my queen's full eyes,
Have taken treasure from her lips—
PAULINA   And left them
More rich for what they yielded.   65
LEONTES   Thou speak'st truth.
No more such wives, therefore no wife. One worse,
And better used, would make her sainted spirit
Again possess her corpse, and on this stage,
Where we offenders now appear, soul-vexed,   70
And begin "Why to me?"
PAULINA   Had she such power,
She had just cause.
LEONTES   She had, and would incense me
To murder her I married.   75
PAULINA   I should so.
Were I the ghost that walked, I'd bid you mark
Her eye, and tell me for what dull part in 't
You chose her. Then I'd shriek, that even your ears
Should rift to hear me, and the words that followed   80
Should be "Remember mine."
LEONTES   Stars, stars,
And all eyes else dead coals! Fear thou no wife;
I'll have no wife, Paulina.
PAULINA   Will you swear   85
Never to marry but by my free leave?
LEONTES
Never, Paulina, so be blest my spirit.
PAULINA
Then, good my lords, bear witness to his oath.
CLEOMENES
You tempt him over-much.

91. **like:** similar to

92. **Affront:** meet

94. **I have done:** In the Folio, these words complete Cleomenes' speech.

96. **No remedy:** i.e., if there is no other way

96–97. **office / To choose:** i.e., duty or function of choosing

99. **walked . . . ghost:** i.e., if the ghost of your first queen were to appear; **it should:** i.e., that ghost would

103. **We:** i.e., I (the royal "we")

107. **gives out himself:** claims to be

111. **What with him:** i.e., what retinue accompanies him

112. **Like:** in a manner appropriate

113. **out of circumstance:** unceremonious

114. **forced:** enforced

115. **What train:** i.e., what retinue

117. **mean:** low in social status

119. **piece of earth:** i.e., person (**Earth** could refer to the human body.)

PAULINA   Unless another   90
  As like Hermione as is her picture
  Affront his eye.
CLEOMENES   Good madam—
PAULINA   I have done.
  Yet if my lord will marry—if you will, sir,   95
  No remedy but you will—give me the office
  To choose you a queen. She shall not be so young
  As was your former, but she shall be such
  As, walked your first queen's ghost, it should take
      joy   100
  To see her in your arms.
LEONTES   My true Paulina,
  We shall not marry till thou bid'st us.
PAULINA   That
  Shall be when your first queen's again in breath,   105
  Never till then.

                    Enter a Servant.

SERVANT
  One that gives out himself Prince Florizell,
  Son of Polixenes, with his princess—she
  The fairest I have yet beheld—desires access
  To your high presence.   110
LEONTES   What with him? He comes not
  Like to his father's greatness. His approach,
  So out of circumstance and sudden, tells us
  'Tis not a visitation framed, but forced
  By need and accident. What train?   115
SERVANT   But few,
  And those but mean.
LEONTES   His princess, say you, with him?
SERVANT
  Ay, the most peerless piece of earth, I think,
  That e'er the sun shone bright on.   120

123. **Above . . . gone:** i.e., as superior to a time past that was actually **better; grave:** i.e., your beauty now in the **grave**

127. **that theme:** i.e., Hermione's beauty, now cold in the grave

129. **shrewdly:** grievously

132. **The one:** i.e., Hermione

134. **tongue:** voice, vote (as the more beautiful)

135. **Would she:** i.e., who, if she chose to; **sect:** religion (devoted to herself as its goddess)

136. **all professors else:** all those who affirmed a belief in other religions

143. **assisted with:** attended by

148. **paired:** matched (so as to form a pair)

"Jupiter became a bull." (4.4.31–32)
From Gabriele Simeoni, *La vita . . . d'Ouidio . . .* (1559).

PAULINA   O Hermione,
  As every present time doth boast itself
  Above a better gone, so must thy grave
  Give way to what's seen now. ⌜*To Servant.*⌝ Sir, you
      yourself   125
  Have said and writ so—but your writing now
  Is colder than that theme—she had not been
  Nor was not to be equalled. Thus your verse
  Flowed with her beauty once. 'Tis shrewdly ebbed
  To say you have seen a better.   130
SERVANT   Pardon, madam.
  The one I have almost forgot—your pardon;
  The other, when she has obtained your eye,
  Will have your tongue too. This is a creature,
  Would she begin a sect, might quench the zeal   135
  Of all professors else, make proselytes
  Of who she but bid follow.
PAULINA   How, not women?
SERVANT
  Women will love her that she is a woman
  More worth than any man; men, that she is   140
  The rarest of all women.
LEONTES   Go, Cleomenes.
  Yourself, assisted with your honored friends,
  Bring them to our embracement.
                          ⌜*Cleomenes and others*⌝ *exit.*
                              Still, 'tis strange   145
  He thus should steal upon us.
PAULINA   Had our prince,
  Jewel of children, seen this hour, he had paired
  Well with this lord. There was not full a month
  Between their births.   150
LEONTES   Prithee, no more; cease. Thou
      know'st
  He dies to me again when talked of. Sure,
  When I shall see this gentleman, thy speeches

156. **Unfurnish:** deprive

158. **print your royal father off:** exactly reproduce the image of your father

160. **hit:** exactly represented

166. **begetting wonder:** i.e., producing admiration (in onlookers)

169. **brave:** worthy

170. **Though . . . life:** i.e., even though I am miserable, I desire to live

174. **at friend:** as a **friend**

175. **but:** i.e., except for the fact that

176. **waits . . . times:** attends on old age

176–78. **something . . . ability:** i.e., somewhat taken prisoner the **ability** he wishes he still had

180. **Measured:** traveled

185. **offices:** kindnesses

186. **rarely:** exceptionally

A man "grown incapable" through "age and alt'ring rheums." (4.4.462–64)
From August Casimir Redel, *Apophtegmata symbolica* . . . [n.d.].

Will bring me to consider that which may   155
Unfurnish me of reason. They are come.

Enter Florizell, Perdita, Cleomenes, and others.

Your mother was most true to wedlock, prince,
For she did print your royal father off,
Conceiving you. Were I but twenty-one,
Your father's image is so hit in you,   160
His very air, that I should call you brother,
As I did him, and speak of something wildly
By us performed before. Most dearly welcome,
And your fair princess—goddess! O, alas,
I lost a couple that 'twixt heaven and earth   165
Might thus have stood, begetting wonder, as
You, gracious couple, do. And then I lost—
All mine own folly—the society,
Amity too, of your brave father, whom,
Though bearing misery, I desire my life   170
Once more to look on him.
FLORIZELL   By his command
Have I here touched Sicilia, and from him
Give you all greetings that a king, at friend,
Can send his brother. And but infirmity,   175
Which waits upon worn times, hath something
    seized
His wished ability, he had himself
The lands and waters 'twixt your throne and his
Measured to look upon you, whom he loves—   180
He bade me say so—more than all the scepters
And those that bear them living.
LEONTES   O my brother,
Good gentleman, the wrongs I have done thee stir
Afresh within me, and these thy offices,   185
So rarely kind, are as interpreters
Of my behindhand slackness. Welcome hither,
As is the spring to th' earth. And hath he too

189-90. **fearful . . . ungentle:** i.e., terrible, or at least rough, **usage**

190. **Neptune:** in Roman mythology, god of the sea

192. **adventure:** risk

195. **Smalus:** No historical source has been found for this name.

200. **friendly:** i.e., being friendly or favorable

201. **charge:** command

202. **My best train:** perhaps, the greatest part of my retinue; or, perhaps, the most noble members of my retinue

204. **for Bohemia bend:** i.e., proceed to Bohemia

210. **climate:** i.e., visit; **holy:** i.e., of high and reverend excellence (The emphasis on Polixenes' sanctity as a monarch continues in the next lines with **graceful** [literally meaning "full of divine grace"] and **sacred**.)

216. **Worthy his goodness:** i.e., who are **worthy** of him and **his goodness**

220. **will bear no credit:** i.e., would not be believed

Exposed this paragon to th' fearful usage,
At least ungentle, of the dreadful Neptune,   190
To greet a man not worth her pains, much less
Th' adventure of her person?
FLORIZELL   Good my lord,
   She came from Libya.
LEONTES   Where the warlike Smalus,   195
   That noble honored lord, is feared and loved?
FLORIZELL
   Most royal sir, from thence, from him, whose
       daughter
   His tears proclaimed his, parting with her. Thence,
   A prosperous south wind friendly, we have crossed   200
   To execute the charge my father gave me
   For visiting your Highness. My best train
   I have from your Sicilian shores dismissed,
   Who for Bohemia bend, to signify
   Not only my success in Libya, sir,   205
   But my arrival and my wife's in safety
   Here where we are.
LEONTES   The blessèd gods
   Purge all infection from our air whilst you
   Do climate here! You have a holy father,   210
   A graceful gentleman, against whose person,
   So sacred as it is, I have done sin,
   For which the heavens, taking angry note,
   Have left me issueless. And your father's blest,
   As he from heaven merits it, with you,   215
   Worthy his goodness. What might I have been
   Might I a son and daughter now have looked on,
   Such goodly things as you?

                Enter a Lord.

LORD   Most noble sir,
   That which I shall report will bear no credit,   220

221. **Please:** i.e., if it please (a deferential phrase)
222. **Bohemia:** Polixenes, king of Bohemia
223. **attach:** arrest, seize
224. **dignity:** rank
229. **amazedly:** in a state of bewilderment, as if in a maze; **becomes:** is appropriate to
239. **Lay . . . charge:** i.e., rightly blame it on him
243. **in question:** under judicial examination
245. **Forswear . . . speak:** i.e., deny under oath everything that they assert
250. **contract:** betrothal; **celebrated:** i.e., completed or ratified in the celebration of our wedding

A handfasting. (4.4.412–52)
From George Wither, *A collection of emblemes* . . . (1635).

Were not the proof so nigh. Please you, great sir,
Bohemia greets you from himself by me,
Desires you to attach his son, who has—
His dignity and duty both cast off—
Fled from his father, from his hopes, and with   225
A shepherd's daughter.
LEONTES   Where's Bohemia? Speak.
LORD
Here in your city. I now came from him.
I speak amazedly, and it becomes
My marvel and my message. To your court   230
Whiles he was hast'ning—in the chase, it seems,
Of this fair couple—meets he on the way
The father of this seeming lady and
Her brother, having both their country quitted
With this young prince.   235
FLORIZELL   Camillo has betrayed me,
Whose honor and whose honesty till now
Endured all weathers.
LORD   Lay 't so to his charge.
He's with the King your father.   240
LEONTES   Who? Camillo?
LORD
Camillo, sir. I spake with him, who now
Has these poor men in question. Never saw I
Wretches so quake. They kneel, they kiss the earth,
Forswear themselves as often as they speak.   245
Bohemia stops his ears and threatens them
With divers deaths in death.
PERDITA   O my poor father!
The heaven sets spies upon us, will not have
Our contract celebrated.   250
LEONTES   You are married?
FLORIZELL
We are not, sir, nor are we like to be.

254. The odds . . . alike: perhaps, the chances (of success or happiness) are the same for people of all social conditions, high and low

256. daughter: Florizell replies (line 258) as if **daughter** had its sense of "daughter-in-law."

261. broken . . . liking: i.e., displeased him

263. worth: rank

265. look up: cheer up

266. visible: i.e., visibly

269–70. since . . . now: i.e., when you were as young as I

270. thought . . . affections: i.e., recalling what your feelings then were

284. Your honor: i.e., since your honor is

"Lady Fortune." (4.4.59; 5.1.266)
From [John Lydgate,] *The hystorye sege and dystruccyon of Troye . . .* [1513].

The stars, I see, will kiss the valleys first.
The odds for high and low's alike.
LEONTES   My lord,   255
Is this the daughter of a king?
FLORIZELL   She is
When once she is my wife.
LEONTES
That "once," I see, by your good father's speed
Will come on very slowly. I am sorry,   260
Most sorry, you have broken from his liking,
Where you were tied in duty, and as sorry
Your choice is not so rich in worth as beauty,
That you might well enjoy her.
FLORIZELL, ⌜*to Perdita*⌝   Dear, look up.   265
Though Fortune, visible an enemy,
Should chase us with my father, power no jot
Hath she to change our loves.—Beseech you, sir,
Remember since you owed no more to time
Than I do now. With thought of such affections,   270
Step forth mine advocate. At your request,
My father will grant precious things as trifles.
LEONTES
Would he do so, I'd beg your precious mistress,
Which he counts but a trifle.
PAULINA   Sir, my liege,   275
Your eye hath too much youth in 't. Not a month
'Fore your queen died, she was more worth such
    gazes
Than what you look on now.
LEONTES   I thought of her   280
Even in these looks I made. ⌜*To Florizell.*⌝ But your
    petition
Is yet unanswered. I will to your father.
Your honor not o'erthrown by your desires,
I am friend to them and you. Upon which errand   285

287. **mark . . . make:** i.e., observe how I remove obstacles to (your) progress

5.2 Autolycus learns from courtiers that Leontes' lost daughter has been found; he then meets the newly elevated shepherd and shepherd's son, who promise to recommend Autolycus to Florizell.

1–2. **this relation:** the telling of this story
4. **deliver:** tell
5. **amazedness:** overwhelming astonishment
9. **issue:** outcome
10. **a broken delivery:** an incomplete statement
12. **notes of admiration:** exclamation marks
13. **staring on:** i.e., staring at
14. **cases:** i.e., lids
16. **as:** i.e., as if
19. **seeing:** i.e., what could be seen; **importance:** import
20. **of the one:** i.e., of one or the other
21. **must needs:** i.e., must
22. **happily:** perhaps
24. **bonfires:** outdoor fires lit on festive occasions

I now go toward him. Therefore follow me,
And mark what way I make. Come, good my lord.

They exit.

Scene 2
Enter Autolycus and a Gentleman.

AUTOLYCUS Beseech you, sir, were you present at this
relation?

FIRST GENTLEMAN I was by at the opening of the fardel,
heard the old shepherd deliver the manner how he
found it, whereupon, after a little amazedness, we   5
were all commanded out of the chamber. Only this,
methought, I heard the shepherd say: he found the
child.

AUTOLYCUS I would most gladly know the issue of it.

FIRST GENTLEMAN I make a broken delivery of the   10
business, but the changes I perceived in the King
and Camillo were very notes of admiration. They
seemed almost, with staring on one another, to tear
the cases of their eyes. There was speech in their
dumbness, language in their very gesture. They   15
looked as they had heard of a world ransomed, or
one destroyed. A notable passion of wonder appeared in them, but the wisest beholder that knew
no more but seeing could not say if th' importance
were joy or sorrow; but in the extremity of the one it   20
must needs be.

Enter another Gentleman.

Here comes a gentleman that happily knows more.—
The news, Rogero?

SECOND GENTLEMAN Nothing but bonfires. The oracle
is fulfilled: the King's daughter is found! Such a   25

27. **ballad makers:** i.e., even writers of ballads (See longer note to 4.4.218, page 246.); **cannot:** i.e., will not

29. **deliver:** tell

33–34. **pregnant by circumstance:** compelling in its details

35. **unity:** agreement; **proofs:** items of physical evidence (listed in the lines that follow)

36. **jewel:** costly ornament of gold, silver, or precious stones

37. **letters:** i.e., letter

38. **character:** handwriting

39. **creature:** i.e., Perdita

40–41. **affection . . . breeding:** i.e., her naturally noble disposition, which surpasses her upbringing

46. **was to:** i.e., needed to

47. **crown:** add the finishing touch to

52. **known by garment:** i.e., recognizable only through their clothing; **favor:** face

57. **worries . . . clipping her:** i.e., vehemently kisses and hugs his daughter (Literally, **worries** means "attacks" or "strangles.") **clipping:** embracing

58. **which:** i.e., who

deal of wonder is broken out within this hour that
ballad makers cannot be able to express it.

Enter another Gentleman.

Here comes the Lady Paulina's steward. He can
deliver you more.—How goes it now, sir? This news
which is called true is so like an old tale that the   30
verity of it is in strong suspicion. Has the King
found his heir?

THIRD GENTLEMAN   Most true, if ever truth were pregnant by circumstance. That which you hear you'll
swear you see, there is such unity in the proofs. The   35
mantle of Queen Hermione's, her jewel about the
neck of it, the letters of Antigonus found with it,
which they know to be his character, the majesty of
the creature in resemblance of the mother, the
affection of nobleness which nature shows above   40
her breeding, and many other evidences proclaim
her with all certainty to be the King's daughter. Did
you see the meeting of the two kings?

SECOND GENTLEMAN   No.

THIRD GENTLEMAN   Then have you lost a sight which   45
was to be seen, cannot be spoken of. There might
you have beheld one joy crown another, so and in
such manner that it seemed sorrow wept to take
leave of them, for their joy waded in tears. There
was casting up of eyes, holding up of hands, with   50
countenance of such distraction that they were to
be known by garment, not by favor. Our king, being
ready to leap out of himself for joy of his found
daughter, as if that joy were now become a loss,
cries "O, thy mother, thy mother!" then asks Bohe-   55
mia forgiveness, then embraces his son-in-law, then
again worries he his daughter with clipping her.
Now he thanks the old shepherd, which stands by

59. **weather-bitten:** weather-corroded; **conduit:** fountain (with reference to his tears); **of many:** i.e., who has lived through many

61–62. **undoes . . . do it:** ruins description's attempt to describe it

65. **Like:** i.e., as in

66. **matter:** subject matter; **rehearse:** recount, narrate; **credit:** belief (in the **tale**)

67. **with a bear:** i.e., by **a bear**

69. **innocence:** simplicity, guilelessness

70. **his:** i.e., Antigonus'

72. **bark:** ship

74. **Wracked:** i.e., shipwrecked at

76. **instruments:** agents

83–84. **she . . . losing:** i.e., Perdita . . . being lost (or, perhaps, Paulina might not again be in danger of losing Perdita)

85. **dignity:** excellence; **act:** performance

89. **angled for:** (1) artfully caught; (2) fished for

90. **water:** i.e., tears

like a weather-bitten conduit of many kings' reigns.
I never heard of such another encounter, which   60
lames report to follow it and undoes description to
do it.

SECOND GENTLEMAN   What, pray you, became of Antigonus, that carried hence the child?

THIRD GENTLEMAN   Like an old tale still, which will   65
have matter to rehearse though credit be asleep and
not an ear open: he was torn to pieces with a bear.
This avouches the shepherd's son, who has not only
his innocence, which seems much, to justify him,
but a handkerchief and rings of his that Paulina   70
knows.

FIRST GENTLEMAN   What became of his bark and his
followers?

THIRD GENTLEMAN   Wracked the same instant of their
master's death and in the view of the shepherd, so   75
that all the instruments which aided to expose the
child were even then lost when it was found. But O,
the noble combat that 'twixt joy and sorrow was
fought in Paulina. She had one eye declined for the
loss of her husband, another elevated that the   80
oracle was fulfilled. She lifted the Princess from the
earth, and so locks her in embracing as if she would
pin her to her heart that she might no more be in
danger of losing.

FIRST GENTLEMAN   The dignity of this act was worth the   85
audience of kings and princes, for by such was it
acted.

THIRD GENTLEMAN   One of the prettiest touches of all,
and that which angled for mine eyes—caught the
water, though not the fish—was when at the rela-   90
tion of the Queen's death—with the manner how
she came to 't bravely confessed and lamented by
the King—how attentiveness wounded his daugh-

94. **from one sign . . . another:** i.e., passing from one visible indication of sorrow to another

96. **marble:** hard-hearted, unfeeling

103. **piece:** work of art; **in doing:** i.e., in the course of its creation

104. **performed:** completed

104–5. **Julio Romano:** a famous Italian artist (See longer note, page 248.)

106–7. **beguile . . . custom:** i.e., deprive the goddess Nature of her customers

107. **ape:** imitator

108–9. **one would:** i.e., an observer of his **statue** (line 102) would be likely to

110. **greediness of affection:** eager love (If **sup** [line 111] means "feed their eyes" rather than "have supper," the word **greediness** would also carry its meaning of "gluttony.")

112. **she:** i.e., Paulina

116. **piece:** join

117. **be thence:** i.e., stay away from there

118. **benefit of access:** advantage of being admitted; **wink:** blink

119. **unthrifty:** harmful

121. **dash:** touch, tinge

123. **Prince:** i.e., Prince's ship

ter, till, from one sign of dolor to another, she did,
with an "Alas," I would fain say bleed tears, for I am   95
sure my heart wept blood. Who was most marble
there changed color; some swooned, all sorrowed.
If all the world could have seen 't, the woe had been
universal.

FIRST GENTLEMAN Are they returned to the court?   100

THIRD GENTLEMAN No. The Princess hearing of her
mother's statue, which is in the keeping of
Paulina—a piece many years in doing and now
newly performed by that rare Italian master, Julio
Romano, who, had he himself eternity and could   105
put breath into his work, would beguile Nature of
her custom, so perfectly he is her ape; he so near to
Hermione hath done Hermione that they say one
would speak to her and stand in hope of answer.
Thither with all greediness of affection are they   110
gone, and there they intend to sup.

SECOND GENTLEMAN I thought she had some great
matter there in hand, for she hath privately twice or
thrice a day, ever since the death of Hermione,
visited that removed house. Shall we thither and   115
with our company piece the rejoicing?

FIRST GENTLEMAN Who would be thence that has the
benefit of access? Every wink of an eye some new
grace will be born. Our absence makes us unthrifty
to our knowledge. Let's along.   120

⌜*The Three Gentlemen*⌝ *exit.*

AUTOLYCUS Now, had I not the dash of my former life
in me, would preferment drop on my head. I
brought the old man and his son aboard the Prince,
told him I heard them talk of a fardel and I know
not what. But he at that time, overfond of the   125
shepherd's daughter—so he then took her to be—
who began to be much seasick, and himself little

129. **remained undiscovered:** i.e., was not then revealed

129–30. **all one to me:** i.e., all the same to me

131. **relished:** found acceptance or favor

136. **past:** i.e., past fathering

137. **gentlemen born:** i.e., born gentlemen, but with continuing comedy about the phrase "gentleman born" (See longer note, page 248.)

142. **were best:** i.e., might as well

143. **Give me the lie:** i.e., call me a liar (a provocation that would, according to those who prescribed rules for duelling, require a gentleman to fight)

146–47. **any time . . . hours:** i.e., for at least **four hours** ("Four" was often used to denote an indefinite number.)

158. **preposterous estate:** i.e., prosperous condition (See longer note, page 248.)

Playing "a tabor and pipe." (4.4.215–16)
From William Kemp, . . . *Kempes nine daies wonder* . . . (1600; 1884 facs.).

better, extremity of weather continuing, this mys-
tery remained undiscovered. But 'tis all one to
me, for had I been the finder-out of this secret, it   130
would not have relished among my other dis-
credits.

Enter Shepherd and ⌜*Shepherd's Son,*
both dressed in rich clothing.⌝

Here come those I have done good to against my
will, and already appearing in the blossoms of their
fortune.   135
SHEPHERD Come, boy, I am past more children, but thy
sons and daughters will be all gentlemen born.
SHEPHERD'S SON, ⌜*to Autolycus*⌝ You are well met, sir.
You denied to fight with me this other day because I
was no gentleman born. See you these clothes? Say   140
you see them not and think me still no gentleman
born. You were best say these robes are not gentlemen born. Give me the lie, do, and try whether I am
not now a gentleman born.
AUTOLYCUS I know you are now, sir, a gentleman born.   145
SHEPHERD'S SON Ay, and have been so any time these
four hours.
SHEPHERD And so have I, boy.
SHEPHERD'S SON So you have—but I was a gentleman
born before my father. For the King's son took me   150
by the hand and called me brother, and then the
two kings called my father brother, and then the
Prince my brother and the Princess my sister called
my father father; and so we wept, and there was the
first gentlemanlike tears that ever we shed.   155
SHEPHERD We may live, son, to shed many more.
SHEPHERD'S SON Ay, or else 'twere hard luck, being in
so preposterous estate as we are.
AUTOLYCUS I humbly beseech you, sir, to pardon me all

161. **me:** i.e., on my behalf
162. **gentle:** generous; mild or forgiving
172. **boors:** peasants; **franklins:** landowners lower in status than gentlemen
174. **If . . . false:** i.e., no matter how **false** it is
176–77. **tall . . . hands:** a strong **fellow** who is formidable with weapons
179. **would:** wish
181. **to my power:** i.e., to the best of **my power**
185. **Princes:** i.e., Perdita and Florizell
186. **picture:** statue

A shepherd. (3.3; 4.4)
From *Hortus sanitatis* . . . (1536).

the faults I have committed to your Worship and to 160
give me your good report to the Prince my master.
SHEPHERD   Prithee, son, do, for we must be gentle now
we are gentlemen.
SHEPHERD'S SON, ⌈*to Autolycus*⌉ Thou wilt amend thy
life? 165
AUTOLYCUS   Ay, an it like your good Worship.
SHEPHERD'S SON   Give me thy hand. I will swear to the
Prince thou art as honest a true fellow as any is in
Bohemia.
SHEPHERD   You may say it, but not swear it. 170
SHEPHERD'S SON   Not swear it, now I am a gentleman?
Let boors and franklins say it; I'll swear it.
SHEPHERD   How if it be false, son?
SHEPHERD'S SON   If it be ne'er so false, a true gentle-
man may swear it in the behalf of his friend.—And 175
I'll swear to the Prince thou art a tall fellow of thy
hands and that thou wilt not be drunk; but I know
thou art no tall fellow of thy hands and that thou
wilt be drunk. But I'll swear it, and I would thou
wouldst be a tall fellow of thy hands. 180
AUTOLYCUS   I will prove so, sir, to my power.
SHEPHERD'S SON   Ay, by any means prove a tall fellow. If
I do not wonder how thou dar'st venture to be
drunk, not being a tall fellow, trust me not. Hark,
the Kings and Princes, our kindred, are going to see 185
the Queen's picture. Come, follow us. We'll be thy
good masters.
They exit.

5.3 Leontes, Polixenes, Perdita, Florizell, and Camillo go with Paulina to view the statue of Hermione. Leontes grieves over her death, and Perdita kneels to entreat her blessing. Paulina tells the Hermione statue that the oracle has been fulfilled and instructs her to come down.

---

3. **What:** i.e., that which
5. **home:** in full
9. **answer:** return in kind
11. **with trouble:** i.e., only by imposing on you pains and exertion
13. **content:** pleasure
14. **singularities:** special excellences; rarities
22. **lively mocked:** vividly imitated
24. **shows off:** displays
26. **near:** i.e., close to lifelikeness

Scene 3
Enter Leontes, Polixenes, Florizell, Perdita, Camillo,
Paulina, ⌜*and*⌝ *Lords.*

LEONTES
O grave and good Paulina, the great comfort
That I have had of thee!

PAULINA   What, sovereign sir,
I did not well, I meant well. All my services
You have paid home. But that you have vouchsafed,   5
With your crowned brother and these your contracted
Heirs of your kingdoms, my poor house to visit,
It is a surplus of your grace which never
My life may last to answer.

LEONTES   O Paulina,   10
We honor you with trouble. But we came
To see the statue of our queen. Your gallery
Have we passed through, not without much content
In many singularities; but we saw not
That which my daughter came to look upon,   15
The statue of her mother.

PAULINA   As she lived peerless,
So her dead likeness, I do well believe,
Excels whatever yet you looked upon
Or hand of man hath done. Therefore I keep it   20
⌜Lonely,⌝ apart. But here it is. Prepare
To see the life as lively mocked as ever
Still sleep mocked death. Behold, and say 'tis well.
⌜*She draws a curtain*
to reveal⌝ *Hermione (like a statue).*
I like your silence. It the more shows off
Your wonder. But yet speak. First you, my liege.   25
Comes it not something near?

LEONTES   Her natural posture!—
Chide me, dear stone, that I may say indeed
Thou art Hermione; or rather, thou art she

30. **tender:** kind, loving, gentle

32. **nothing:** not at all

36. **lets go by:** i.e., indicates the passage of

37. **As she:** i.e., as if she

44. **more stone:** i.e., more unfeeling; **piece:** work of art; masterpiece

46. **conjured:** magically invoked

47. **admiring:** astonished; **spirits:** i.e., "animal spirits" that were thought to mediate between mind and body and to be the source of motion

50. **superstition:** an idolatrous religious observance (Perdita's kneeling before a statue to ask for a blessing might well have reminded audiences in Shakespeare's day that the Church of England attacked as **superstition** the Roman Catholic practice of kneeling in prayer before statues of Christ or of saints.)

55. **patience:** wait a little

56. **fixed:** put in place (See longer note, page 249.) **the color's:** i.e., the paint is (Greek statues, as well as effigies in Shakespeare's day, were painted so as to look lifelike.)

58. **sore:** intensely; **laid on:** inflicted, imposed ("**Laid on**" could also mean "applied as a coat of paint." This meaning—along with the words "**blow away**" and "**dry**" in the following lines—may pick up on the reference to the paint on the statue.)

60. **So . . . dry:** i.e., nor can sixteen **summers** dry up **your sorrow** (line 58)

In thy not chiding, for she was as tender   30
As infancy and grace.—But yet, Paulina,
Hermione was not so much wrinkled, nothing
So agèd as this seems.
POLIXENES   O, not by much!
PAULINA
So much the more our carver's excellence,   35
Which lets go by some sixteen years and makes her
As she lived now.
LEONTES   As now she might have done,
So much to my good comfort as it is
Now piercing to my soul. O, thus she stood,   40
Even with such life of majesty—warm life,
As now it coldly stands—when first I wooed her.
I am ashamed. Does not the stone rebuke me
For being more stone than it?—O royal piece,
There's magic in thy majesty, which has   45
My evils conjured to remembrance and
From thy admiring daughter took the spirits,
Standing like stone with thee.
PERDITA   And give me leave,
And do not say 'tis superstition, that   50
I kneel, and then implore her blessing. ⌈*She kneels.*⌉
                                   Lady,
Dear queen, that ended when I but began,
Give me that hand of yours to kiss.
PAULINA   O, patience!   55
The statue is but newly fixed; the color's
Not dry.
CAMILLO, ⌈*to Leontes, who weeps*⌉
My lord, your sorrow was too sore laid on,
Which sixteen winters cannot blow away,
So many summers dry. Scarce any joy   60
Did ever so long live; no sorrow
But killed itself much sooner.

64–66. **Let . . . himself:** Polixenes refers to himself as the **cause** of Leontes' pain.   **piece up:** perhaps, repair or patch up

69. **wrought:** agitated
72. **draw:** i.e., close
73. **fancy:** imagination
83. **fixture:** fixed position
84. **mocked with:** deceived by
89. **together:** i.e., in a row
90. **No . . . world:** i.e., no calm mind in the world

POLIXENES   Dear my brother,
Let him that was the cause of this have power
To take off so much grief from you as he   65
Will piece up in himself.
PAULINA   Indeed, my lord,
If I had thought the sight of my poor image
Would thus have wrought you—for the stone is
      mine—   70
I'd not have showed it.
LEONTES   Do not draw the curtain.
PAULINA
No longer shall you gaze on 't, lest your fancy
May think anon it moves.
LEONTES   Let be, let be.   75
Would I were dead but that methinks already—
What was he that did make it?—See, my lord,
Would you not deem it breathed? And that those
      veins
Did verily bear blood?   80
POLIXENES   Masterly done.
The very life seems warm upon her lip.
LEONTES
The fixture of her eye has motion in 't,
As we are mocked with art.
PAULINA   I'll draw the curtain.   85
My lord's almost so far transported that
He'll think anon it lives.
LEONTES   O sweet Paulina,
Make me to think so twenty years together!
No settled senses of the world can match   90
The pleasure of that madness. Let 't alone.
PAULINA
I am sorry, sir, I have thus far stirred you, but
I could afflict you farther.
LEONTES   Do, Paulina,
For this affliction has a taste as sweet   95

96. **cordial:** restorative
97. **an air:** a breath
103. **painting:** paint
108. **presently:** at once
108–9. **resolve you / For:** i.e., make up your minds (to experience)
114. **What:** i.e., whatever
120. **unlawful business:** i.e., witchcraft, which was outlawed and punishable by death
124. **Strike:** i.e., strike up
127. **come away:** i.e., come
128. **Bequeath:** assign, hand over; **him:** i.e., it (death)

"Methinks I play as . . . in Whitsun pastorals." (4.4.158–59)
From Charles Grignion, Morris dancers . . . [n.d.].

As any cordial comfort. Still methinks
There is an air comes from her. What fine chisel
Could ever yet cut breath? Let no man mock me,
For I will kiss her.
PAULINA   Good my lord, forbear.   100
The ruddiness upon her lip is wet.
You'll mar it if you kiss it, stain your own
With oily painting. Shall I draw the curtain?
LEONTES
No, not these twenty years.
PERDITA, ⌈*rising*⌉   So long could I   105
Stand by, a looker-on.
PAULINA   Either forbear,
Quit presently the chapel, or resolve you
For more amazement. If you can behold it,
I'll make the statue move indeed, descend   110
And take you by the hand. But then you'll think—
Which I protest against—I am assisted
By wicked powers.
LEONTES   What you can make her do
I am content to look on; what to speak,   115
I am content to hear, for 'tis as easy
To make her speak as move.
PAULINA   It is required
You do awake your faith. Then all stand still—
⌈Or⌉ those that think it is unlawful business   120
I am about, let them depart.
LEONTES   Proceed.
No foot shall stir.
PAULINA   Music, awake her! Strike!
                              ⌈*Music sounds.*⌉
'Tis time. Descend. Be stone no more. Approach.   125
Strike all that look upon with marvel. Come,
I'll fill your grave up. Stir, nay, come away.
Bequeath to death your numbness, for from him
Dear life redeems you.—You perceive she stirs.

130. **Start not:** i.e., don't shy away; **holy:** sinless
133. **double:** i.e., a second time
138. **Lawful:** i.e., as lawful
147. **Mark:** observe
150. **pray:** entreat, ask for
160. **in being:** alive
161. **issue:** outcome
163. **push:** provocation

A turtledove on a "withered bough." (5.3.166–67)
From Konrad Gesner, . . . *Historiae animalium* . . . (1585–1604).

⌈*Hermione descends.*⌉

Start not. Her actions shall be holy as   130
You hear my spell is lawful. Do not shun her
Until you see her die again, for then
You kill her double. Nay, present your hand.
When she was young, you wooed her; now in age
Is she become the suitor?   135
LEONTES   O, she's warm!
If this be magic, let it be an art
Lawful as eating.
POLIXENES   She embraces him.
CAMILLO   She hangs about his neck.   140
If she pertain to life, let her speak too.
POLIXENES
Ay, and make it manifest where she has lived,
Or how stol'n from the dead.
PAULINA   That she is living,
Were it but told you, should be hooted at   145
Like an old tale, but it appears she lives,
Though yet she speak not. Mark a little while.
⌈*To Perdita.*⌉ Please you to interpose, fair madam.
    Kneel
And pray your mother's blessing. ⌈*To Hermione.*⌉   150
    Turn, good lady.
Our Perdita is found.
HERMIONE   You gods, look down,
And from your sacred vials pour your graces
Upon my daughter's head! Tell me, mine own,   155
Where hast thou been preserved? Where lived? How
    found
Thy father's court? For thou shalt hear that I,
Knowing by Paulina that the oracle
Gave hope thou wast in being, have preserved   160
Myself to see the issue.
PAULINA   There's time enough for that,
Lest they desire upon this push to trouble

164. **like relation:** i.e., stories like the one you have just requested from Perdita

165. **precious winners:** i.e., winners of what you value as precious

166. **Partake:** communicate; **turtle:** turtledove, symbolic of fidelity in love (See page 232.)

167. **wing me:** fly

168. **My mate:** i.e., Antigonus

169. **lost:** destroyed, dead

171–73. **Thou . . . vows:** Although the audience has heard Leontes agree to marry only at Paulina's direction, these lines are the first mention of Paulina's agreeing to marry a husband of Leontes' choosing.

178. **For him:** i.e., as for him

181. **Is:** i.e., are; **richly:** fully; **justified:** maintained as true

182. **Let's:** i.e., let's go

185. **holy:** sinless

186. **ill:** evil

187. **whom heavens directing:** i.e., who, as directed by heaven

188. **troth-plight:** betrothed, engaged

190–91. **demand . . . Performed:** i.e., ask questions and provide answers about the parts we have **performed**

Your joys with like relation. Go together,
You precious winners all. Your exultation   165
Partake to everyone. I, an old turtle,
Will wing me to some withered bough and there
My mate, that's never to be found again,
Lament till I am lost.
LEONTES   O peace, Paulina.   170
Thou shouldst a husband take by my consent,
As I by thine a wife. This is a match,
And made between 's by vows. Thou hast found
    mine—
But how is to be questioned, for I saw her,   175
As I thought, dead, and have in vain said many
A prayer upon her grave. I'll not seek far—
For him, I partly know his mind—to find thee
An honorable husband.—Come, Camillo,
And take her by the hand, whose worth and honesty 180
Is richly noted and here justified
By us, a pair of kings. Let's from this place.
⌜*To Hermione.*⌝ What, look upon my brother! Both
    your pardons
That e'er I put between your holy looks   185
My ill suspicion. This your son-in-law
And son unto the King, whom heavens directing,
Is troth-plight to your daughter.—Good Paulina,
Lead us from hence, where we may leisurely
Each one demand and answer to his part   190
Performed in this wide gap of time since first
We were dissevered. Hastily lead away.
                                        They exit.

Longer Notes

1.2.0 SD. Camillo: The immediate re-entry of this character (unusual in Shakespearean drama) has led some editors to believe that even though the Folio marks a new scene here, the action may be continuous, with Archidamus and Camillo simply stepping aside while the two kings, the queen, and Mamillius enter.

There is general agreement that this play was printed from a transcript made by the professional scribe Ralph Crane. It is possible that Crane introduced the scene break, along with Camillo's exit and re-entry. Some editors have Camillo wait to re-enter until well along in 1.2, but there are strong indications in the dialogue that he overhears much of what happens from the beginning of the scene.

1.2.13–16. I am . . . truly: Polixenes' lines have defied editorial attempts to provide convincing explanations of their meaning. There is agreement that Polixenes compares his kingdom to a garden where plants may **breed,** and that he fears his garden-kingdom may be threatened by cold **sneaping** winds. However, it is not clear why the blowing of the winds "make us [i.e., me] say, / 'This is put forth too truly,'" and the meaning of **This** is particularly unclear. Our paraphrase of "I am questioned" as "I am tormented" depends on a legal meaning of the noun "question" as "the application of torture as part of a judicial examination."

1.2.56–108. No, madam . . . with us: From line 56 to line 108, Leontes takes no part in the conversation between Hermione and Polixenes. Some critics

237

who are intent upon finding in the play a rational explanation for Leontes' sudden fit of jealousy (first evident at
line 139) imagine him eavesdropping or inadvertently
overhearing parts of the dialogue between Hermione
and Polixenes and interpreting their words as evidence
of a sexual liaison. Most critics find this way of reading
the play problematic and think that the play offers no
rational explanation for Leontes' jealousy.

1.2.168. blacks: Black fabric could be **false** or unstable for a number of reasons. The process of dyeing
the wool black could in itself weaken the cloth. Further,
since legislation required that wool first be dyed red or
blue, all black fabric was overdyed with additional dye
and hence could be considered "false." Funeral clothing and hangings were called **blacks,** and Leontes may
be calling into doubt the sincerity of mourners, especially the widow who has buried more than one husband and hence has "overdyed" her mourning wear. It
has also been suggested that the phrase "false as
o'erdyed blacks" may refer to contemporary attitudes
toward black people, who were considered licentious
and who were thought by some to be dyed black by the
sun.

1.2.175. Affection . . . center: This line contains two
abstract nouns (**affection, intention**) and the figurative
term **the center.** The history of commentary includes a
variety of reasonable interpretations of the line. Some
trace **affection** to the Latin *affectio* and see Leontes as
commenting abstractly on the power of emotion (or of a
disturbed mind) to find out the truth, or (again abstractly) on the power of passionate love to pierce the
soul and "make possible things not so held" (line 176).
Others think that Leontes is addressing his own

affection—his emotions, or passions; more specifically, his jealousy of Hermione. On this interpretation, **intention** could refer to the "intensity" of his feeling, or to the "attentive observation" (of Hermione and Polixenes) that his feeling has provoked, or to the "meaning" (his notion of an affair between Hermione and Polixenes) to which his feeling has led him. The figurative term **the center,** according to this way of reading the passage, could mean the "truth" about his wife and friend, or it could mean Leontes' **center** (his heart, which is wounded by his jealousy), or it could even mean the **center** of the universe, which is shaken, for him, by his belief in Hermione's adultery.

Still others think that Leontes addresses what he believes to be Hermione's lust (**affection**). In this case the sense of **intention** is probably limited; it would mean "purpose," or "import." **The center,** in this reading of the line, probably refers to Leontes' heart, but possibly means the center of the universe.

Almost all readings of this difficult speech agree that its obscurity reflects Leontes' disturbed mind, and that its central point is that the impossible (**things not so held, dreams, what's unreal, nothing** [lines 176–79]) has been made **possible.**

1.2.269. **They're here with me:** A similar expression is to be found in *May Day*, a play by Shakespeare's contemporary George Chapman: "As often as he turns his back to me, I shall be *here* [*makes V*] *with him;* that's certain." The "V" stands for two fingers held up to make the V shape of the pair of horns that the cuckold is said to wear. Thus Leontes' words "They're *here with me* already" may mean he thinks that people in his court already know he is a cuckold and that they are already making mocking gestures behind his back.

**1.2.511–12. Swear his thought over / By each par-
ticular star:** Though the general sense is fairly clear—
i.e., "even if you swear by every star in heaven"—there
is no agreement about the meaning of the phrase "swear
his thought over." Suggestions about "swear over"
range from "overswear" (i.e., "persuade by the superior
power of oaths" or "swear so as to overcome") to
"outswear" (i.e., "be more vehement in denial than he is
in accusation"). There is general agreement that "his
thought" refers to lines 499–502: "He thinks . . . that
you have touched his queen / Forbiddenly."

2.1.161–63. If . . . her: This passage presents several
puzzles. Editors have been unable to agree, for example,
on what Antigonus means by his allusion to keeping his
stables where he lodges his wife. Suggested meanings
include "I'll guard my wife as carefully as my horses"
and "I'll separate my wife from all other men, just as I
keep my mares apart from my stallions." Another puzzle
is his "I'll go in couples with her." One possible meaning is "I'll harness or leash myself to her as if we were
horses or dogs," a reading that depends on **couples**
meaning "pairs." "Couple" could, however, also mean
"leash."

2.1.221. Delphos: Delos, the legendary birthplace of
Apollo, was famous in classical culture and one of the
places that the wandering Aeneas visits in Virgil's *Aene-
id*. By the sixteenth century, the already deserted island had come to be called Delphos by analogy with
Delphi, the mainland site of Apollo's more celebrated
oracle.

2.3.112. as . . . stands: As Stephen Orgel points out
(in a note to the Oxford edition), were Leontes not the

king, Hermione (under English law of Shakespeare's time) could sue him for slander: "To defame a woman's honour was actionable in both civil and ecclesiastical courts. . . . 'As the case now stands' Leontes cannot be sued for slander only because no court has jurisdiction over the King" (p. 136).

2.3.198. **midwife:** Stephen Orgel points out (in a note to the Oxford edition) that Leontes' use of this term for Paulina "implicates [her] in both the birth of the child and the concealment of its true paternity." He quotes from the midwife's oath, part of the sixteenth-century licensing process, the midwife's "promise not to 'permit or suffer that woman being in labour or travail shall name any other to be the father of her child, than only he who is the right true father thereof' " (p. 139).

3.2.11. **Silence:** This word is printed in the First Folio in italic as if it were a stage direction, but there is no precedent for such a stage direction in other Shakespeare plays and no certain precedent in any other play of the period. (The only possible precedent may be in George Chapman's *Monsieur d'Olive*.) Ralph Crane, the scribe who is widely thought to have prepared the manuscript from which *The Winter's Tale* was set into type, used the italic hand in order to emphasize particular words. Although we are far from certain about whether "Silence" should be printed as part of the dialogue or as a stage direction, the combination of Crane's habit of using italic for emphasis and the absence of any such stage directions in Shakespeare's other plays has led us to incorporate the word into the dialogue.

4.1.0 SD. **Time, the Chorus:** In Robert Greene's *Pandosto,* a novel that *The Winter's Tale* in part dramatizes, the subtitle reads: "The Triumph of Time. Wherein is discovered . . . that although by the means of sinister fortune truth may be concealed, yet by time . . . it is most manifestly revealed." (See page xviii.)

4.1.8–9. **law . . . custom:** The speaker, Time, may here be understood to refer to all laws and customs, since both are the products of time and are subject to change in time; but Time has been understood to refer particularly to one of the West's dramatic conventions, the "unity of time." This convention may be traced back to Aristotle's *Poetics*, although there it was not yet the **law** or **custom** that it later came to be. Aristotle simply described a particular Greek tragedy as having a plot duration of only a single day and observed that tragedy was set in a more limited time span than epic. Some of Shakespeare's contemporaries—neoclassical critics, like Sir Philip Sidney in his *Apology for Poetry* or like Ben Jonson, a dramatist who criticized Shakespeare's use of time in plot construction—represented Aristotle as prescribing, rather than merely describing, that a tragic plot not exceed twenty-four hours' duration. As a prescription, the requirement became known later as the "unity of time." The speaker Time may here be addressing this emerging dramatic convention, announcing that he may violate it because all law and custom are under his control.

4.1.22. **I mentioned a son o' th' King's:** The reference here is to the discussion of Polixenes' son in 1.2.205–13. Time as Chorus here presents all of the previous stage action as his own narrative.

4.2.20. **the heaping friendships:** When Polixenes assures Camillo that he will **be more thankful to**

Camillo, and then speaks of the **profit** to be expected from this increase in gratitude, it seems that Polixenes is thinking that Camillo owes him something in return— an increase in friendly services—as we have explained. But the play's language is, as so often, irreducibly ambiguous. **The heaping friendships** could also mean an increase in the friendship between Camillo and Polixenes; or an increase in the friendships, or alliances, that Camillo, as Polixenes' agent, will make for the king with others; or even an increase in the friendship of Polixenes for Camillo—friendship that puts Camillo under a still greater obligation to serve Polixenes.

4.3.24. **Autolycus:** The name comes from Greek mythology, in which **Autolycus** is the son of the god Hermes—or, in Roman mythology, Mercury. In Ovid's *Metamorphoses* (book 11) one reads (in Arthur Golding's 1567 translation) that Chione bears Mercury "a son that hight [was called] *Awtolychus*, who proved a wily pie [magpie, a thieving bird], / And such a fellow as in theft and filching had no peer. / He was his father's own son right [truly]; he could men's eyes so blear [deceive] / As for to make the black things white, and white things black appear" (lines 360–63, spelling modernized).

4.3.31 SD. **Shepherd's Son:** In the Folio text, this character is throughout designated as "Clown." Such a designation probably means both that the role was played by the theatrical company's comic actor and that the character is to be viewed as a rustic simpleton.

4.3.36 SD **He lies down:** At this point Autolycus begins to enact a version of the story of the Good Samaritan (Luke 10.30–37), a parable about a man beaten and robbed who is helped by a passing stranger. Here Autolycus *pretends* to be beaten and robbed, and uses the stranger's charity as an opportunity to pick his purse. Robert Greene, in one of his late-sixteenth-century pamphlets about the tricks of thieves and con men (the "Conny-catching Pamphlets"), tells of a similar trick played on a wealthy visitor to St. Paul's Cathedral.

4.3.48. **out of my note:** While it is extremely unlikely that a shepherd in Shakespeare's England would have been able to read, we have included at line 39 the stage direction *"He reads a paper"* and have given as one meaning of "out of my note" "i.e., not on my list." Our reasons for doing this are twofold. First, the Shepherd's Son responds to the list of ingredients given him by his sister to purchase as if he is reading rather than remembering ("five pound of currants, rice—what will this sister of mine do with rice?"). Second, there are several indications in 4.4 that not only the Shepherd's Son but also Mopsa and Dorcas (rural serving girls) are literate. (Mopsa, for example, loves "a ballad in print," and both girls are shown reading the words to "Two Maids Wooing a Man.") The shepherds in this play, in other words, seem to participate in the tradition of the literary pastoral in which shepherds are often portrayed as literate.

4.3.105. **rogue:** While Shakespeare had used the word *rogue* in earlier plays in some of its looser senses, here it seems to carry a rather specific meaning, as if it were one of the "knavish professions" practiced by Autolycus. The word came into English in 1561 as the name given a beggar who uses as his excuse for being on the road the tale that he has come to seek a kinsman. It then was used as well to describe beggars who got money by pretending to be sick. By 1572 it had become the term used in legal statutes to refer to those who, though healthy, were unemployed and who had no other source of income. To be a rogue—i.e., to be unemployed and destitute—was to be a criminal liable to severe punishment. In 1604 King James' first parliament specified, in addition to such punishments as whippings, that "rogues . . . shall be branded in the left shoulder with a great Roman R . . . [so] that the letter R be seen and remain for a perpetual mark upon such rogue during his or her life." (See Barbara A. Mowat, "Rogues, Shepherds, and the Counterfeit Distressed," in Further Reading.)

4.4.31–34. Jupiter . . . swain: Although Apollo is not recorded in classical mythology as having transformed himself into a country laborer (**swain**) in order to pursue a woman, he is represented (in Ovid's *Metamorphoses*) as having done so in the tapestry woven by Arachne: "In likeness of a country clown was Phebus [Apollo] pictured there. . . . And how he in a shepherd's shape was practising a wile / The daughter of one *Macarie* dame *Issa* to beguile" (6.152–55, Arthur Golding's translation [1567], spelling modernized).

4.4.48. forced: In the period in which Shakespeare was writing, the word *forced* was strongly associated with violence and torture, including pressing, the most violent coercion of the subject by the monarch to bring the subject to conform to royal will.

4.4.80 SD. to Polixenes: In adding this direction (and that at line 82) for Perdita's speeches of welcome, we are assuming that though in disguise, the king's costume will indicate that he is socially superior to Camillo.

4.4.97. **bastards:** Streaked gillyflowers were, according to Sir Francis Bacon, a kind of natural hybrid, appearing in different colors and with different stripes depending on the soil in which the seeds were planted. In lines 102–4, Perdita seems to question the naturalness of the process that produces "streaked gillyvors" (line 96), claiming that she has "heard it said" that their "piedness" is the result of horticultural "art."

4.4.218. **ballads:** The reference here is to what are called "broadside ballads," sensational stories told in rough verse and printed on one side of a large sheet of paper. These ballads were often sung to popular tunes.

4.4.442. **Take . . . bargain:** In Shakespeare's time, couples who clasped hands and exchanged vows before witnesses performed a ceremony called "handfasting," after which they were regarded as legally married. Hence Polixenes refers to what appears about to happen in this scene as his son's **nuptial** (line 460 below).

4.4.540 **Where no priest shovels in dust:** According to the 1549 *Book of Common Prayer* of the Church of England, the priest was to cast earth on the corpse during a proper burial service; here the play slips for a moment from pagan Bohemia to Shakespeare's England.

4.4.727. **geld a codpiece of a purse:** Like the word **placket** (line 726), the words **geld, purse,** and **codpiece** all had sexual connotations. A **codpiece** was a showy appendage to the front of a man's breeches (and, by extension, a man's private parts); a **purse** was both a wallet and a name for the scrotum. In line 728, the word **keys** continues the sexual wordplay, since the word "key" was slang for the penis.

4.4.752. change garments: Editors have puzzled over just what garments are exchanged between Florizell and Autolycus. Perdita describes Florizell's garments as "a swain's wearing" (4.4.10). A "swain" was usually a rustic laborer, often a shepherd, and Perdita's concern that Florizell has "obscured" himself (line 9) in the clothes he wears would support the idea that he is dressed humbly. However, Autolycus is greatly delighted at being given these very clothes in exchange for his own—"What a boot [profit] is here with this exchange!" (lines 798–99). Furthermore, the Shepherd later says of Autolycus in the same clothes "His garments are rich" (line 879). This discrepancy is for directors to resolve; one possible expedient is to have Florizell wear his "swain's wearing" over his royal attire and then strip off the disguise once Polixenes has left, so that the garments Florizell gives Autolycus are a prince's suit.

There is also some question about what kind of clothes Autolycus gives Florizell; at least in terms of the standards of realism in force in the modern theater, Autolycus cannot appear at the sheepshearing in the rags he wore in 4.3 without being identified by the Shepherd's Son. Autolycus' peddler's costume is therefore entirely at the modern director's discretion.

4.4.770. The truth of your own seeming: Critics have noted that Camillo is here given a rather awkward phrase, which they read as dramatic irony. This irony arises because the characters on stage cannot know that Perdita is royal by birth, but the audience can and does. At this point Perdita is still dressed up, as she was for the feast, in the costume of a queen (4.4.5 and 528). Her royal appearance (**seeming**) thus reveals the truth of her birth—**the truth of** [her] **own seeming.**

5.1.69–70. and on . . . soul-vexed: The Folio reads: "and on this Stage / (Where we Offendors now appeare) Soule-vext." The lines have been variously emended by editors through the centuries. Among the proposed emendations of line 70 are "(*Were* we offenders now) appear soul-vexed"; "(Where we *offend her* now), . . ."; "Where *we're* offenders now, . . ."; "Where we offenders *move*, . . ."; and "(Where we offenders *mourn*)."

5.2.104–5. Julio Romano: This Italian artist (who lived c. 1499–1546) was best known in Shakespeare's England for his painting and his architecture, but his epitaph, quoted in Vasari's *Lives of the Artists,* reads "Jupiter saw sculpted and painted bodies breathe . . . by the skill of Giulio Romano." There is no agreement among scholars about why Shakespeare included Romano's name in a play set in an age when kings turned to the Delphic oracle for answers.

5.2.137. gentlemen born: In Elizabethan usage, a "gentleman born" was one "descended from three degrees of gentry, both on the mother's and father's side" (William Segar, *The Booke of Honor and Armes* [1590], p. 36). Technically, then, the Shepherd misuses the term. His son comically misuses it in every possible way.

5.2.158. preposterous estate: The word **preposterous** is the Shepherd's Son's comic error. Derived from the Latin word meaning "reversed," cart-before-the-horse, the word **preposterous** is even more comic: when the Shepherd's Son said "I was a gentleman born before my father" (lines 149–50), he defined his condition as literally **preposterous** by putting a necessarily earlier event—his father's birth—after a necessarily later one—his own. (See Patricia Parker, "Preposterous Events," *Shakespeare Quarterly* 43 [1992], 186–213.)

5.3.56. **The statue is but newly fixed:** Many editors interpret this line as meaning "the color has only recently been made fast." If so, Shakespeare uses the word "fixed" in this sense some fifty years before the earliest usage recorded in the *Oxford English Dictionary*.

Textual Notes

The reading of the present text appears to the left of the square bracket. Unless otherwise noted, the reading to the left of the bracket is from **F,** the First Folio text (upon which this edition is based). The earliest sources of readings not in **F** are indicated as follows: **F2** is the Second Folio of 1632; **F3** is the Third Folio of 1663–64; **F4** is the Fourth Folio of 1685; **Ed.** is an earlier editor of Shakespeare, beginning with Rowe in 1709. No sources are given for emendations of punctuation or for corrections of obvious typographical errors, like turned letters that produce no known word. **SD** means stage direction; **SP** means speech prefix; *uncorr.* means the first or uncorrected state of the First Folio; *corr.* means the second or corrected state of the First Folio; ~ stands in place of a word already quoted before the square bracket; ∧ indicates the omission of a punctuation mark.

1.1　　10. Beseech] F ('Beseech)
　　　　19. Believe] F ('Beleeue)
1.2　　21. sev'nnight] F (Seue'night)
　　　　25. beseech] F ('beseech)
　　　　41. proclaimed.] ~, F
　　　　64. "verily"] F (Verely')
　　　　85. twinned] F (twyn'd)
　　　　133. And] F2; A F
　　　　133. thyself∧] ~, F
　　　　165. full∧] ~, F
　　　　174. be?—] ~∧ F
　　　　175. Affection,]~? F
　　　　178. unreal∧] ~: F
　　　　199. do] Ed.; do's F

251

257. they] F2; *omit* F
315. forth. . . . lord,] ~∧ . . . ~. F
338. hobby-horse] Ed.; Holy-Horse F
370. wife's] F (Wiues)
430. thousands] F (thousand's)
474. aught] F (ought)
474. behoove] F (behoue)
552. off∧] ~, F

2.1   0. SD *Enter Hermione, Mamillius, Ladies:*
            Leontes, Antigonus, Lords. F
3, 6, 18, 21. SP FIRST LADY] Ed.; *Lady* F
15. this] F ('this)
29. Pray] F ('Pray)
52. venom,] ~: F
53. infected;] ~)∧ F
136, 141. Beseech] F ('beseech)
194. true∧ . . . suspicion,]~, . . . ~∧ F
220. have] hane F

2.2   0. SD *Enter Paulina, a Gentleman, Gaoler,*
            Emilia. F
27. gracious] gtacious F
57. presently] presenrly F
64. let 't] F (le't)

2.3   0. SD *Enter Leontes, Seruants, Paulina, An-*
            tigonus, and Lords. F
2. thus, . . . weakness.] ~: . . . ~, F
46. What] F2; Who F
74. good, so∧] ~∧~, F
94. dotard;] ~, F
181. can, . . . liege.] ~: . . . ~, F
185. beseech] F (beseech')
236. Please] F (Please')

3.2   0. SD *Enter Leontes, Lords, Officers: Hermio-*
            ne (as to her Triall) Ladies: Cleomines,
            Dion. F

11. Silence] *printed in F as SD at end of line 10.*
161. strike] stiike F
168. Beseech] F ('Beseech)
212. done 't] F (don't)
220. sweet'st,] ~. F
263–64. appear, . . . perpetual.] ~(. . . ~) F

3.3   0. SD *Enter Antigonus, a Marriner, Babe, Sheepeheard, and Clowne.* F
8. wills] F (wil's)
33. thrower-out] Thower-out F
83 *and hereafter.* SD *Shepherd's Son*] This ed.; *Clowne* F
84 *and hereafter.* SP SHEPHERD'S SON] This ed.; *Clo., Clow, Clowne* F
90. sky;] ~, F
126. made] F (mad)
142. Marry] F ('Marry)

4.1   19. himself,] ~. F
4.2   53. Prithee] F ('Prethe)
57. SD *They exit*] Ed.; *Exit* F
4.3   1. SP AUTOLYCUS] Ed.; *omit* F
5. *bleaching*] *bleachiug* F
10. *With heigh, with heigh*] F2; *With heigh* F
37. counters] F (Compters)
40. currants] F (Currence)
59. offends] F2; offend F
65. detestable] derestable F
124. SD *One line earlier in* F
130. *Sings*] Ed.; *Song.* F
4.4   0. SD *Enter Florizell, Perdita, Shepherd, Clowne, Polixenes, Camillo, Mopsa, Dorcas, Seruants, Autolicus.* F
13. it] F2; *omit* F
14. swoon] Ed.; sworne F
69. afire] F (o'fire)

116. your] F2; you F
125. wi' th'] F (with')
176. shepherd] Sphepherd F
190. out] Ed.; on't F
225. customers] cnstomers F
236. Believe] Beleeee F
254. SP AUTOLYCUS] Ed.; *omit* F
273. than] rhen F
275. Maybe] F ('May be)
281. kiln-hole] F (kill-hole)
285. promised] ptomis'd F
305. midwife's] F (Midwiues)
305–6. Mistress] F (Mist.)
308. Pray] F ('Pray)
311. things] rhings F
335–37. you. | *Song* | AUTOLYCUS *Get . . . go* |
         Where] Ed; you: | Song *Get . . . goe* |
         Aut. *Where* F
353. gentlemen] F (Gent.)
355. me.—Wenches,] ~, ~∧ F
360. *cape*] *Crpe* F
411. who] F2; whom F
439. better.] ~∧ F
493. acknowledged] F2; acknowledge F
504. shalt] Ed.; shalt neuer F
507. Far'r] Ed.; Farre F
514. thee—] ~. F
516. hoop] Ed.; hope F
553. your] F2; my F
572. am, . . . fancy.] ~: . . . ~, F
573. obedient,] ~: F
591. our] Ed.; her F
599. Perdita.—] ~, F
652. the son] F3; there Sonne F
693. rear] F (reare')
727. could] Ed.; would F

727. filed] F3; fill'd F
728. off] F (of)
758. flayed] F (fled)
783. Pray] F ('Pray)
792. SD *Camillo . . . exit.*] Ed.; *Exit.* F
837. Pray] F ('Pray)
857. like] lke F
862. and] Ed.; at F
907. sheep-whistling] Sheepe-whistiing F
918. aqua vitae] F (Aquavite)
975. *He exits.*] Ed.; *Exeunt.* F

5.1   0. SD *Enter Leontes, Cleomines, Dion, Pauli-na, Seruants: Florizel, Perdita.* F
13–14. of. | PAULINA True, too true] Ed.; of, true. | *Paul.* Too true F
49. human] F (humane)
73. just cause] F3; just such cause F
93–95. madam— | PAULINA I have done. | Yet] Ed.; Madame, I haue done. | *Paul.* Yet F
151. Prithee] F ('Prethee)
181. bade] F (bad)
199. his,] ~∧ F

5.2   97. swooned] F (swownded)
120. SD *The . . . exit.*] Ed.; *Exit.* F
162. Prithee] F ('Prethee)

5.3   0. SD *Enter Leontes, Polixenes, Florizell, Perdita, Camillo, Paulina: Hermione (like a Statue:) Lords, &c.* F
21. Lonely] Ed.; Louely F
76. already—] ~. F
81. Masterly] F ('Masterly)
120. Or] Ed.; On F
159. the] rhe F
162. time] ttme F

The Winter's Tale:
A Modern Perspective

Stephen Orgel

For modern audiences and critics *The Winter's Tale* is a strangely discordant play. The title declares it a fable—a winter's tale is a trifle, a fairy tale to enliven long winter nights. Yet the first half presents, in the depiction of Leontes' jealousy, one of Shakespeare's most brilliant and deeply felt studies of human psychology, uncompromising in its intensity and realism. It is also a pointed and powerful dramatization of the dangers and responsibilities of monarchy, a logical corollary to *King Lear*. But why, then, the change of direction for the conclusion? Why does Shakespeare set up the tragic momentum of the first three acts, only to disarm it with fantasy and magic? And if the tragedy is to be disarmed, why is the happy ending so partial—why is Mamillius not restored along with Hermione and Perdita? Why, indeed, is the death of Leontes' young son, the heir to the throne, so much less of an issue dramatically than the loss of his infant daughter? Most puzzling of all, why does Shakespeare—quite uncharacteristically, if one thinks of his earlier plays about bad kings—preserve and finally exonerate Leontes? Why not let him atone for his crimes by dying, and resolve the tragic issues through the succession of a new and innocent generation, on the models of *Henry IV, Macbeth, King Lear*? Reconciliations are the stuff of Shakespearean comedy; but why does Shakespeare want this play to be a comedy?

These questions may express modern critical concerns, but for the history of the play on the stage, they are not at all new. From the time *The Winter's Tale* was first revived in the mid–eighteenth century, revisers and performers have set to work to diminish the play's tragic aspects, to soften and rationalize Leontes' jealousy, to focus the play more clearly on the pastoral scenes and the young lovers (Garrick's adaptation was even called *Florizel and Perdita*). At the same time, the statue scene has always been the play's emotional center: however illogical or frankly incredible, the conclusion has always been theatrically foolproof.

Though the play has a family setting, its issues are deeply informed by the political and legal history of Jacobean England—by questions of the perquisites and responsibilities of the monarch, the relation between royal authority and the will of the people, the limits of protocol, and what sanctions may be brought to bear on the actions of a criminal king. All these issues were being actively debated throughout the first decade of King James I's reign, and the play's focus on the king is certainly a reflection of the world of contemporary politics. At the same time, however, the play's political issues were ones that had concerned Shakespeare in his deepest tragedies throughout his career, and even overtly political tragedy, for Shakespeare, invariably starts in the family. It is Richard II's behavior toward his uncles and cousins that prompts the rebellion that deposes him; the tragedy of Hamlet begins with fratricide and incest, and takes shape around the complex relations of parents and children; Macbeth, assassinating Duncan at the urging of his wife, is murdering his cousin; Lear's tragedy is from beginning to end a family matter. It is to the point that when

James I came to the English throne in 1603, there was a fully constituted royal family at the center of English society for the first time since the death of Henry VIII.

Leontes' jealousy of his wife's affection for his oldest friend seems to appear, dramatically, out of nowhere. It springs, paradoxically, from his wife's ability to persuade Polixenes to extend his stay in Sicily, when Leontes' own pleas had failed. In doing so, she is fulfilling his wishes, acting as his agent—being a good wife—and Leontes' response obviously includes a large measure of ambivalence toward both his marriage and his best friend. Criticism has widely regarded Leontes' jealous rage as unmotivated, and critics and editors have often attempted to provide the play with a rational basis for his delusion, arguing that Hermione, though certainly innocent, must have presented the appearance of impropriety. Directors, similarly, often give Hermione and Polixenes some suspiciously intimate stage business to justify Leontes' outburst. But in Shakespeare's text, the motivation comes from within— the play's psychology, indeed, is strikingly modern in its recognition of the self-generating nature of Leontes' passion and the compulsiveness of paranoid behavior.

Shakespeare's explanation for Leontes' behavior is rooted in childhood and in the complex tensions between male bonding and heterosexual love. The king turns from his wife and friend to his child, and this provides the rationale for his evident dismay:

> Looking on the lines
> Of my boy's face, methoughts I did recoil
> Twenty-three years, and saw myself unbreeched,
> In my green velvet coat, my dagger muzzled

Lest it should bite its master and so prove,
As ornaments oft do, too dangerous.

                                (1.2.194–99)

He finds himself in the seven-year-old Mamillius, and
the return to childhood is a retreat from sexuality
and the dangers of masculinity represented by un-
muzzled daggers. He sees himself "unbreeched," not
yet in breeches—Renaissance children of both
sexes were dressed in skirts until the age of seven
or so, and the "breeching" of boys was the formal
move out of the world of women and into man-
hood. Polixenes, questioned by Hermione, describes
his childhood with Leontes as both Edenic and pre-
sexual:

                        What we changed
        Was innocence for innocence. We knew not
        The doctrine of ill-doing, nor dreamed
        That any did. Had we pursued that life,
        . . . we should have answered heaven
        Boldly "Not guilty," the imposition cleared
        Hereditary ours.

                                (1.2.86–94)

The world of their childhood was without vice or
temptation, innocent even of original sin, of whose
"imposition" we are guilty by heredity. Hermione point-
edly observes, "By this we gather / You have tripped
since." Polixenes concurs; the fall from grace was
the fall into sexuality—the entrance of women, and
thereby of sin, into the garden: "Temptations have
since then been born to 's, for / In those unfledged
days was my wife a girl" (98–99). The temptations
are the prelude to marriage. But this is not a happy

ending: Hermione draws the logical inference, that "Your queen and I are devils" (104). The banter is lighthearted, but her teasing account of wedlock as a continuing state of sin with diabolical women confirms the view of sexuality implied in the men's fantasy.

The entry of women into the childhood Eden is also, of course, a disruptive element in the perfection of male friendship. The tension between friendship and marriage is a recurrent Shakespearean theme: think of Portia's elaborate strategy to undo Bassanio's allegiance to Antonio, or Othello's automatic assumption of his friend's honesty as against his wife's. Leontes' sudden, violent spasm of jealousy is triggered by nothing— "nothing," indeed, becomes a key word in his litany of evidence against his wife ("Is whispering nothing?," etc.)—but the transformation of the best friend into a rival and the faithful wife into a whore is part of the same fantasy, its worst-case scenario. Marriage is a dangerous condition in Shakespeare, and in agonizing over whether his wife is chaste, his children legitimate, Leontes is articulating a critical subtext that resonates throughout the patriarchal culture of early modern Europe.

The women in this world have their own society too. Hermione's prison is also the birth chamber, and she has as her champion not some heroic knight of romance but the fearless Paulina, whose challenge to Leontes' authority provides some of the most thrilling moments of the play. Her shrewish tongue is the agent of reconciliation and restoration, but she is also a half-comic figure, one whom the play refuses to take entirely seriously: what she restores, after all, is the culpable Leontes' equanimity and some—not all—of his losses.

Hermione's trial is not really a trial, since there is no evidence; or more precisely, no agreement about what constitutes evidence. What for Leontes is empirical is to Hermione merely "surmises, all proofs sleeping else / But what your jealousies awake" (3.2.119–20). The appeal to the oracle itself acknowledges the radical fallibility of human justice, the impossibility of determining truth through the processes of reason. The play certainly assumes the oracle's infallibility, though this, for a Renaissance audience, may have constituted one of its many improbabilities. There was, by Shakespeare's time, a considerable literature denying any divine inspiration to the ancient oracles, and Leontes' rejection of Apollo's word is entirely consistent with orthodox Christian opinion. For Shakespeare's audience, the crucial testimony, the word of the oracle, would have been rather like the word of the ghost in *Hamlet*—something the play requires you to believe but that you knew, as a good Reformation Christian, you were supposed to reject.

The oracle minces no words, but neither does Leontes in his reaction; nor is any evidence necessary in declaring the oracle false. What brings Leontes to his senses is not Apollo's word but the sudden report of the death of Mamillius:

> The Prince your son, with mere conceit and fear
> Of the Queen's speed, is gone.
>
> .   .   .
>
> > Is dead.
>
> LEONTES
> Apollo's angry, and the heavens themselves
> Do strike at my injustice.
>
> (3.2.156–61)

There is no reason for Leontes to realize he is mistaken at this point. He takes Mamillius' death as a judgment of Apollo, but he need not give it this interpretation. Indeed, the messenger has offered a perfectly satisfactory physiological explanation: the boy died from fear and grief over his mother's situation. It is Leontes who supplies an alternative explanation that gives Mamillius' death a metaphysical meaning, that implies a providential universe, a world of rewards and punishments, and perhaps most important, a world that contains a mechanism enabling you to determine whether you are actually right or wrong, that solves the problem of your skepticism. Leontes sees this particular event as part of a larger scheme. But the process by which he arrives at this conviction is no different from that by which he had convinced himself of Hermione's guilt. Being released from one's delusions and restored to one's senses has nothing to do with a return to rationality.

Leontes' reaction to all this is worth pausing over. To Hermione's swoon at the announcement of the death of Mamillius, his response is remarkably casual: "Her heart is but o'ercharged." Mamillius has been represented as the joy of his life, and also as his twin (they are "almost as like as [two] eggs") and the hope of the kingdom. His reaction to the boy's death produces not a recognition of the limits of human physiology under grief, and the acknowledgment of his responsibility for the most profound of losses, but the conviction that "Apollo's angry"—and therefore can be appeased. He accommodates himself to his losses very easily. Hermione is to be revived, heaven is squared with an apology, and all past errors are assumed to be easily rectifiable:

> Apollo, pardon
> My great profaneness 'gainst thine oracle.
> I'll reconcile me to Polixenes,
> New woo my queen, recall the good Camillo,
> Whom I proclaim a man of truth, of mercy.
> (3.2.170–74)

It is significant that nothing here is said about Mamillius. This is, in a sense, Leontes' ultimate salvation: his ability both to ignore what it does not suit him to recognize and to make metaphysical leaps of faith, to move beyond the immediacies of facts and evidence. It is an ability that Paulina will invoke in the final scene as an essential element in the restoration of Hermione: "It is required / You do awake your faith" (5.3.118–19).

To call Leontes' accommodation to the death of his child (and later that of his wife) easy is not to deny the realities of the feeling involved, but it is to see it as a psychological strategy that, morally, leaves the king unpleasantly intact. Even in coming to his senses, Leontes' ego remains relentlessly unbruised: "I have too much believed mine own suspicion" (3.2.167)—as if there were some difference between the belief and the suspicion, and some lesser degree of credulity would have been warranted. The death of his son and wife, the loss of his daughter, are to be lessons for him—terrible lessons—but that is all they will be. It is Antigonus who suffers death for the abandonment of Perdita; Leontes remains at the center of the play's moral universe. The restored Hermione accepts him back at the play's end; Perdita reappears to provide him with the heir his actions have destroyed; Mamillius, the twin/rival/successor, remains safely dead: the preservation and continuance of the king is throughout the critical issue.

We can, if we wish, describe Leontes' transformation, with its recognition of the reality of divine intervention, as the affirmation of a religious vision (critics often account for the miraculous endings of the late plays by invoking Shakespeare's supposed belief, in his old age, in a transcendent Christianity—his age, remember, was forty-six in 1611), but I doubt that there is much about it to comfort the religious sensibility. What Leontes constructs is a version of events in which God has killed his innocent child in order to teach him a terrible lesson; the child was in no way at fault, but the sins of the father are here visited on the son in the worst possible way. It may well be true that Shakespeare is expressing a religious doctrine in this, but if so, it should serve to remind us that religion in Shakespeare's age was not at all a comforting matter. The church was not the infinitely welcoming mother you could always return to, but a fierce and angry father—people were still being burned alive for heresy, for believing the wrong version of Christianity, in Shakespeare's time.

For all the ultimate restorations, Mamillius is really dead, and nothing restores that loss. To stress the effectiveness of the fantastic reconciliations at the end of Shakespeare's career is surely to ignore Mamillius. The play itself is curiously compliant about the matter: Paulina is as hard as the severest moralist could wish in recalling to Leontes' attention his responsibility for the loss of his wife and daughter, but Mamillius is scarcely mentioned. It is as if the death of the son, the heir—the rival—really *solves* all the play's problems, leaving the transcendent resolution to the unthreatening, infinitely accommodating daughter and wife.

Indeed, in Leontes' quick speech of repentance at
3.2.170–74, nothing is said about Antigonus and
Perdita either. Out of sight, for this hero, is out of
mind. It is Paulina who expresses the realities that
Leontes is unaware of—that everything does not take
place inside his head, that losses cannot be restored
simply by apologizing, that feelings have no effect on
facts:

> O thou tyrant,
> Do not repent these things, for they are heavier
> Than all thy woes can stir. Therefore betake thee
> To nothing but despair.
>
> (3.2.228–31)

But even she, at his merest gesture of repentance,
withdraws the charge, declares herself "a foolish woman" (line 252), and asks forgiveness. Even for the best of
women, speaking the truth to the king is going too
far.

Paulina is presented in one sense as a heroic figure,
intensely serious, the one person who is utterly un-
afraid of Leontes, willing to say, and keep saying, the
hardest truths to his face. But she is also, obviously, a
figure of fun, the butt of a series of jokes about women
who talk too much and do not know their place, and
about men who cannot control their wives—about
women who behave, in the deepest sense, inappropri-
ately. Leontes, in the height of his exasperation, sums it
up by calling her "a mankind witch" (2.3.84). "Mankind" means mannish, masculine: witches are traditionally female, but Paulina violates the gender
boundaries as well.

In a patriarchal society, the position of women is a
basic issue; Leontes' charge against Paulina is obvi-

ously related to his sense of his inability to control his own wife, his power within his family as a microcosm of his power over his kingdom, his potency in the largest sense. Paulina in this scene sums up everything this patriarchal culture finds dangerous in women: she is shrewish, refuses to obey her husband, meddles in the affairs of men, has no respect for the king's authority. Leontes charges her in addition with the female vice that is predicated on the notion of women who do not know their place: she is "a most intelligencing bawd" (2.3.85)—a spying whore. Unbridled language is a sure sign of both lechery and sedition. If we put this together with the assertion that she is a "mankind witch," one who behaves like a man, we can see the gender confusions at the heart of the play and, indeed, of the culture: what is most quintessentially female about women, their sexuality, is most masculine—or perhaps more precisely, is most clearly a projection of masculine fears about women. Sex is something that men do; anything that forces men to acknowledge a specifically female sexuality (the fact, for example, that Hamlet's mother likes to sleep with her husband) is profoundly disturbing.

So far, we would say, Paulina is a recognizable and even commonplace figure for the Renaissance, descending from the view of women Shakespeare dramatized at the beginning of his career in *The Taming of the Shrew*. The trouble is, however, that to call a woman masculine in the period, while it is the worst thing that can be said about her, is also the best. When Ben Jonson wants to idealize his patron the Countess of Bedford, he gives her "a manly soul" (*Epigrams* 76); Queen Elizabeth addressing her troops before the engagement with the Spanish Armada told them that though she had the body of a weak and feeble woman, she had the heart and stomach of a king; and after all the jokes about Paulina, by the end of Act 3 Leontes is deferring to her. Even the charge of witchcraft gets turned around: Leontes says at the revelation of Hermione's statue, "If this be magic, let it be an art / Lawful as eating." To see Paulina as masculine, then, is ultimately a way of idealizing her; and her masculinity is the essential, enabling agent of Hermione's female virtues of obedience and humility—her willingness to lay down her life because of her husband's displeasure, however unmerited. These are the two sides of Shakespeare's women, and together they epitomize the culture's deep ambivalence about both gender and patriarchy.

But the other side of Paulina, the side that somehow gets forgotten, is her relation to her husband. Where is Antigonus in this world of heroic female masculinity? In fact, Antigonus is disposed of quite as coldbloodedly as Mamillius, and his death is another of the play's unrestored losses. He is the faithful servant to an irrational and vindictive master. He has been criticized for obeying Leontes, but however barbarous the king's orders may be, the alternative to obeying them is to see Perdita burned. He commits himself and the infant to the protection of Providence—naively, no doubt, but that is the point. Paulina essentially writes him off as soon as he leaves (see 3.2.255–56), and when, at the play's end, Camillo is offered as a replacement, there is no question of her remaining true to her husband's memory, as Leontes has remained true to his wife's. Antigonus is, in the play's terms, a total loss.

Hermione's death is one of Shakespeare's most daring pieces of stagecraft. There is no question that, at the

end of act 3, the queen is dead—as dead as Mamillius. The evidence for both deaths is the same, the
report of an eyewitness; but Shakespeare does not
leave the matter there. Leontes not only demands to
view the bodies but says he will see them buried
together in the same grave. Shakespeare could have left
Leontes in silence, or sent him into seclusion, unable
to face the evidence of his crimes; but we are allowed
no doubt about the reality of the deaths. What this
means is that if at the play's end Leontes is being
deceived by Paulina about the reality of death, so by
the same token are we being deceived by Shakespeare.

The move to pastoral and the young lovers, and that
geographical figment the seacoast of Bohemia, comes
via the most notorious of Shakespearean gimmicks, the
bear that devours Antigonus—an impossible problem
for directors, a tragic moment that always gets a laugh.
The tragedy becomes comedy—black comedy initially,
though as act 4 continues, it is clear that even within
the world of shepherds and romance there is a great
deal that is threatening. Indeed, the very presence of
aristocrats in the world of pastoral is ominous and
disruptive. Florizell woos Perdita by comparing himself to a series of divine lovers bent on the rape of their
mortal mistresses; Perdita invokes the flowers that fell
from Proserpina's arms as the god of the Underworld
carried her off to an enforced marriage in Hades.
Polixenes' fury at his son's wish to choose his own
bride would have seemed less irrational to Shakespeare's audience than it does to us—princes' mar-
riages were matters of state—but even so, the play has
little to say in favor of romance. The only reason the
elopement constitutes a happy ending is that Perdita is
not only not a shepherdess, but the very princess

Proserpina being abducted in "Dis's wagon." (4.4.139–41)
From Claude François Menestrier, *L'art des emblemes* . . . (1684).

Polixenes would have chosen as his son's wife, the one bride who can heal the wounds of the previous generation.

It is to the point, too, that the happy ending depends on the manipulations of both Autolycus and Paulina, and on an egregious piece of theatrical artistry. In this case the line between the artist and the con-artist is a very fine one. The faith that Paulina demands from Leontes for her *tableau vivant* is only a courtly version of the gullibility Autolycus's ballads exact from his rural clientele. Hermione's statue itself is invented out of old tales, out of Vasari's *Life* of Giulio Romano (which seems to imply, erroneously, that this painter, renowned for the lifelike quality of his work, was also a sculptor), and out of Ovid's account of the sculptor Pygmalion, whose statue of the perfect wife answered his prayers by coming to life. The catharsis engineered by Paulina depends on sixteen years of suffering and penance on Leontes' part. Nothing is said, however, of what Hermione has undergone during the sixteen years; and indeed, the play's stagecraft renders the question irrelevant: she has been dead. For modern audiences, the reunion of husband and wife is an essential element in what is, theatrically, an overwhelming conclusion, but this is probably an anachronistic reaction: Leontes' courtiers continually urge him to remarry, and Paulina prevents him from doing so precisely because Hermione could have been produced at any time, the royal family reconstituted, new heirs born. The oracle would not thereby have been fulfilled, but clearly no one at court except Paulina believes that it needs to be. For Shakespeare's age, the restoration of Perdita, the finding of the heir, the continuance of the royal line, is the crucial element; even Hermione says she has preserved herself to see Perdita, not Leontes. And once the losses are restored, Paulina returns to her proper status of obedient wife—to somebody, to anybody, to whomever the king chooses. Grace and wonder inhere only in kingship. *The Winter's Tale* is very much a royalist, patriarchal vision, and the extent to which it succeeds for modern audiences and readers is a measure of the extent to which we are still willing to buy into that ideology.

Further Reading

The Winter's Tale

Adelman, Janet. "Masculine Authority and the Maternal Body: The Return to Origins in the Romances." In *Suffocating Mothers: Fantasies of Maternal Origin in Shakespeare's Plays, Hamlet to the Tempest*, pp. 193–238, esp. pp. 219–38. New York and London: Routledge, 1991.

In her feminist psychoanalytic study of *The Winter's Tale (WT)*, Adelman traces the movement from "a sterile court in which the maternal body and the progeny which bear its signs" must be exorcised to a court in which that body is radically recuperated, "its regenerative sanctity recognized and embraced." The shift from a male pastoral (static and nostalgic) to a female pastoral (creative and full of hope), with the corresponding shift in presiding deities from Apollo to the goddess Nature, epitomizes the turn from tragedy to romance. Where Leontes and Polixenes base their masculine identity on separation from the female (1.2.85–101), Florizell finds his in the fertile promise of Perdita (4.4.49–53, 134–56, and 569–70). Patriarchy is affirmed in the final scene, but it is "grounded in a benignly generative maternal presence": Leontes' power remains contingent on the return of Hermione.

Bartholomeusz, Dennis. *The Winter's Tale in Performance in England and America, 1611–1976*. Cambridge and New York: Cambridge University Press, 1982.

In addition to analyzing the earliest performances of *WT* at the Globe and Whitehall in the first part of the seventeenth century and David Garrick's adaptation in the eighteenth, this examination of sixty-two produc-

273

tions pays special attention to revivals by J. P. Kemble, William Charles Macready, Samuel Phelps, Charles Kean, Herbert Beerbohm Tree, Harley Granville-Barker, Peter Brook, and Trevor Nunn. Bartholomeusz observes the interactive influence of critics and actors/directors in interpreting the play, particularly its mix of diverse elements and its treatment of Leontes' jealousy and the "resurrection" of Hermione. While modern productions have achieved a certain brilliance in their emphasis on symbolism, "there has been no automatic rising curve of progress" since Granville-Barker's effort in 1912 to recover "the Elizabethan principles at work in Shakespeare's theatrical art."

Barton, Anne. "Leontes and the Spider: Language and Speaker in Shakespeare's Last Plays." In *Shakespeare's Styles: Essays in Honour of Kenneth Muir*, edited by Philip Edwards, Inga-Stina Ewbank, and G. K. Hunter, pp. 131–50. Cambridge and New York: Cambridge University Press, 1980. Reprinted in Barton's *Essays, Mainly Shakespearean*, pp. 161–81. Cambridge: Cambridge University Press, 1994.

Barton finds in Leontes' spider passage (2.1.47–63) the stylistic key to Shakespeare's late plays in general and *WT* in particular. In these plays Shakespeare subordinates character to plot, deliberately destroying the "close relationship between language and dramatic character" he had so successfully forged in the tragedies. Language is used no longer to reveal a character's nature and intentions but to emphasize the "impersonal quality" of the dramatic occasion; as a result of this gap between language and speaker, characters remain unaware of what is clear to the audience—the primary, but to the speakers "involuntary," meaning of their words. "The involuntary plays a significantly new part in the Last Plays."

Bethell, Samuel L. *The Winter's Tale: A Study*. London: Staples Press, 1947.

In this first book-length study of the play, Bethell reads *WT* as a dramatic illustration of Christian humanism. Numerous anachronisms combine with the pervasive presence of such concepts as grace, sin, penance, conscience, redemption, and the Pauline view of a "resurrected life" to result in "a timeless Christian story in no place and every place." The dramatic synthesis of natural and supernatural, medieval and classical, sacred and secular, and symbolic and realistic makes *WT* "the supreme literary expression of the Baroque." The playwright's great achievement is his fusion of Hellenic-medieval romance (the Florizell-Perdita story) and the "unromantic otherworldliness of orthodox medieval religion" (the Leontes-Hermione story) to reveal "the work of Providence in individual and national history."

Biggins, Dennis. " 'Exit pursued by a Beare': A Problem in *The Winter's Tale*." *Shakespeare Quarterly* 13 (1962): 3–13.

After agreeing with those who claim that the beast in the stage direction at 3.3.64 was first impersonated by an actor rather than played by a real bear, Biggins turns his attention to the structural, tonal, thematic, and, most important, symbolic significance of Antigonus' "disposal." By pursuing the agent of tyranny and sparing the innocent baby, the bear functions as the symbol of "destruction, broken integrity, and Heavenly vengeance" and thus makes possible a more serious than comic response to this "atmospherically ticklish moment."

Cavell, Stanley. "Recounting Gains, Showing Losses (A Reading of *The Winter's Tale*)." In *Disowning Knowledge in Six Plays of Shakespeare*, pp. 196–206. Cambridge and

New York: Cambridge University Press, 1987. Reprinted in Cavell's *In Quest of the Ordinary Lines of Skepticism and Romanticism,* pp. 76–101. Chicago: University of Chicago Press, 1988.

Cavell examines *WT* in the context of philosophical skepticism, finding in Leontes "a portrait of the skeptic as fanatic." What interests the author is the "intersection of the epistemologist's questioning of [the] existence . . . of the external world . . . with Leontes' perplexity about knowing whether his son is his." Neither knowing by telling (language) nor knowing by observing (empiricism) can confirm or deny his paternity. Cavell considers the complex relationship between Leontes and Mamillius to be a variation on the Oedipal conflict: instead of being initiated by the son's wish to remove or replace the father, the conflict in *WT* "seems primarily generated by the father's wish to replace or remove the son." The son's death functions as wish fulfillment, thereby enabling Leontes to disown his role in the procreative act, free himself of the responsibilities of fatherhood, and cling to fantasies of childhood innocence. The first half of *WT* constitutes a study of skepticism; the second, a study of the search for recovery from it. The final scene is one of "issuing" in which Leontes and Hermione each awaken and create one another, thus showing "what it may be to find in oneself the life of the world."

Clubb, Louise G. "The Tragicomic Bear." *Comparative Literature Studies* 9 (1972): 17–30.

Clubb shows how Shakespeare's use of a man-eating bear in the stage direction at 3.3.64 to effect the transition from tragedy to comedy "accords with the ambiguity attached to the bear and distinguishing it from other beasts in sixteenth-century Italian pastoral tragicomedy." The animal traditionally thought of as unformed at birth and licked into shape is "both more and less terrible" than other wild beasts; savage and yet tamable, potentially tragic or comic, the bear served as an "emblematically appropriate" figure for playwrights experimenting with mixed genres. "For transitions, especially, the bear is a tragicomic beast *par excellence*," ensuring "the tempering of pain or laughter."

Greene, Robert. *Pandosto. The Triumph of Time* (1588). In *Narrative and Dramatic Sources of Shakespeare,* edited by Geoffrey Bullough, vol. 8, pp. 156–99. London: Routledge & Kegan Paul; New York: Columbia University Press, 1975.

This prose romance, first published in 1588, was the primary source for Shakespeare's *WT*. While clearly indebted to its plot, especially in the first three acts of his play, Shakespeare changed names, reversed locales (Leontes' counterpart presides over Bohemia, while Polixenes' rules Sicilia), introduced new characters (e.g., Paulina, Antigonus, and Autolycus), treated Leontes' jealousy as a surprising explosion rather than something building over time, quickly passed over the interval of sixteen years, and developed the sheepshearing festival from a brief allusion into a full-blown scene. Shakespeare's decision to "resurrect" Hermione, eliminate attempted incest by Leontes, and forgo his suicide resulted in multiple reunions and a tonal atmosphere far different from that of Greene's conclusion. Minor sources include Greene's "Conny-Catching" pamphlets, which carry significance for the creation of Autolycus, and book 10 of Ovid's *Metamorphoses*, which deals with the Pygmalion story of a statue come to life.

Hunt, Maurice, ed. *The Winter's Tale: Critical Essays.* New York: Garland Publishing, 1995.

The first part of this anthology (following an introductory overview of the scholarship and performance history related to *WT*) provides nineteen critical commentaries spanning the years 1817 to 1995; the second part is devoted to theater reviews covering productions between 1802 and 1988. Along with observations by William Hazlitt, Samuel Taylor Coleridge, Harley Granville-Barker, and Sir Arthur Quiller-Couch, the critical essays contain F. David Hoeniger's "The Meaning of *The Winter's Tale*," Northrop Frye's "Recognition in *The Winter's Tale*," Edward W. Tayler's "Shakespeare's *The Winter's Tale*" (from *Nature and Art in Renaissance Literature*), Inga-Stina Ewbank's "The Triumph of Time in *The Winter's Tale*," Robert G. Hunter's "*The Winter's Tale*" (from *Shakespeare and the Comedy of Forgiveness*), Joan Hartwig's "The Tragicomic Perspective of *The Winter's Tale*," Peter Lindenbaum's "Time, Sexual Love, and the Uses of Pastoral in *The Winter's Tale*," Howard Felperin's "Our Carver's Excellence: *The Winter's Tale*" (from *Shakespearean Romance*), Carol Thomas Neely's "*The Winter's Tale*: The Triumph of Speech," Patricia Southard Gourlay's " 'O my most sacred lady': Female Metaphor in *The Winter's Tale*," Richard Proudfoot's "Verbal Reminiscence and the Two-Part Structure of *The Winter's Tale*," Russ McDonald's "Poetry and Plot in *The Winter's Tale*," Kay Stockholder's "From Matter to Magic: *The Winter's Tale*" (from *Dream Works: Lovers and Families in Shakespeare's Plays*), Maurice Hunt's "The Labor of *The Winter's Tale*," and David Bergeron's "The Apollo Mission in *The Winter's Tale*." In addition to nineteenth-century productions by J. P. Kemble, Samuel Phelps, and Charles Kean, the theater reviews relate to revivals by Granville-Barker (1912), Peter Brook (1951), Trevor Nunn (1969), John Barton and Trevor Nunn (1976),

Jane Howell (for the BBC in 1981), Terry Hands (1986), David William (1986), and Peter Hall (1988).

Morse, William R. "Metacriticism and Materiality: The Case of Shakespeare's *The Winter's Tale*." *English Literary History* 58 (1991): 283–304.
This materialist-metacritical approach to *WT* questions the New Historicist claim of an absolute cultural hegemony in Shakespeare's time that completely contained subversive tendencies. Morse views the "seemingly apolitical" *WT* as a site of conflict between dominant and emergent ideologies. Whatever the commitment of James I's court to the ideology of absolutism in 1610, *WT* shows that the emergent anti-absolutist ideology "is already passing into a kind of cultural dominance, consigning the absolutist culture of the court to a residual status thirty years before political events confirm the shift." Shakespeare's self-conscious appropriation of the genre of romance disengages the audience and demystifies authority "through the deconstruction of the transcendent conceptions of metaphysics and rationality that privilege and sustain it." *WT*'s conflicting modes of representation, its equal criticism of medieval analogical discourse and modern analytical-referential discourse, and its "incomplete" containment of subversive elements reveal a play of "radical political openness" and, by extension, a world "teeter[ing] in the gap" between contending ideologies.

Mowat, Barbara A. "Rogues, Shepherds, and the Counterfeit Distressed: Texts and Infracontexts in *The Winter's Tale*." *Shakespeare Studies* 22 (1994): 58–76.
Mowat analyzes the matrix of printed discourse stratifying and complicating the surface meaning of *WT* 4.3 (Autolycus' encounter with the Shepherd's Son). One set

of contexts—the Greek myth of the "master thief" Autolycus (the son of Mercury), Greene's *Second Part of Conny-Catching*, vagabond songs, and picaresque tales—"makes of the dramatic moment a variously nuanced celebration of the cunning of the trickster." Another set—a vast body of "rogue" literature that contributed to a century-long socioeconomic debate on the issue of vagrancy and the need to distinguish between the genuinely distressed and the counterfeit distressed—"makes the moment instead an enactment of frightening social conflict." An intertextual reading of 4.3 allows one to recover the scene's embedded complexity and "to exchange [its] amusing surface context . . . for a supercharged contextual world." Mowat calls attention to the darker and more specific (even legal) semantics in Shakespeare's time of the word "rogue," the term used to characterize Autolycus in the list of *dramatis personae*.

Orgel, Stephen. "The Poetics of Incomprehensibility." *Shakespeare Quarterly* 42 (1991): 431–37.

Orgel considers four obscure passages from *WT* (1.2.13–16 and 175–83, 3.2.46–51 and 111–13) to argue that "linguistic opacity" is a basic feature of the play. He cautions against imposing an arbitrary clarity where, even for Shakespeare's audience, ambiguity was the desired end. Some lines, while definitely intended to mean something, are nevertheless meant to resist "paraphrasable meaning." *WT* speaks "incomprehensibly."

Schalkwyk, David. " 'A Lady's "Verily" Is as Potent as a Lord's': Women, Word, and Witchcraft in *The Winter's Tale*." *English Literary Renaissance* 22 (1992): 242–72.

Schalkwyk views the exchange between Hermione

and Polixenes at 1.2.50–70 as a microcosm of *WT*'s exploration of "the radical instability, for patriarchy, of [the female] word." Informing both Sicilian and Bohemian society is the recognition that legitimacy of the bloodline, so crucial to patriarchal authority, depended on the woman's word concerning paternity—a word, however, that was less trustworthy than man's because "women . . . will say anything" (1.2.166–67). Accusations of witchcraft directed at women who "transgress the patriarchal order" further devalue female speech and erotic power. Rather than offering a regenerated world that recognizes the dignity of women, the final scene "rehearses the political need for men to escape their ideological impasse through the [containment and] appropriation of the potency of the female word and the concomitant silencing of women." By justifying female virtue (i.e., asserting a woman's chastity), "a pair of kings" (5.3.182) guarantees the honesty and worth of Hermione and Paulina, thus fulfilling male desires and furthering the ends of patriarchy.

Traub, Valerie. "Jewels, Statues, and Corpses: Containment of Female Erotic Power." In *Desire and Anxiety: Circulations of Sexuality in Shakespearean Drama*, pp. 25–49, esp. pp. 42–49. London and New York: Routledge, 1992. [An earlier version of this chapter appeared in *Shakespeare Studies* 20 (1988): 215–38.]

Traub explores the meaning of masculine anxiety toward female power within the context of recent feminist, psychoanalytic, and New Historicist criticism. Focusing on female chastity in *Hamlet*, *Othello*, and *WT*, she maintains that male anxiety toward female eroticism "is channeled into a strategy of containment; the erotic threat of the female body is psychically contained by means of a metaphoric and dramatic transformation of women into jewels, statues, and corpses." Instead of privileging feminist values (see Adelman above), the final scene presents the return of Hermione, her sexuality "monumentally" displaced into a statue, as "wish-fulfillment" for Leontes, who recovers a virtuous wife and patriarchal authority over "all social relations." Traub's reading challenges the prevailing psychoanalytic interpretation of the romances as "reconstituting the broken families" of the tragedies: "the restraints of genre do not contain the erotic anxieties of gender."

Shakespeare's Language

Abbott, E. A. *A Shakespearian Grammar*. New York: Haskell House, 1972.

This compact reference book, first published in 1870, helps with many difficulties in Shakespeare's language. It systematically accounts for a host of differences between Shakespeare's usage and sentence structure and our own.

Blake, Norman. *Shakespeare's Language: An Introduction*. New York: St. Martin's Press, 1983.

This general introduction to Elizabethan English discusses various aspects of the language of Shakespeare and his contemporaries, offering possible meanings for hundreds of ambiguous constructions.

Dobson, E. J. *English Pronunciation, 1500–1700*. 2 vols. Oxford: Clarendon Press, 1968.

This long and technical work includes chapters on spelling (and its reformation), phonetics, stressed vowels, and consonants in early modern English.

Houston, John. *Shakespearean Sentences: A Study in Style and Syntax.* Baton Rouge: Louisiana State University Press, 1988.

Houston studies Shakespeare's stylistic choices, considering matters such as sentence length and the relative positions of subject, verb, and direct object. Examining plays throughout the canon in a roughly chronological, developmental order, he analyzes how sentence structure is used in setting tone, in characterization, and for other dramatic purposes.

Onions, C. T. *A Shakespeare Glossary.* Oxford: Clarendon Press, 1986.

This revised edition updates Onions's standard, selective glossary of words and phrases in Shakespeare's plays that are now obsolete, archaic, or obscure.

Robinson, Randal. *Unlocking Shakespeare's Language: Help for the Teacher and Student.* Urbana, Ill.: National Council of Teachers of English and the ERIC Clearinghouse on Reading and Communication Skills, 1989.

Specifically designed for the high-school and undergraduate college teacher and student, Robinson's book addresses the problems that most often hinder present-day readers of Shakespeare. Through work with his own students, Robinson found that many readers today are particularly puzzled by such stylistic devices as subject-verb inversion, interrupted structures, and compression. He shows how our own colloquial language contains comparable structures, and thus helps students recognize such structures when they find them in Shakespeare's plays. This book supplies worksheets—with examples from major plays—to illuminate and remedy such problems as unusual sequences of words and the separation of related parts of sentences.

Williams, Gordon. *A Dictionary of Sexual Language and Imagery in Shakespearean and Stuart Literature*. 3 vols. London: Athlone Press, 1994.

Williams provides a comprehensive list of the words to which Shakespeare, his contemporaries, and later Stuart writers gave sexual meanings. He supports his identification of these meanings by extensive quotations.

Shakespeare's Life

Baldwin, T. W. *William Shakspere's Petty School*. Urbana: University of Illinois Press, 1943.

Baldwin here investigates the theory and practice of the petty school, the first level of education in Elizabethan England. He focuses on that educational system primarily as it is reflected in Shakespeare's art.

Baldwin, T. W. *William Shakspere's Small Latine and Lesse Greeke*. 2 vols. Urbana: University of Illinois Press, 1944.

Baldwin attacks the view that Shakespeare was an uneducated genius—a view that had been dominant among Shakespeareans since the eighteenth century. Instead, Baldwin shows, the educational system of Shakespeare's time would have given the playwright a strong background in the classics, and there is much in the plays that shows how Shakespeare benefited from such an education.

Beier, A. L., and Roger Finlay, eds. *London 1500–1800: The Making of the Metropolis*. New York: Longman, 1986.

Focusing on the economic and social history of early modern London, these collected essays probe aspects of metropolitan life, including "Population and Disease,"

"Commerce and Manufacture," and "Society and Change."

Bentley, G. E. *Shakespeare's Life: A Biographical Handbook.* New Haven: Yale University Press, 1961.
This "just-the-facts" account presents the surviving documents of Shakespeare's life against an Elizabethan background.

Chambers, E. K. *William Shakespeare: A Study of Facts and Problems.* 2 vols. Oxford: Clarendon Press, 1930.
Analyzing in great detail the scant historical data, Chambers's complex, scholarly study considers the nature of the texts in which Shakespeare's work is preserved.

Cressy, David. *Education in Tudor and Stuart England.* London: Edward Arnold, 1975.
This volume collects sixteenth-, seventeenth-, and early-eighteenth-century documents detailing aspects of formal education in England, such as the curriculum, the control and organization of education, and the education of women.

Dutton, Richard. *William Shakespeare: A Literary Life.* New York: St. Martin's Press, 1989.
Not a biography in the traditional sense, Dutton's very readable work nevertheless "follows the contours of Shakespeare's life" as he examines Shakespeare's career as playwright and poet, with consideration of his patrons, theatrical associations, and audience.

Fraser, Russell. *Young Shakespeare.* New York: Columbia University Press, 1988.
Fraser focuses on Shakespeare's first thirty years, paying attention simultaneously to his life and art.

De Grazia, Margreta. *Shakespeare Verbatim: The Repro-duction of Authenticity and the 1790 Apparatus*. Oxford: Clarendon Press, 1991.

De Grazia traces and discusses the development of such editorial criteria as authenticity, historical periodi-zation, factual biography, chronological development, and close reading, locating as the point of origin Edmond Malone's 1790 edition of Shakespeare's works. There are interesting chapters on the First Folio and on the "legendary" versus the "documented" Shakespeare.

Schoenbaum, S. *William Shakespeare: A Compact Doc-umentary Life*. New York: Oxford University Press, 1977.

This standard biography economically presents the essential documents from Shakespeare's time in an accessible narrative account of the playwright's life.

Shakespeare's Theater

Bentley, G. E. *The Profession of Player in Shakespeare's Time, 1590–1642*. Princeton: Princeton University Press, 1984.

Bentley readably sets forth a wealth of evidence about performance in Shakespeare's time, with special atten-tion to the relations between player and company, and the business of casting, managing, and touring.

Berry, Herbert. *Shakespeare's Playhouses*. New York: AMS Press, 1987.

Berry's six essays collected here discuss (with illustra-tions) varying aspects of the four playhouses in which Shakespeare had a financial stake: the Theatre in Shore-ditch, the Blackfriars, and the first and second Globe.

Cook, Ann Jennalie. *The Privileged Playgoers of Shakespeare's London*. Princeton: Princeton University Press, 1981.

Cook's work argues, on the basis of sociological, economic, and documentary evidence, that Shakespeare's audience—and the audience for English Renaissance drama generally—consisted mainly of the "privileged."

Greg, W. W. *Dramatic Documents from the Elizabethan Playhouses*. 2 vols. Oxford: Clarendon Press, 1931.

Greg itemizes and briefly describes many of the play manuscripts that survive from the period 1590 to around 1660, including, among other things, players' parts. His second volume offers facsimiles of selected manuscripts.

Gurr, Andrew. *Playgoing in Shakespeare's London*. Cambridge: Cambridge University Press, 1987.

Gurr charts how the theatrical enterprise developed from its modest beginnings in the late 1560s to become a thriving institution in the 1600s. He argues that there were important changes over the period 1567–1644 in the playhouses, the audience, and the plays.

Harbage, Alfred. *Shakespeare's Audience*. New York: Columbia University Press, 1941.

Harbage investigates the fragmentary surviving evidence to interpret the size, composition, and behavior of Shakespeare's audience.

Hattaway, Michael. *Elizabethan Popular Theatre: Plays in Performance*. London: Routledge & Kegan Paul, 1982.

Beginning with a study of the popular drama of the

late Elizabethan age—a description of the stages, performance conditions, and acting of the period—this volume concludes with an analysis of five well-known plays of the 1590s, one of them (*Titus Andronicus*) by Shakespeare.

Shapiro, Michael. *Children of the Revels: The Boy Companies of Shakespeare's Time and Their Plays.* New York: Columbia University Press, 1977.

Shapiro chronicles the history of the amateur and quasi-professional child companies that flourished in London at the end of Elizabeth's reign and the beginning of James's.

The Publication of Shakespeare's Plays

Blayney, Peter. *The First Folio of Shakespeare.* Hanover, Md.: Folger, 1991.

Blayney's accessible account of the printing and later life of the First Folio—an amply illustrated catalog to a 1991 Folger Shakespeare Library exhibition—analyzes the mechanical production of the First Folio, describing how the Folio was made, by whom and for whom, how much it cost, and its ups and downs (or, rather, downs and ups) since its printing in 1623.

Hinman, Charlton. *The Printing and Proof-Reading of the First Folio of Shakespeare.* 2 vols. Oxford: Clarendon Press, 1963.

In the most arduous study of a single book ever undertaken, Hinman attempts to reconstruct how the Shakespeare First Folio of 1623 was set into type and run off the press, sheet by sheet. He also provides almost all the known variations in readings from copy to copy.

Hinman, Charlton. *The Norton Facsimile: The First Folio of Shakespeare*. Second Edition. New York: W. W. Norton, 1996.

This facsimile presents a photographic reproduction of an "ideal" copy of the First Folio of Shakespeare; Hinman attempts to represent each page in its most fully corrected state. The second edition includes an important new introduction by Peter Blayney.

Key to
Famous Lines and Phrases

A sad tale's best for winter.   [*Mamillius*—2.1.33]

I am a feather for each wind that blows.

          [*Leontes*—2.3.191]

When daffodils begin to peer,
With heigh, the doxy over the dale . . .

          [*Song*—4.3.1–12]

. . . a snapper-up of unconsidered trifles.

          [*Autolycus*—4.3.26]

Jog on, jog on, the footpath way,
And merrily hent the stile-a . . .   [*Song*—4.3.130–33]

. . . Flora
Peering in April's front.   [*Florizell*—4.4.2–3]

. . . nature is made better by no mean
But nature makes that mean.   [*Polixenes*—4.4.106–7]

Daffodils,
That come before the swallow dares, and take
The winds of March with beauty; violets dim,
But sweeter than the lids of Juno's eyes . . .

          [*Perdita*—4.4.141–52]

        When you do dance, I wish you
A wave o' th' sea, that you might ever do
Nothing but that . . .   [*Florizell*—4.4.166–68]

. . . she is
The queen of curds and cream.

                        [*Camillo*—4.4.190–91]

The Folger Shakespeare Editions combine expertly edited texts with illuminating explanatory notes and images to help you discover the works of William Shakespeare in exciting new ways.

ALL PLAYS NOW AVAILABLE

FOLGER Shakespeare Editions Library

All's Well that Ends Well	Julius Caesar	Richard II
Antony and Cleopatra	King John	Richard III
As You Like It	King Lear	Romeo and Juliet
The Comedy of Errors	Love's Labor's Lost	Shakespeare's Sonnets
Cymbeline	Macbeth	Shakespeare's Sonnets
Coriolanus	Measure for Measure	and Poems
Hamlet	The Merchant of Venice	The Taming of the Shrew
Henry IV Part 1	The Merry Wives of	The Tempest
Henry IV Part 2	Windsor	Timon of Athens
Henry V	A Midsummer Night's	Titus Andronicus
Henry VI Part 1	Dream	Troilus and Cressida
Henry VI Part 2	Much Ado About Nothing	Twelfth Night
Henry VI Part 3	Othello	The Two Gentlemen
Henry VIII	Pericles	of Verona
		The Two Noble Kinsmen
		The Winter's Tale

FOLGER Shakespeare Library Presents: Audio Editions

Folger Theatre brings Shakespeare to life with unabridged, full-cast dramatizations.